Water Ethics

This book introduces the idea that ethics are an intrinsic dimension of any water policy, program, or practice, and that understanding what ethics are being acted out in water policies is fundamental to an understanding of water resource management. Thus, in controversies or conflicts over water resource allocation and use, an examination of ethics can help clarify the positions of conflicting parties as preparation for constructive negotiations.

The author shows the benefits of exposing tacit values and motivations and subjecting these to explicit public scrutiny where the values themselves can be debated. The aim of such a process is to create the proverbial "level playing field," where values favoring environmental sustainability are considered in relation to values favoring short-term exploitation for quick economic stimulus (the current problem) or quick protection from water disasters (through infrastructure which science suggests is not sustainable).

The book shows how new technologies, such as drip irrigation, or governance structures, such as river basin organizations, are neither "good" nor "bad" in their own right, but can serve a range of interests which are guided by ethics. A new ethic of coexistence and synergies with nature is possible, but ultimately depends not on science, law, or finances but on the values we choose to adopt. The book includes a wide range of case studies from countries including Australia, India, the Philippines, South Africa, and the United States. These cover various contexts including water for agriculture, urban, domestic, and industrial use, the rights of Indigenous Peoples, and river, watershed, and ecosystem management.

David Groenfeldt is the founder and Director of the Water-Culture Institute in Santa Fe, New Mexico, and Adjunct Associate Professor, Department of Anthropology, University of New Mexico, USA. He has previously worked on irrigation research at the International Water Management Institute (Sri Lanka), the design and management of irrigation projects for the World Bank, and rural development consulting for various international agencies. More recently, he directed a watershed NGO in New Mexico, and in 2010 founded the Water-Culture Institute to address the underlying causes of unsustainable water manageme

D1153578

Water Ethics

A Values Approach to Solving
the Water Crisis

David Groenfeldt

Routledge
Taylor & Francis Group

LONDON AND NEW YORK

First published 2013
by Routledge
2 Park Square, Milton Park, Abingdon, Oxon OX14 4RN

Simultaneously published in the USA and Canada
by Routledge
711 Third Avenue, New York, NY 10017

Routledge is an imprint of the Taylor & Francis Group, an informa business

© 2013 David Groenfeldt

British Library Cataloguing-in-Publication Data
A catalogue record for this book is available from the British Library

Library of Congress Cataloging in Publication Data
Groenfeldt, David.
Water ethics : a values approach to solving the water crisis /
by David Groenfeldt.
pages cm
"Simultaneously published in the USA and Canada"–Title page verso.
Includes bibliographical references and index.
1. Water-supply–Moral and ethical aspects. 2. Water-supply–Government policy. 3. Water resources development–Moral and ethical aspects.
4. Water resources development–Government policy.
5. Environmental ethics. I. Title.
TD353.G76 2013
178–dc23
2013009093

ISBN: 978-0-415-62644-6 (hbk)
ISBN: 978-0-415-62645-3 (pbk)
ISBN: 978-0-203-10266-4 (ebk)

Typeset in Goudy
by Taylor & Francis Books

MIX
Paper from
responsible sources
FSC
www.fsc.org   FSC® C013604

Printed and bound by CPI Group (UK) Ltd, Croydon, CR0 4YY

Contents

Acknowledgments   vi
Preface – Why Water Ethics?   viii

1   Introduction to Water Ethics   1

2   Manipulating Rivers   17

3   Water for Agriculture: The Ethics of Irrigation   50

4   Ethics in Urban and Domestic Water Use   68

5   Water for Industry: What is Responsible Use?   86

6   The Ethics of Water Governance   106

7   Indigenous Water Ethics   135

8   Towards a New Water Ethic   155

9   Conclusions   175

Bibliography   183
Index   197

Acknowledgments

This book combines three genealogical strands of my professional experience which deserve to be acknowledged separately. The first strand is my graduate studies in anthropology and most especially my PhD field research along the northern fringe of the Thar Desert in Rajasthan and Haryana, India. My interest then focused on the cultural values that gave a particular stamp to the farming communities I studied, and how those values changed when irrigation canals brought new agricultural opportunities. My mentors during that period have already been thanked once in the acknowledgments to my dissertation, but warrant a renewed recognition here, both my professors, and even more importantly, my mentors in the study villages whose lives were temporarily intertwined with my own. The village life I experienced as pastoral and romantic (depicted in the cover photograph) can also be viewed as limiting and backward, yet there was no doubt in my mind that village life contained deeply important qualities that faded in the face of economic development. Was development simply incompatible with that pastoral quality, or could the two coexist with a more nuanced approach to development?

The second strand of experience leading to this book is my professional work in the social dimensions of irrigation management, and particularly on farmers' management participation in irrigation systems. Here I want to recognize my mentors and colleagues within the orbit of the International Water Management Institute in Sri Lanka, and later at the World Bank: Tom Wickham, Roberto Lenton, David Seckler, and Robert Chambers, who introduced me to the idea that management principles could be applied to an understanding of how irrigation networks operated; Doug Merrey, Namika Raby, Bob Yoder, Ed Martin, and my late wife, Pam Stanbury, whose work on a range of social issues in irrigation expanded my horizons; and many others, including Jean Verdier, Lucas Host, Geert Diemer, Ruth Meizen-Dick, Doug Vermillion, Bryan Bruns, Uraivan Tan-kim Yong, Walt Coward, Jayanta Perera, Shamila Abeyratne, Abdullah Herzenni, Rachid Abdelloui, Nyoman Sutawan, Prachanda Pradhan, Ujjwal Pradhan, Romana de los Reyes, and Sylvia Jopillo. During my time at the World Bank (1994–2001) my thinking about the roles and levels of participatory irrigation management was broadened by Hatsuya Azumi, Peter Sun, Keith Oblitas,

Ashok Subramanian, Richard Reidinger, and outside the Bank, Jose Trava, Atef Hamdy, Mark Svendsen, Paul Van Hofwegen, Peter Mollinga, Karin Roelofs, Raymond Peter, Sithapathi Rao, and Linden Vincent. The basic question that all these people helped me address was, "What is irrigation for?" Clearly it had utility beyond the raw production of food, to include social and even environmental benefits.

The third strand of experience reflected in this book has to do with cultural values, which I later came to label as "ethics." My foray into the indigenous world of water was facilitated by Rutgerd Boelens, Darlene Sanderson, Tom Goldtooth, Vicki Corpuz, Joji Carino, Vernon Masayesva, Jose Lucero, Ellen Lutz, Ameyali Ramos Castillo, Zheng Xiao Yun, and Emigdio Ballon. My understanding of agricultural values and multi-functionality owes much to discussions with Kazumi Yamaoka, Riota Nakamura, and Itaru Minami. The direct impetus for this book, however, comes from the nearly four years (2006–09) I spent as Executive Director of the Santa Fe Watershed Association in New Mexico. Here I encountered the limits of cultural romanticism in the cold reality of local water policies, and the cultural values supporting those policies. I would like to acknowledge particularly Paige Grant, Francois-Marie Patorni, Dale Lyons, Claudia Borchert, Sandy Hurlocker, Jerrey Jacobi, Mayor David Coss, Staci Matlock, Melissa Savage, Laura McCarthy, Neil Williams, John Horning, Terry Sullivan, Alan Hamilton, Steve Harris, and Mark Smith. With so many talented people working to restore their local river, why was it so difficult? The answer that slowly emerged in my mind was, and still is, "cultural values." I founded the Water-Culture Institute (http://www.waterculture.org) to explore the dynamics between values and water policies, and discovered that others had already been working on that relationship under the name of "water ethics." This is where I owe a debt of gratitude for their intellectual inspiration, to Sandra Postel, Jerry delli Priscoli, Jeremy Schmidt, Peter Brown, Adrian Armstrong, Dieter Gerten, Martin Kowarsch, Cynthia Barnett, Irene Klaver, Janos Bogardi, Ramon Llamas, Bill Cosgrove, Kathryn Kintzele, and Curt Meine.

The actual writing of the book was made possible through financial support from the Kalliopeia Foundation, moral support from my colleagues, friends, and family, and the personal support from my wife, Annette and our children, Margot, Julia, Leah, and Naomi. Helpful comments on earlier drafts were provided by Jeremy Schmidt, Tom Groenfeldt, Jennifer Archer, Luzma Nava, and my editor, Tim Hardwick.

During the overly long process of writing, I took inspiration from two very different water ecosystems with "whom" I feel a deep personal connection. One is the dammed and usually dry Santa Fe River near my home, and the other is the voluminous but also stressed Lake Michigan where my family spends time each year on the Wisconsin shore. To both these ecosystems I feel a debt of responsibility to try to right, or at least to mitigate, the many wrongs of the past. I hope this book might make some small contribution to that effort.

Preface
Why Water Ethics?

In March 2008, I was in a conference room in Santa Fe, New Mexico, listening to a discussion about the water laws of the western United States. Those laws were born out of the California Gold Rush in the 19th Century and designed to avoid bloodshed when miners fought about who had priority to divert the streams needed for mining operations. The courts came up with a solution based on the mining law itself. The first person to divert the stream and use the water for beneficial use (i.e. for his mining operations) could claim that water for his own use. If another miner started a mine upstream, he could also claim the right to divert water from the same stream, but his diversion could not interfere with the water supply of the earlier claimant downstream. This is more or less how the legal principle of "prior appropriation" began in the American West. The same solution that helped miners avoid killing each other in water disputes was applied to irrigation disputes as well, and later on it was applied to the water rights of towns and cities.

There were, and still are, two big problems with water law based on prior appropriation. The first is equity. The lucky few who staked early claims, appropriated most of the water rights. (The customary water claims of the Native Americans were totally ignored when these laws were being developed and were later retrofitted in.) The second problem is environmental. Under Western water law the entire flow of water in a given stream could be claimed by people (and corporations and municipalities that the law also considers to be "persons"). The rivers that the water comes from have no claim to their own water. Miners, farmers, and cities are legally entitled to scoop out the last bit of water in the river, if they possess priority water rights.

The discussion I was listening to that evening was being led by a water law expert from a national environmental organization. I had invited her to speak in Santa Fe, because I thought she could offer insights about our local Santa Fe River. I was director of the Santa Fe Watershed Association at the time, and our river had just been declared as the "Most Endangered River" in the country.[1] I had nominated our river to draw national attention to its plight. Dammed upstream of the historic state capitol of New Mexico, only a dry dusty ditch marked the path of the once vibrant river, a tributary to the Rio Grande. The city-owned water utility had the legal right to dam the river and suck out all the water because of the principle of water rights based on prior appropriation. If water law was the problem, the solution, it seemed to me, would be to change the laws. That's the question I asked.

"What do you see as the long-term evolution of our water laws," I asked the speaker, "How will the principle of prior appropriation be overturned?" My question assumed that this principle is so dysfunctional for sensible water management, that eventually it will simply have to change. The speaker did not share my views. It cannot change, she said. There is too much institutional and political inertia, too many interests vested in the way things are; it will not change and we will just have to accept it and try to work around it as best we can.

That, coming from a fellow environmentalist, who was personally committed to using the law for environmental ends, was not what I wanted or expected to hear. Are we born to serve the imperfect laws our forefathers came up with 150 years ago just because it is too inconvenient to change them? The answer, incredibly, seemed to be, "Yes." We will live with the social inequity and environmental destruction of our water laws because, overall, the system works well enough. We will reform the edges but we will not challenge the core principles because we would almost certainly fail.

The conundrum facing rivers in the American West is an extreme form of the conundrum facing rivers around the globe. The laws and policies governing water seem incompatible with the sustainable stewardship that we know is needed, but changing those policies is simply too big a task. The policies are not stagnant; they are evolving and becoming greener overall. Particularly in Europe, but even in the American West and in the emerging powers of China, India, and Brazil, water policies are shifting to acknowledge the importance of flowing rivers and relatively clean water. But the changes are too small, too slow, and most critically, too "shallow." With some important exceptions, the changes are not rooted in fundamentally new principles; rather, the new and slightly greener policies are being grafted onto the existing principles that caused the current crisis. The response to supply shortages emphasizes efficiencies, new technologies, and more investment in water infrastructure: dams, pipelines, desalination plants, and wastewater treatment facilities. The response to floods is bigger levees; the response to water-starved crops is bigger canals.

Most of my professional water experience has been international in focus, and I felt reasonably confident that the professional water world was evolving along the right track. The rise of major water research institutes and UN water centers, the sophistication of professional associations and the involvement of universities, think tanks, and environmental organizations were encouraging signs that bright minds and well-intentioned political forces would keep our water resources reasonably well governed. The World Water Forum held in The Hague in 2000 reinforced the message that the world was on track to preserve our freshwater resources. The World Water Vision produced for the Forum laid out a 40-year vision for balancing the needs of nature, people, agriculture, and industry. There was much work to do, but we have the vision and the specifics can be worked out as we go along. Yes, there is a water crisis, but we can handle it. That was the basic message I derived from the Water Forum.

Since that Water Forum in 2000, I have changed my views for two reasons. One is that I moved to New Mexico where I experienced the extremes of water policies that promote dewatered rivers, while local Pueblo Indian culture reveres those same rivers as sacred. Which worldview makes more sense from a water perspective? The second reason is the way climate change is reframing water policy discourse. Who is going to support living rivers as the climate becomes hotter and drier, without carefully considered ethical principles already in place that recognize a human responsibility to nature?

My view of water in the American West, as well as globally, is that the incremental policy changes we are making will not be enough to avert disaster. We are using water too fast, protecting it too little, and meanwhile the climate is going to make everything even more challenging. We need to manage water not only differently, but on the basis of different principles – ethical principles.

We face a water crisis, but not because of a lack of water. It is a moral crisis that is being expressed through fear-based water management. The picture, of course, is complicated, and along with moral crisis there are a great many moral success stories of innovative pilot programs and even some elements of national and global water policies. What we are experiencing as a "crisis" is a manifestation of weak, bad, or ignored ethical principles. By addressing those ethics directly, identifying what they are, asking ourselves whether those are the ethics we wish to live by, and then figuring out what our improved set of ethics might be and how to operationalize them through policy and legal reforms, by doing all these things, I believe we will discover that we no longer have a water crisis! We will face shortages, but we will be clear about how to meet those shortages. We will not face scarcity because we will already be living within our means. And I don't think we will have to be water-poor either, because we do have technology. With carefully adjusted water ethics, we will be clear about how best to incorporate technology into our water management strategies to produce enough water for ourselves, and for nature as well.

This is my vision which has inspired this book. This vision hinges on getting the ethics right as the first step, which then helps determine the specifics of planning, managing, and overall water governance. It starts with ethics.

David Groenfeldt

Note

1 This was an annual designation by American Rivers, a national environmental group (http://www.americanrivers.org).

1   Introduction to Water Ethics

What do you call the principles, the values, that form the basis of water policies, or that motivate us to use or not use water in certain ways? How do we judge whether our use of water – whether for brushing our teeth or irrigating a farmer's field – is wasteful or necessary? When we read about the proposed dam that the government of Laos wants to build on the Mekong river, what determines whether we feel that is a good idea or a terrible one? I use the term "water ethics" to denote these underlying principles that influence our own water behavior and our reaction to other people's behaviors.

The kind of ethics I am talking about are rarely black and white. We usually need more information to form a judgment about the dam, or even about whether we are using too much water in brushing our teeth: What is the source of the water flowing our of the tap, and what will happen to it when it goes down the drain? What sort of dam is being proposed on the Mekong? What will be the impacts on the river's fish, and on the traditional communities and cultures that depend on fishing? What will the electricity from the dam be used for and what are the alternative energy options? What will happen to the people who live in the proposed reservoir area?

The questions we ask in our inquiry about whether the dam is desirable or not, or whether we are using too much water in our own homes, reflect our values about what is important. What information is relevant to our support or opposition to the dam proposal? Does it matter if fish can navigate around the dam through fish ladders? Does it matter if local communities have to give up fishing and work in a factory powered by the dam's electricity? Does it matter what is being produced in the factory that uses the electricity from the dam? What about the labor conditions? Where do water ethics end and other ethics begin?

The American conservationist, Aldo Leopold, believed that an extension of ethics beyond our immediately obvious self-interest, to include the well-being of nature, is "an evolutionary possibility and an ecological necessity" (Leopold 1970 [original 1949]:167). Our civilization has already made good progress on our ethical path and embracing nature is the next step. In his most famous essay, *The Land Ethic*, Leopold illustrates how far we've come in our ethical evolution, by relating the Greek myth of Odysseus returning after twenty years away from home (ten years fighting the Trojan War and another ten years finding his way back). His wife and son have been loyally awaiting his return, but what about his slaves, and particularly the female slaves? Had they been loyal too? Just to be sure, Leopold tells us, paraphrasing Homer, "he hanged all on one rope a dozen slave-girls of his household whom he suspected of misbehavior during his absence." What would today be considered mass murder was then seen as justified house-cleaning. "The girls were property. The disposal of property was then, as now, a matter of expediency, not of right and wrong ... " (Leopold 1970 [original 1949]:167).

Leopold's story has been recounted many times not only because of the powerful imagery, but also because there are two deep truths in his example. The first truth is that we have made incredible progress over the past few millennia, and particularly in the past century, in extending our ethical boundaries. While we continue to give special attention to our immediate families and communities ("Charity begins at home"), we have also embraced an ethical concern about people we do not know and will never meet. Through the United Nations, we have endorsed resolutions proclaiming the rights of people and cultures. In 2010, we (again through the UN) even recognized the right of every person to have safe water to drink. Clearly, we are making progress!

The second truth in Leopold's account is that for all our recent progress in caring for the larger human community we have not yet made room for nature in our ethical sphere. The way we treat our rivers, lakes, aquifers, wetlands, and estuaries is largely, if not entirely, governed by expediency. The easiest place to discharge industrial waste is the river that is flowing by, and the easiest way to expand urban water supply is to build a reservoir on that river upstream of the factory where the water quality is still good.

The environmental movement of the 1970s and the new paradigm of sustainable development, which emerged with the report of the Brundtland Commission in 1987 (World Commission on Environment and Development 1987) and the Rio Conference in 1992, seemed to demonstrate that the ethical evolution Leopold anticipated was now taking place. Yet 20 years later, at the time of the Rio+20 meetings, the path to an ecological ethic seemed neither immanent nor inevitable. There is no dearth of analytical tools and concepts (e.g. ecosystem services, green economy, etc.) but these very concepts, like "sustainability" are too easily twisted into the old concepts with new names.

The problem, it seems to me, lies more in "how" we are thinking than "what" we are thinking; how we are using the analytical tools. There is nothing wrong with the tools themselves. Ecosystem services is a powerful concept with far-reaching implications. But then, cost-benefit analysis is also a powerful and valuable tool which has been around for many decades, but has not really helped us along the Leopoldian path of evolution. What's missing? In a word, *ethics*. We have ethics, personally, and there are normative ethics in every society (which is what we anthropologists like to study); we have them, but we are not using those values when it comes to water.

Somehow we have gotten used to the idea that water management is a technical subject better left to the experts. That's partly right; water management is technical, but there are lots of value assumptions embedded in the technical choices. Moreover, the *governance* of water, the laws, policies, and institutions which set the context for technical water management, is anything but technical. Water governance is all about values, and if we don't take the trouble to offer our own values to the water discourse, we are going to be living with the values of the people who do take (and often make!) trouble.

Imposing our personal ethics onto water discussions in our home communities is not necessarily going to get us very far along Leopold's path either. What I believe Leopold had in mind (and he was rather vague about the details) was that through reflecting on both the moral and practical implications of alternative courses of action (e.g. whether to build the dam to provide more water or, alternatively, to start a water conservation campaign to create water savings), we would learn to discern the better choice. Eventually we would also realize that interfering with natural processes, like flowing rivers, has limits, and if those are exceeded (e.g. taking too much water out of the river) we will undermine the natural productivity that our self-interest relies on. Bringing nature into our ethical sphere is not necessarily an act of altruism, though it can be. It is also, I believe, in the long-term self-interest of our civilization, and our very survival as a species.

The message of this book is that an awareness of ethics can contribute to better decisions about water management and governance. My assumption is that the process of thinking through the ethical implications of alternative water policies and practices will favor outcomes that are better for us as people, and for the planet on whose health we ultimately depend. If our management of water becomes more sustainable, we will be further along Leopold's path, and further away from a water crisis. It is in this sense that water ethics has the potential to "solve" the water crisis.

Ethics and Values

In our everyday speech, and in this book, the words "values" and "ethics" are used interchangeably but it is sometimes helpful to make a distinction. Values refer to "standards or criteria to guide not only action but also judgment, choice, attitude, evaluation, argument, exhortation, rationalization, and, one might add, attribution of causality" (Rokeach 2000:2). Ethics refers to a coherent system of values. For example, an environmental ethic is built upon a set of values about how we ought to relate to nature in small, practical ways (e.g. don't step on ants) as well as big conceptual ways (e.g. awe and respect).

But the word, "ethics," also refers to "the discipline dealing with what is good and bad and with moral duty and obligation."[1] My intent is to promote the application of ethics as a discipline to the process of making decisions about water. Rather than living with the fiction that decisions about water are made through objective logic unencumbered by subjective values, I am suggesting that we start with the opposite assumption: Every decision about water reflects values and sets of values (ethics) about the relative importance of different water uses, impacts, and outcomes. Making an effort to understand what tacit values we are bringing to our water decisions (e.g. whether to build the dam) will help us make better decisions because we will understand our own motivations more clearly.

Ethics about What?

Ethics can be applied to just about anything, but it needs to be applied to something. One cannot be simply "ethical" without putting those ethics to the test. To me, this is what makes ethics, as a subject, so fascinating; it is designed for action and application. We can have beliefs about water, that it is sacred, or healing, or beautiful, or even dangerous, but those qualities are not ethics; rather, they are the basis for values which become organized into ethics. Ethics is what we do or how we respond to our concept of water as dangerous (we put a fence around the swimming pool) or beautiful (we frame a photograph and put it on our living room wall).

If we conceive of nature as important to preserve in as "natural" a state as possible, we will try to protect the natural state of a river. If we view the river's flooding as dangerous we might decide to build a levee along the river to protect people and property. If we consider flooding as dangerous but also value the natural river, we will look for a solution to the flooding that does not compromise the river's ecological functions. For example, we might opt for low levees set far away from the river channel to protect against major floods, but allow the river freedom to "be a river" within that zone. The decisions we make about the best way to manage the river depend on how we value different outcomes, and flood management strategies are a rich topic for exploring competing values and ethics.

The various categories of ethics and water management provide the conceptual framework of this book. The chapter themes are organized around how water is managed and used. These provide the context for discussing how different values and ethics play out in practical decisions within those management categories. We will consider four basic contexts of water management. The first, in Chapter 2, is the management of rivers and other water ecosystems through dams, levees, or water pollution standards. The second management context is how we use water and what we use it for, whether in agriculture (Chapter 3), urban water supply (Chapter 4), and industry (Chapter 5). The third management context we consider (Chapter 6) is the governance of water and choices about the kinds of institutions we create to handle governance. A fourth context discussed in Chapter 7 is water management within Indigenous societies where cultural values take on particular importance. Exploring the cultural implications of water management in Indigenous settings also helps us to see more clearly the cultural values and ethics influencing water decisions within our globalized, ostensibly rational, Western-inspired society. We all operate according to an internal value compass which we had better become aware of if we are going to take decisions which are indeed rational!

Table 1.1 depicts these four contexts of water management along the left-hand column: (1) ecosystem management, (2) water use, (3) water governance, and (4) indigenous water management. Within each of these management categories, this book considers how values and ethics influence management decisions in a particular direction. Some values are explicit and are clearly invoked in explaining management decisions, while other values are tacit; they influence decisions, but they are not acknowledged. This mix of explicit and tacit value assumptions masks a confusion of motives that provide a wobbly foundation for water management decisions. Untangling the mess of contradictory values starts with sorting out the values into categories that we can call "ethics categories." What categories should we use? The most obvious value/ethics category is economic. How can water management help the economy? What will be the economic benefits of a particular water project? Economic values are well studied and economics is almost always invoked in water decisions. The persistent confusion about the economic implications of water decisions stems from choosing which economic values/costs to count and how to weigh different kinds of economic values. For example, the economic costs of environmental impacts, e.g. water pollution, are often ignored or downplayed, particularly when big infrastructure projects are at stake.

The reason that only some economic costs are considered and others are ignored, has to do with the influence of conflicting values in other ethics categories. In this book we recognize three additional categories of values/

Table 1.1 Domains of water management (left) and domains of values/ethics (top)

	Environmental values/ethics	Social values/ethics	Cultural values/ethics	Economic values/ethics
Ecosystem Management				
Water Use (Agriculture, Water Supply, Industrial)				
Governance Arrangements				
Indigenous Water Mgmt				

ethics: (1) ethics about the environment, (2) ethics about people and society, and (3) ethics about culture and cultural diversity. These four categories (including economic ethics) are depicted on the top row of Table 1.1. In the real world, of course, there are no clear lines separating these categories; they spill into each other often within a single thought. "We need to protect the economic services of wetlands" simultaneously invokes environmental and economic values. In this book we will try to separate categories which are actually linked and interactive. It is the interactions that are most interesting, and also where the potential lies for bridging conflicts and finding creative solutions. In the final two chapters we will try to put the value categories back together again and see how a deeper understanding of the way values actually function in water decisions can help us create a better water future.

Additional types of values could also be distinguished, such as spiritual values, psychological values, and aesthetic values. In certain contexts these or other types of values could be important to consider. For example, in addressing the pollution of the sacred Yamuna River in India, it is difficult to imagine a type of value that is *not* relevant (Haberman 2006). Another way of categorizing ethics is in terms of whose interests are being prioritized. Carolyn Merchant (2010, original 1997) identifies three categories of ethical intention: egocentric (self-interest), homocentric (utilitarian social interest), and ecocentric (pure environmentalism). What we really need, she concludes, is a hybrid of homocentric and ecocentric ethics which she terms, *partnership ethics*, a "moral consideration for both humans and other species." This seems like a good compromise position, but these three categories are not necessarily mutually exclusive. Distinctions among self, society, and nature fade into insignificance when we consider the prospect of a warming planet and increasingly insecure, and locally scarce, water supplies. We need an ethic that will help us and the next seven generations survive and thrive. Our current ethic of what Leopold calls "expediency" has gotten us into trouble.

This is where the Odysseus story provides hope. Our society no longer accepts slavery; it is ethically taboo. There are no international conferences to consider alternative social policies that would re-instate slavery as an institution. Ethics can and do change. An historically more relevant example, also related to slavery, is the civil rights movement in the United States. We have compelling evidence of changing ethics from the fact that an African American, Barak Obama, was twice elected as President. Precisely how ethics change is not the focus of this book, because I would be moving beyond my field of claimed expertise, though I do provide some suggestions in Chapter 8. This book has the more modest goal of promoting ethics awareness and the application of ethics analysis to water decisions. My expectation, based more on hope than theory, is that by becoming more aware of the ethical dynamics, our collective ethics around water will change for the better.

A Brief History of Water Ethics

The interest in water ethics from within the ranks of the water profession has been very much linked to initiatives of UNESCO through its Commission on the Ethics of Scientific Knowledge and Technology (COMEST). In 1998 this Commission formed a working group on the ethics of freshwater use which issued an initial report, *The Ethics of Freshwater Use: A Survey* two years later (Selborne 2000). This was followed by a series of fourteen reports on various aspects of water ethics, ranging from gender to groundwater to environment. Under the title, "Water and Ethics" the reports were published by UNESCO in 2004 with an introductory volume providing a concise overview (Delli Priscoli et al. 2004). An additional report, *Best Ethical Practice in Water Use*, identified "some fundamental principles ... as essential components" of ethical water use, including human dignity, participation, solidarity, human equality, common good, stewardship, transparency, inclusiveness, and empowerment" (Brelet and Selborne 2004). More recently, the Bangkok office of UNESCO produced a report on *Water Ethics and Water Resource Management* (UNESCO 2011) as part of the Project on "Ethics and Climate Change in Asia and the Pacific."

The UNESCO initiatives had the dual purpose of highlighting how ethics plays a role in decisions about water use and management, and also prescribing what that role should be. A more scholarly approach to water ethics was adopted by the Botin Foundation in Spain, which sponsored two seminars on water ethics in 2007 and 2010. The proceedings from the 2007 seminar are available as the book, *Water Ethics* (Llamas et al. 2009) while the 2010 seminar papers were published in a special issue of the journal, *Water Policy* in 2012.[2]

More recently, UNESCO published a book on *Water, Cultural Diversity, and Global Environmental Change* (Johnston et al. 2012) which provides a series of case studies showing the interplay of cultural values and water management and governance. And finally, mention should be made of the work of David Feldman whose book, *Water Resources Management: In Search of an Environmental Ethic*, pioneered the application of ethics to water management within the United States (Feldman 1991).

In addition to the interest in ethics from inside the water profession, there are a great many more strands of interest from other disciplines (law, development studies, philosophy, history, religion, geography, anthropology, etc.) and professions (business, social and environmental NGOs, academics, journalists, etc.). But in my view, the most significant contribution to water ethics awareness has come not from scholars or business associations but from Indigenous Peoples' organizations such as Tebtebba in the Philippines, and the Indigenous Environment Network in the United States. As discussed in Chapter 7, the Indigenous Peoples' statements and declarations about water offer an important counter-narrative to the consensus positions of the global water establishment. This divide takes visible form at the triennial World Water Forum, where, since the 2006 meetings in Mexico City, it has become standard procedure for an "NGO Forum" to be held nearby as a protest against the neo-liberal consensus represented by the World Water Forum. While it is tempting to regard that divide as political, which it is, there is also a strong cultural element based less on power politics than on cultural values about nature, society, and "The Right to Be Different" (Boelens 1998:30).

The intellectual ancestry that I would like to claim for this book includes Aldo Leopold, his son, Luna Leopold, and though too young to qualify as an ancestor, Sandra Postel. Aldo Leopold's characterization of a Land Ethic (Leopold 1949) was applied to rivers by his hydrologist son, Luna (Leopold 1977). Sandra Postel breathed new life into the concept with her book, *Last Oasis: Facing Water Scarcity* (Postel 1997, original 1992). The common message, which is echoed in the present book, is that ethics about protecting and respecting water ecosystems are not only abstractions, but have very real practical ramifications. Working backwards, the implication is that the current unsustainable patterns of water behavior and policies could be reformed by changing the ethics that promote those behaviors. If the water crisis is caused by behaviors, which in turn are driven by ethics, then let's find a way to change those ethics!

Related Concepts

The water crisis has sparked a number of new ways of conceptualizing water use and policies, and which have important overlaps with water ethics. Three examples of such conceptual approaches are described briefly here to illustrate the range of approaches: (1) water footprint, (2) water stewardship, and (3) the soft path approach to water management.

1. Water footprint concept

Water footprinting refers to calculating the water used in a manufacturing process, a company as a whole, a city, or country. The importance of the process is partly in raising awareness, but also as a practical planning and monitoring tool. The current version (Hoekstra et al. 2011, Hoekstra 2013) provides a sophisticated analysis of water use by a company and its suppliers, broken down into sub-operations, and including data on water quality from the various sources, plus use of gray water and green water (soil moisture) for agriculture. Footprinting services are performed by consultants, or conducted in-house for larger corporations or municipalities. The goals may be to cut production costs or help the environment, or to support a marketing campaign about their responsible water use. The Water Footprint Network (http://www.waterfootprint.org) is a non-profit think tank which continues to refine the measuring methods and reporting standards. Its mission is "to promote the transition towards sustainable, fair and efficient use of fresh water resources worldwide."[3]

2. Water stewardship

The Alliance for Water Stewardship (http://www.allianceforwatersteward-ship.org) brings together environmental organizations (e.g. WWF and The Nature Conservancy), businesses, water utilities, research institutes, and others to agree on standards of what water stewardship means. The aim is to enlist the support of key water users, and particularly industries, to adopt voluntary standards which they themselves have had input in developing. The generic standard addresses four themes: water governance, water balance, water quality, and "important water areas" (usually conservation areas), with detailed scoring for each theme. Specific standards are also being applied for key water sectors by regions. For example, the European branch of AWS has developed specific standards for agriculture and industry.[4]

3. The soft path of water management

The "soft path" concept was popularized by the Pacific Institute (http://www.pacinst.org) and its director, Peter Gleick. The soft path refers to non-structural solutions to conserving water, and to relieving human-induced pressure on water ecosystems. The approach provides an important new way of thinking about rivers and rebalancing the needs of people and nature (Brooks et al. 2009). At its core, the soft path is economic, but it is revolutionary by virtue of advocating full cost accounting, including the costs and benefits to ecosystems, in making choices about water development. The soft path points out that it is far cheaper, to people and to nature, to obtain new sources of water by lowering demand for water through investments in efficiency and conservation, rather than by trying to keep up with that demand by increasing supply. New water supplies will become increasingly expensive, rendering investments in efficiency and conservation increasingly profitable.

In addition to these three examples of "brands" of quasi-water ethics, the larger environmental crisis has prompted the development of new ways to value the natural environment, including water ecosystems. The concept of *ecosystem services* which recognizes, and typically places a monetary value on, the benefits society derives from natural ecosystems, offers a way to account (literally) for nature's services. A more radical concept, which does not fit so neatly within the dominant economic paradigm is *rights of nature*. No longer the exclusive domain of philosophers specializing in environmental ethics (e. g. Nash 1989), the idea that we should recognize nature's intrinsic rights has entered the constitutions of Ecuador and Bolivia, and receives serious attention within the United Nations.[5]

The net impact of these approaches – footprint, stewardship, the soft path, and ecosystem services and rights of nature – are advancing the discourse about how to think about water and how to respond to increasing water stress and climate change. The "water footprint" concept is both economic and environmental in its goals. By reducing water use, companies or cities can save money while also helping the environment. "Stewardship" is primarily an environmental concept, though it implies a concern about social justice as well. Similarly, the goals of the "soft path" combine economic efficiency, environmental impact mitigation, and social justice. Ecosystem services is, of course, environmentally focused, while the deeper issue of "rights of nature" goes beyond environmental ethics per se to the ethics of respecting indigenous cultures who see nature as sacred. It is no coincidence that the two countries to adopt "rights of nature" provisions into their constitutions, Ecuador and Bolivia, also have majority indigenous populations.

What is new about the approach to water ethics presented in this book is not any of the details. The literature on water ethics cited above has already provided numerous examples and case studies, and there are more than enough concepts, such as the water footprint and water stewardship, or rights of nature, with which to analyze the specifics. Where the present book has something new to offer is in prioritizing ethical analysis as a crucial step in the water management process: planning, designing projects, setting policies, or negotiating conflicts. The ethics proposed here is not merely a perspective to be applied for better understanding why things are the way they are. Ethics can be used as a practical tool for changing the way things are, for identifying gaps between what we really want for our future, and the trajectory of ecocide that our policies are actually creating.

Analyzing our water ethics can help us to confront what we are really doing to water ecosystems and the people and cultures whose lives are interconnected with those ecosystems, but the purpose is not to make us feel badly for all the harm we are inflicting in the name of water development. The reason to explore our water ethics is to discover new ways of framing our problems and creative ways of addressing those challenges.

Box 1.1 Water for Nature or Economic Development?

Conserving water can relieve pressure on water ecosystems, which is an environmental benefit, but this is not necessarily the case. Household water conservation programs in my city of Santa Fe, New Mexico, for example, have been pursued as a way of providing "new" water to support the construction of more houses and businesses in this water-scarce city. Economically, the community is better off because the same amount of water is providing more net benefit, at the same cost, but the river and aquifer from which the water is taken have not benefited from the increased efficiency.

Benefiting the river through urban water conservation would require a deliberate shift in priorities away from economic values to environmental ethics. For example, the community could adopt a policy of reducing the amount of water diverted from the river by

10%. A soft path of water conservation would then be pursued with the aim of meeting the present (and perhaps future) water demand from houses and businesses plus a 10% water rebate to the river.

Economics is a tool for management which can be usefully applied to finding efficient solutions to the challenge of meeting nature's own water demands. But the questions of how saved water should be allocated, and whether the river deserves a rebate for her (his?) many years of faithful service to the community, are fundamentally ethical decisions.

What is Responsible Use of Water?

How much water is it ethical to use and for what purposes? Food produced by industrial methods of agriculture has a much higher total water footprint than food produced by small farms and marketed locally. Coal that is mined through mountaintop removal, or gold that is mined and processed with water-polluting methods, or electricity produced by hydropower dams that have severely altered water ecosystems are examples of indirect consumption of water. Whether we use water directly, as in growing food or taking a shower, or indirectly for manufacturing processes or energy production, the effects are the same. Water is being used, and to some extent, "consumed."

Water use and water consumption are not exactly the same thing. We can "use" water to take a shower, and the drainage water can be used to irrigate your garden. Your garden plants might consume about half that water, and the other half will either infiltrate into the subsurface aquifer (where it is theoretically available to be pumped out and used again) or it will evaporate to return as rain someplace else, and landing either on land (where it will add to local freshwater supplies) or on the ocean (where it is effectively lost by merging with the saltwater). Theoretically you don't consume any water when you take a shower, since all of it can be recaptured and reused. If you want to get very technical about it, water is not truly consumed by plants, either, or at least not very much. The carrot plant in you garden transforms some of the water from your shower into a carrot, plus some other roots and a leafy top. When you eat the carrot, you are also eating carrot-water, while the other roots remain in the soil, to be evaporated, and the leafy top goes into your compost, eventually to return to the garden where some will evaporate and the rest will contribute to the water content of next season's vegetables and the cycle starts all over.

Water is both finite and infinite. The stock of water does not expand, but neither does it diminish, at least in theory. We cannot really destroy water, but depending on how we use it, we can make it very difficult, and practically impossible, to reuse it for something else. This is where ethics comes into play. The way we use water should incorporate some consideration for the next person (or fish) who wants to use that water. And that next person will, hopefully, think about the other future users of that same water.

One of the big problems with water use is that, practically speaking, it's often just not possible to use water without consuming it. When water is diverted from a river to irrigate fields of tomatoes destined for market, those tomatoes will be taking some of the river to wherever that market is. For all practical purposes, that water has disappeared from the river, even though some of it may fall as rain and flow into other rivers somewhere (or the tomato will be eaten and the water content excreted into a toilet, and then a wastewater treatment plant and finally a river!). Similarly, the irrigation water that never gets to the tomato but evaporates out of the soil, or the water that gets to the tomato plant but is lost from the leaves through evapotranspiration, is not going to get back into the river from which it was diverted. This "lost" water can be said to be consumed, because, like Humpty Dumpty, it's just not practicable to recapture that water and put it back into the river.

Water is also consumed, practically speaking, when it becomes contaminated through some kind of industrial process. Water used to process gold ore, for example, can be tainted by mercury, either from the processing procedure itself or from mercury in the gold-containing ore. Water may be used directly, as part of the mining process, and become contaminated in this way, or water can be indirectly contaminated with mercury, through the leaching of mine tailings, or from mercury emitted into the atmosphere and falling into streams and lakes, where it bio-accumulates in fish, as the little fish are eaten by bigger fish. In this case, we might say that water is "consumed" without actually being used! The water still exists, but it is no longer available for anyone else to use unless it is first treated to remove the mercury.

Other forms of water consumption through contamination include nuclear power plants that use large amounts of water for cooling. The water in this case is thermally contaminated (i.e. it's warm). It is available to use again, but only if heat is not a problem. For the purpose of providing fish habitat, for example, heat is a big problem. Fish adapted to cool rivers are likely to die if the water becomes too warm.

The single biggest source of water contamination in most developing countries is human waste, an easily preventable problem which has lately attracted global attention through the Millennium Development Goals. In the industrial countries, in contrast, human waste is no longer a major concern. The biggest problems are not, surprisingly, industrial pollutants, but agricultural ones, especially nitrates from fertilizer applications and poor management of animal wastes. Water polluted by nitrogen can be reused for irrigation, but is no longer suitable for many other very important uses such as drinking. Agriculture is also the source of many other pollutants such as pesticides and good old-fashioned dirt from soil erosion. Dirt, however, is a lot easier to deal with than, say, Atrazine or Roundup, the two most popular herbicides, but more on these later in the agriculture section.

Water use and consumption should be looked at in cultural context, because ethics are derived from cultural norms; ethics are operative rules that make sense within a set of cultural assumptions. We shouldn't be too hard on ourselves not because we really shouldn't, but because if we try to be too different, we will define ourselves out of the mainstream and lose our leverage in trying to change our water ethics. In that case we would rely on the demonstration effect, showing the mainstream culture that there is a different, and presumably better, way. This is what "counter-culture" means, and when it is applied to water use it means people like my Santa Fe neighbor, Louise Pape, who very carefully minimizes her water use. Whereas most Americans use about 100 gallons a day for cooking, bathroom flushes, and bathing, Louise averages about 10. "I conserve water because I feel the planet is dying, and I don't want to be part of the problem," she said in a National Geographic blog.[6]

Americans use two to three times as much water per capita as Europeans, but perhaps even the Europeans are using too much. Africans use far less, particularly West Africans living in the Sahel. Cultural values and a whole system of culturally inspired ways of doing things are intertwined with water use decisions. What John Muir said about the nature of the universe is also true of water ethics: "When we try to pick out anything by itself, we find it hitched to everything else in the Universe" (Muir 1911:110).

Water Scarcity

The idea that water is scarce is one of those things that is hitched to lots of other things in our culture. The notion that there is only so much water to go around, and that supplies are fixed, seems so obvious that no further explanation is required. But water scarcity has taken on more urgency than, for example, food. In many parts of the world, food is just as scarce as water, and the production and distribution of food pose huge logistical and developmental challenges. Yet we don't speak of "food scarcity" as the general state of affairs. Rather, food scarcities are seen as problems to be solved. Water scarcity, on the other hand, seems very much like a problem that we actually do *not* want to solve; there are too many vested interests in keeping scarcity, like terrorism, as a background fear.

In tracing the history of the scarcity concept in water policy discourse, Schmidt (2012) identifies 1977 as the turning point for reframing water as basically scarce, rather than basically abundant. The occasion was a major UN conference on water, held in Mar del Plata, Argentina, which endorsed the then-new paradigm of "Integrated Water Resources Management" (IWRM) as a response to the challenge of water scarcity. Since then, an entire professional discipline has grown up around the idea that water scarcity is the problem and IWRM is the solution.

Critics like Schmidt (2012) and Linton (2012) have suggested that the concept of scarcity is just that – a concept. It is no more real than food scarcity is to a gluttonous child dissatisfied with his small portion of choco-late cake. It would not be heartless to label the child's demands as subjective and without real merit, nor would such an observation deny that very real food scarcity can and does exist in the world, just not at that particular table. A similar claim might be made that water scarcity is a misleading character-ization of the water supply of Phoenix, Arizona. This metropolis of 3.2 million, constructed at the confluence of three important desert rivers, whose water supply is supplemented by huge water transfers from the Colorado River, suffers only from a very subjective water scarcity. It is a water scarcity resulting from profligate water consumption averaging 173 gallons per capita per day[7] and from an influx of residents lured by local developers to make the desert city their new home.

Economists define water scarcity as the condition when demand for water exceeds the supply. When demand is low and the supply is high, there's enough for everyone. As the demand increases, e.g. from more people moving into Phoenix and installing lawn sprinklers, the buffer between demand and supply gets thinner; we are approaching scarcity. What happens next is a moral choice. Is the scarcity a result of too much demand, or not enough supply? As we ascribe causes to the increasing scarcity, we char-acterize the problem in certain ways. If we see the problem as caused pri-marily by too much demand, we might focus on the profligate behavior of the people using too much water on their lawns. This definition of the pro-blem will lead us toward solutions aimed at lowering the demand for water, perhaps through awareness campaigns, or by increasing the price of water to discourage wastage, or by imposing a tax on lawns, or incentive programs to replace the lawns with gravel, etc. But if we see the problem as basically one of not enough supply, our proposed solutions will aim at finding new sources of water that can keep up with rising demands.

In practice, supply-focused and demand-focused strategies are usually pursued in combination, but the underlying framing of the issue typically gives more weight to one side than the other. In my home city of Santa Fe, New Mexico, the local water planners don't even have a plan for decreasing demand. Instead, they have a very detailed plan, years in the making, describing how total water supplies will be augmented over the next several decades in order to meet the projected demand. Efforts to reduce demand, such as through awareness campaigns promoting water conservation, are included in the supply plan but in a minor supporting role.

Water resources planners have been schooled in supply management. Engineering textbooks refer to urban water *supply*; "water supply and sani-tation" (WS&S) has become a popular term in development circles because so many people in development countries lack access to safe drinking water. Supply is clearly important. Demand seems less so. Even economists, who specialize in connecting the two concepts, show a professional bias in finding supply-based solutions where everyone can be better off (defined as "more" and not "less"). A water utility is a "water supply utility" providing, we hope, safe and secure water. Water utility managers live in fear that they might not be able to deliver enough supply to meet the demand, though from an economic efficiency perspective, water capacity is over-built if those conditions are met. Water utilities promote water conservation not because they want people to use less water, but because they want to ensure that the supply can meet the demand.

Dryland farmers who depend on the rains, and on residual soil moisture, know all about managing the water demands of their crops to fit within the available supply. Traditional dryland farmers in Rajasthan India, for example, learned many generations ago to plant their millet and sorghum as soon as the monsoon rains started, so the crops could benefit from the wet soil for as long as possible. Adjusting the supply of water was not an option before canal irrigation was introduced. Indeed, even with canal irrigation, farmers often had insufficient water to meet even quite minimal demands. The British engineers who set the initial design standards for warabandi-based (rotational turns) canal zones designed-in water scarcity. Each farmer's turn in receiving the canal flow would be enough to irrigate no more than half his fields, thus incentivizing him to use the water frugally. Today the descendants of these farmers have grown up with more supply options; in addition to the unreliable canal, they have installed tubewells powered by electricity or diesel. The farmers have found ways to augment their water supply to meet their growing water demands. No one likes to manage the demand when there is a possibility for managing the supply instead.

While it is easy to sympathize with small farmers seeking more water to increase their production, the plight of Phoenix residents having to curtail the intensity of their lawn watering sounds more like the overweight child wanting more cake. Yet from a supply management perspective, Phoenix suffers from water scarcity. The residents would like to have bigger and greener lawns, and are willing to pay what it takes to make that happen. As they enjoy telling visitors, in this region, water flows uphill towards money.

Conclusions

The ethical basis for our decisions about nature, development, and water, is constantly evolving. We no longer condone slavery or child labor no matter how tempting the profits might be. Our ethics are already influencing our behavior. But more often than not, the ethics we manifest are subconscious, creating a wobbly, and potentially catastrophic, basis for decision-making. We can see this in hindsight easily enough. The systematic destruction of America's rivers was not implemented with malice, but with "hubris" (McCool 2012) which my dictionary defines as "exaggerated pride or self-confidence." It was the swagger of the engineer, as much as the swagger of the cowboy, that tamed the wild West, but this was not only an American phenomenon. A similar hubris among European engineers was busy taming the Rhine (Blackbourn 2006), and still exists today from the Mekong to the Nile. The 21st-Century version of engineering hubris is somewhat tempered by considerations of ecosystem services and human rights, but hubris, when backed by a few billion dollars from investors, still tends to carry the day.

There is an interesting, if tragic, disconnect between what the water profession "knows" to be true on the one hand, from science, economics, and UN resolutions about social and cultural justice, and what actually happens when rivers are dammed, polluted, or otherwise impacted. Standards of best practice only go so far in determining outcomes that are actually decided through politics, lobbying, and, too often, corruption. Those pressures are so powerful that they can easily overwhelm the best intentions of water planners. Readers of this book have probably long ago become inured to stories of bad decisions taken not for lack of knowledge but through the power of vested interests.

The promise, or at least the potential, of water ethics is that clarity about ethical principles can strengthen the resolve of the technical professionals, as well as of the citizen-stakeholders who, of course, have a very strong long-term interest in sustainable water management. Just as importantly, clarity about ethics can also weaken the resolve of vested interests lobbying for a dam or mine that violates broadly held ethical principles. So long as the ethical implications of a proposed water decision remain fuzzy and ill-defined, the proponents are protected from being held accountable by the supposed beneficiaries, the public at large, or even themselves. Careful analysis of the values that will be advanced or violated by a proposed project helps all sides become a little more honest. Clarity about the ethics will not dispel disagreements, but will help focus debate about the deeper values that the project will impact.

Notes

1 Source: Merriam Webster online dictionary 2012.
2 See Llamas (2012) and Delli Priscoli (2012) for an overview of the 2010 seminar. The full set of papers from *Water Policy*, vol. 14, suppl. 1 is available on the "Water Observatory" page of the Botin Foundation website, http://www.fundacionbotin.org/international-seminar-books_publications_water-observatory_trend-observatory.htm.
3 From the website, http://www.waterfootprint.org/?page=files/WFN-mission.
4 See the website of the European Water Stewardship, http://www.ewp.eu/activities/water-stewardship/.
5 Following the Rio+20 meetings in 2012, the United Nations launched a "Harmony with Nature" website featuring examples of national legislation aimed at protecting nature, http://harmonywithnatureun.org/.
6 See http://ngm.nationalgeographic.com/2010/04/last-drop/royte-text.
7 Source: Western Resource Advocates, http://www.westernresourceadvocates.org/azmeter/phoenixsumm.pdf.

2 Manipulating Rivers

The prevailing ethic about how we should manage rivers is in the process of a slow but profound shift from command-and-control to a more peaceful coexistence with nature. The goal of river engineering used to be the transformation of a river's natural meanders into a straight channel confined within its banks by equally uniform levees to protect against flooding. It was considered our ethical duty to tame unruly rivers and harness their waters for irrigation, transportation, flood control, and hydropower.

Today the goals of river management are more complex, because the interactions and trade-offs are better understood. Some rivers that had been straightened at enormous cost, such as the Kissimmee River in Florida, are now being re-naturalized to put those meanders back, at even greater cost (McCool 2012:35ff). Experience convinced the engineers what biologists had warned, that the ecological functions of the river depended on those meanders. But it was the economists who showed that it was worth the cost of trying to correct the mistakes, even though the restored river will never be as valuable, in terms of its ecosystem services, as it used to be. A wounded river is still far more valuable than a dead river.

Around the world, there are examples of dams being removed to allow fish passage (Lejon et al. 2009), levees being moved further from the river channel to provide "room for rivers" (de Groot and de Groot 2009), and flows being partially restored to support basic river function (Arthington 2012). There is no question that rivers are being appreciated and valued for their natural functions far more today than was the case just a few decades ago. In spite of deep controversies surrounding most major water development projects even today, the direction of the trend is unmistakable. Nature is slowly gaining greater support, and the once dominating engineering mentality is being routinely questioned and alternatives debated. Is this because of a new environmental ethic, or just a more sophisticated type of economic analysis which monetizes ecosystem services? I suggest that both trends are happening simultaneously: On one hand there is a shift in values towards recognizing some inherent rights of rivers to exist regardless of their economic value, and at the same time, our understanding of ecological processes is starting to influence how benefit-cost ratios are calculated.

Rivers are also being newly appreciated for their social and cultural values. From riverfront renewal programs to water festivals, rivers have become urban assets. The economic value of rivers underscores the political importance of good river governance. But is the purpose of river governance to create more economic value, or do democratic forms of river governance serve broader interests of society through strengthening civic participation? Water policies which acknowledge ethics of social justice and participatory governance or which respect the customary water rights of Indigenous Peoples (cultural ethics) typically reflect a mix of ethical motivations. They typically make good political, social, as well as economic sense, so what ethics are being promoted by a specific water policy?

It is not mere semantic quibbling to try to identify the ethical categories at work in a policy which has overlapping types of benefits. The reason for analyzing the precise classification is that if the policy of participatory governance, for example, is motivated exclusively by economic ethics, then it leaves open the question of whether there might also be some missed opportunities for meeting additional social or cultural goals. Perhaps a bigger investment in organizational training for a local water cooperative would be justified on the basis of social benefits even if an economic cost-benefit analysis would not justify the additional training costs.

Following the ethical trail of motivations can uncover intertwined and multidimensional logics operating behind seemingly mundane water decisions, whether we are consciously aware of the ethics or not. Why bother with such investigations? Because unless we understand what the motivations (ethics) really are, we will make decisions based on false assumptions rather than on solid information. The importance of good quantitative data is patently obvious. Is qualitative information about motivations and ethics any less important? When millions, and sometimes billions of dollars or Euros are being invested in flood control levees, isn't it important to know whether we are trying to protect property, or revitalize the river's floodplain, or both? And if both, what the relative priorities are?

In this chapter we examine the ethics operating within three broad categories of river management practices: (1) dams, which have gained a well-deserved reputation as a lightning rod for conflicting interests, (2) flood control, a topic which deserves far more environmental attention than it has received thus far, and (3) river protection policies related to environmental flow, pollution standards, and climate change adaptation. While all three of these river management categories could be considered "environmental," the ethics expressed through specific policies are a mix of economic, social, cultural, and environmental values and goals. Specifying the values as precisely as possible within any given situation sharpens governance decisions and helps improve management outcomes (Groenfeldt and Schmidt 2013). This is the rationale for putting on your ethical lenses as we consider the choices involved in how rivers are managed.

Historical Background

Human civilizations have co-evolved with bodies of water, usually rivers, and often very large rivers: the Nile, the Tigris and Euphrates, the Yangtze, the Mekong. Manipulating rivers through engineering projects is as ancient as civilization itself. Indeed, the social requirements of river engineering projects – mobilizing a labor force, a surplus of material on-hand for the construction, not to mention the planning and decision-making involved – may have been the spark (or sparks) that brought our great ancestral civilizations into being. To the oft-quoted mantra, "Water is life" might be added "Manipulating water is civilization!"[1]

The dams and canals constructed by the ancient civilizations were significant accomplishments which defined their identity and character. The ancient Egyptians built not only pyramids, but also a network of levees and canals to retain the floodwaters of the Nile on which their agriculture was totally dependent. The ancient Sumerians did the same thing, though with slightly smaller rivers to deal with, they were able to construct diversions from the Tigris and Euphrates to feed a network of canals. On the other side of the world, the ancient Incas did not have large rivers which they could bring to the land. Instead they manipulated their mountainous lands into a network of terraces and diverted small streams to irrigate the terraced fields. The ancient kingdoms of South India and Sri Lanka took a hybrid approach of constructing dams along small streams and rivers. The reservoir water irrigated their crops in the dry season, and provided insurance against uncertain monsoons.

The engineering works developed by the ancient Romans and their Chinese contemporaries took on a character that seems familiar to us today. The Dujiang irrigation project in China was one of the largest irrigation systems in the world, around 200 BC, is still functioning today, and has been recognized as a UNESCO World Heritage Site.[2] The Roman contribution to water engineering was not so much irrigation as urban water supply, with many of the aqueducts they constructed still functioning today. The Roman technology freed cities from the constraints of local topography, allowing them to pull water from vast hinterlands and grow unencumbered by water constraints. The Romans also developed ways of removing water through drainage canals, starting with draining the valleys of Rome itself, and making the city a much healthier environment in the process. The famous Roman Forum was drained by the Cloaca Maxima ("the big drain") which Lewis Mumford called, "The perfect public works project" (cited in Sura 2010). This carefully constructed, monumentally sized stone drain is still in use today. A perhaps not unrelated feature of this drain is that it was, in antiquity, presided over by a statue of the goddess Venus (Sura 2010).

This "Venus of the Drain" (Venus cloaca) attests to the blending of religion and everyday life in ancient Rome, and to the sanctity accorded to the management of water.

How did the manipulation of rivers and swamps shift from being a sacred task worthy of divine oversight to the image, still current today, of a war against nature? David Blackbourn (2006) traces one strand of what we might call the anti-nature ethic to the Prussian experience of draining swamps in the mid-18th Century. Swamps were associated with dark, malevolent, and mysterious forces, which could be transformed into tamed and productive lands through drainage projects. The massive influx of settlers into the newly drained lands of the Odenbruch (northwest of Berlin), for example, transformed and civilized the region (Blackbourn 2006:49–62). The utilitarian ethic of taming nature for the benefit of people, forged through swamp reclamation, was later applied to the much greater challenge of taming the Rhine River. Napoleon's empire established the enabling conditions for launching large-scale engineering projects without worrying about national boundaries, but the engineering vision was rooted in the belief that the river needed to be tamed for the well-being of the towns and cities along the way. The Prussian engineer, Johann Gottfried Tulla, was the man with that vision, convincing the Napoleon-appointed Magistracy of the Rhine in 1812 to make the first six cuts through the meandering river channel. Though not fully realized for another 60 years, the "rectification" (straightening) process had begun. Dozens of cuts later, the river was shortened nearly 25%, from 220 miles to 170 miles (Blackbourn 2006:97).

Meanwhile, a similar engineering ethic was developing in America where the focus started with construction of transportation canals in the early 1800s and then, with competition from railroads in the latter part of that century, and the growing colonization of the arid West, the focus of water engineering shifted to dams and reservoirs that could be used for irrigation. By the beginning of the 20th Century, the dam-building era was underway in the American West. The twin (and often competitive) national agencies, the US Bureau of Reclamation, and the US Army Corps of Engineers, operated according to a common formula of constructing dams in response to politically influential land and water speculators eager to transform the Western landscape into profits. Donald Worster's landmark book, *Rivers of Empire*, traces the major construction dam projects that collectively tamed the waters of the West (Worster 1985).

Alternatives to Water Imperialism

The prevailing ethic of transforming rivers into profits did not go unchallenged at the time, as Worster shows, but the alternative voices were overwhelmed by the forces of capitalistism coupled with both patriotic (the love of country) and professional (the romance of engineering) boosterism. Who comprised the counter-chorus? Worster recounts the story of Mary Hallock

Foote, a writer and wife of an engineer who designed dams and irrigation networks in Idaho and elsewhere in the West. Her 1892 novel, *The Chosen Valley*, depicts the tensions between the capitalists who financed the irrigation projects and the engineers (like her husband) who both envisioned and designed them, but to what end? As one of her characters asks, "Isn't there land enough, with water belonging to it, without spending millions to twist the rivers out of their courses?" (quoted in Worster 1985:145).

In addition to the intuitive romanticism that nature deserves more respect than she was being accorded, two alternative schools of thought can be discerned in the water history of the American West, which have broad implications for water ethics today. First is what I will call the natural history school, embodied by John Wesley Powell, famous for exploring the Colorado River and later serving as the director of the US Geological Survey. Powell saw the arid landscape of the West as requiring a qualitatively different approach to land and water, and to participatory democracy (deBuys 2001). Since water is the critical, defining resource, development planning should be based on science to ensure the optimal use of scarce supplies, with agriculture being limited to only the best and most easily irrigated soils. Governance should be on the basis of watershed units to facilitate wise management.

The second type of alternative development vision for the West was offered by the conservationist, John Muir, who shared Powell's love of natural science, but infused his interest in nature with a strong spiritual dimension. Known today as the founder of the Sierra Club and a driving force behind the establishment of the national park system, "Muir's sense of the sacredness of nature as the ground for environmental protection may be his most enduring legacy" (Taylor 2010:62). Taking inspiration from the New England Transcendentalists, particularly Henry David Thoreau, Muir applied these principles to specific conservation campaigns. A defining battle for Muir, and emblematic of the conservation movement, was the unsuccessful effort to save the Hetch Hetchy Valley. Originally included as part of Yosemite National Park in California, the US government withdrew the Valley's protected status to allow construction of a reservoir to supply the growing city of San Francisco. Muir argued that there were many other potential sources of water for San Francisco, but only one Hetch Hetchy Valley: "Dam Hetch Hetchy! As well dam for water-tanks the people's cathedrals and churches, for no holier temple has ever been consecrated by the heart of man" (Muir 1912:262).

Neither the aesthetics of romanticism, nor scientific logic, nor spiritual appeals could counter the juggernaut of Western water development fueled by a combination of greed and self-serving visions of manifest destiny. There seemed to be nothing that could stop the consumptive form of progress that took hold of the American West, annihilating the Native American tribes, the herds of buffalo, and the virgin forests, to create a tabula rasa on which to construct a new nation (see Limerick 1987). The legal code governing water in the Western states was written in response to facts on the ground in the wake of the California Gold Rush of 1849. Faced with tens of thousands of gold miners illegally occupying federal lands and diverting water (needed for the mining operations) from public streams, the federal government yielded authority of water to the individual states. Within two decades, the Western states had followed the lead of Colorado in legalizing existing water claims based on "prior appropriation" and "beneficial use." Those who diverted water earliest, and could show that they were using the water for a beneficial activity (e.g. mining, irrigation, or municipal drinking water) were given legal title to the water they were using, with priority of use based on the date they first started diverting the water for the stated use (Hundley 1988).

The ethos of exploitation in the western United States was reinforced by this legal framework based on prior appropriation. This set the stage for a 20th-Century construction boom in manipulating rivers unprecedented at the time, and only recently surpassed in the 21st Century by China's river engineering projects. While the rate and scale of river exploitation in the United States was unique between, say, the 1870s to the 1970s, the drive to dominate nature was broadly shared with other developed countries, particularly those in Europe, and the language about "conquest" and "domination" is easily interchangeable. Consider these quotes from German engineers around 1900 (from Blackbourn 2006:191): "To dam a river was 'to place shackles on a gift of nature and make it useful for our purposes,' 'to compel natural forces to serve the economy,' 'to force the unregulated hydrological cycle of nature into ordered channels' ... "

The evolution of water ethics in Germany and the western United States, however, also reveal important differences. The strong tradition of romanticism within German thought during the 17th and 18th Centuries provided a refuge for critical questioning of the prevailing paradigm which equated human progress with the embrace of technology. More so than their American contemporaries, Germans were concerned about what was being lost in the blind rush to manipulate rivers. Perhaps because the American landscape was so much more vast and seemingly uninhabited, the power of nature appeared more frightening and dominance even more necessary. Or perhaps the disruptive history of modern Germany during the course of two World Wars rendered the logic of technology and dominance over nature less self-evident. Certainly there was a strain of naturalism that ran through Hitler's National Socialism and which was absorbed by the mainstream political parties after the war. The American conservation movement, meanwhile, was largely ineffectual during and immediately after World War II, becoming a force in policies (though never very effectively in politics) only in the 1970s.

American environmentalists struggled to promote legislative reforms to air and water standards in the late 1960s and 1970s, with some success, but their track record in blocking dam projects for environmental reasons was mixed.

Echo Park Dam, proposed for a major tributary of the Colorado River, was defeated, but Glen Canyon Dam went ahead on the Colorado River main stem. Meanwhile in Germany, the environmental debate shifted dramatically in the early 1970s. Water development issues started to be debated in terms of "renaturing." "The question now was not whether to preserve, but how best to do it. By the 1980s the environmental imperative was built into West German public debate ... to a degree that was probably unmatched in any other large developed nation" (Blackbourn 2006:334). Today, "good ecological status" is the required standard for rivers under the EU Water Framework Directive, and programs for re-naturalizing rivers are becoming routine.

A similar trend can be discerned in the United States, but the process was slower and more superficial. In his masterful history of water development in the West, *Cadillac Desert*, Marc Reisner pleads for leaving rivers intact for posterity (Reisner 1993 [original 1986]). In a later book, *Overtapped Oasis*, Reisner (Reisner and Bates 1990) reviews the history of Western water development up to that time, and note that the bleak picture he had painted only a few years earlier in *Cadillac Desert* was already looking better. The era of new dam construction in the United States had come to a close, partly because the best locations for dams already had them, but also because the environmental costs were being more carefully assessed through economic cost-benefit analyses.

Today, it is clear that Reisner's hope for more environmental awareness about water management is being at least partly realized. Restoration projects aimed at mitigating the ecological damage from unfortunate construction projects of the past have become almost routine.[3] The conventions of water management are shifting toward more emphasis on sustainability and ecosystem services, but there is far more rhetoric than action in adopting ecological principles. The conventional paradigm that views water management as a series of physical challenges to be solved through engineering, remains in place, but cracks are starting to appear. Choices about how best to respond to the increased intensity of droughts and floods resulting from climate change will test the resilience of the nascent ecological paradigm.

The new paradigm of Ecological Water Management which has already been largely adopted in Europe appears to be slowly taking hold in the United States as well. The real unknown is how "ecological" the new paradigm will turn out to be and how fully we will be willing to put our trust in nature, particularly amidst the fears of growing water scarcity. Will a new generation of ecologically oriented engineers view themselves as allies and not enemies of natural forces?

Ecological Water Management

The ecological approach to water management builds on natural riparian principles and ecological relationships that are becoming increasingly well understood (Richter et al. 2003, Postel and Richter 2003, Brierley and Fryirs 2008, Arthington 2012, Arthington et al. 2006). Articulated at the World Water Forum in 2000 as *A Vision for Water and Nature*, the ecological water management model is predicated on sustainable ecosystems.[4] The fundamental feature of ecological water management, in contrast to "command-and-control" approaches, is a commitment to maintaining the health of the water ecosystem so that both the river and the people along the way can enjoy the benefits of its services: "we believe that the compatible integration of human and natural ecosystem needs ... should be presumed attainable until conclusively proven otherwise" (Richter et al. 2003:207). This position assumes that sustainable economies and social systems can best be supported, and indeed can only be realized, through healthy and sustainable ecosystems. Managing rivers on the basis of ecosystem principles becomes the means for implementing the "triple bottom line" of sustainability, bringing the environment, the economy, and communities into balance. River management focuses on how to work with the natural dynamics of the river to enhance both the social and environmental benefits from those services. Economics plays an important role in finding the right balance, but so too do aesthetics, recreation, and cultural values about wildlife habitat, religious ceremonies, etc.

Ecological management is distinguished from conventional command-and-control approaches on the basis of goals, process, and outcomes. The goal of ecological management reflects an ethical starting point that the needs of nature are co-equal with society's interests. In contrast, the command-and-control approach puts people first and foremost, and sees the river as a resource which can, and indeed "should," be controlled and exploited for human benefit. In this view, ecological concerns enter into the equation only at the operational level, where the deciding factor will be whether the interests of people are advanced, or not, through environmental protection (e.g. regulating pollution to protect the fishing industry).

Proponents of ecological water management believe in a "sweet spot" between the interests of people and nature. Taking measures to support ecosystem health will ultimately help the people who depend on a healthy natural ecosystem. The management decisions involved in implementing an ecological approach follow from this assumption. Rather than damming or constricting the river with levees, which would protect people and property, but harm the river, an ecological approach looks for alternative solutions to meeting both human and riparian needs. As part of this process, "soft" solutions are explored that rely on indirect measures to relax pressure on the natural systems, while providing human benefits. Instead of conventional flood control levees, for example, other alternatives would be considered: smaller levees set back further from the river, or no levees at all, and instead an insurance program to pay compensation when farms, residences, and businesses are inundated by floodwaters. The outcomes of ecological management are institutional as well as physical; insurance schemes as well as levees and diversions, along with education and disaster planning for the stakeholders.

The following section discusses ecological approaches to three key challenges of river management: (1) the question of dams, whether or not to construct them under particular conditions, and what to do with the more than 50,000 large dams already in operation worldwide; (2) flood management and ways of mitigating flood risk through eco-friendly approaches; and (3) environmental flow and options for ensuring at least a minimum of water to meet the ecological requirements for riparian health.

The Ethics of Dams

There are more than 50,000 large dams (defined as dams higher than 15m) in the world today, an astounding number considering that there were only 5,000 in 1949. Dams have caused huge disruptions to natural systems, but have also delivered huge benefits of irrigation water, electricity, flood control, and water supplies for cities and industry. Along the way, dams have sparked high profile controversy by displacing some 40 to 80 million people, obliterating indigenous communities and sometimes entire cultures, and squandering scarce development resources that might have been spent far more usefully in other ways.

Emotions about dams run strong on all sides. Dams are uniquely destructive and uniquely beneficial. The higher the dam, the more efficient it becomes in generating electricity, but the environmental impacts are magnified as well. Dams can be boons for democracy by sharing the resources of one region with an entire country through distributing the water and power produced. And dams can be monuments to despots who gratify their political egos with the grandiose projects which Western development banks agree to finance. Are the benefits of dams justified by their tremendous environmental, social, and economic costs? As economists like to say, "It depends!"

Given the rapid pace of dam construction after World War II, it is hardly surprising (but was vehemently denied at the time) that many dams were constructed at great economic, social, and environmental cost, which should never have seen the light of day. The controversies surrounding some of these dams, such as India's mega-scheme of building dams along the Narmada river in the 1990s, brought enough pressure on global financial institutions, particularly the World Bank, to start to question the whole reliance on building large dams as a central feature of economic development. With ever more examples of hugely expensive dams leaving the developing world worse off than before, something was clearly amiss, but what exactly was wrong? Was it a case of a few problem projects giving all dams a bad name, or was there something inherently flawed in dam-building as an approach?

Analyses of dam-related resettlement by social scientists, such as Elizabeth Colson, Thayer Scudder, Michael Cernea, and others, and a growing body of work by environmental historians (e.g. Worster 1985) suggested problems at every phase of dam projects. The process of assessing the problems that dams were intended to solve, such as urban flooding, or water scarcity for agriculture or lack of electrical power, and then estimating benefits, was too often based on unexamined assumptions. The very real costs to people forced to move out of the reservoir areas, or to the communities nearby who depended on the forests that would be forever altered by the construction of the dams and related roads, were conveniently excluded from the cost calculations of dams until well into the 1980s when "resettlement" started to become a recognized concern. The environmental impacts of dams, though closely linked to the human and cultural costs, took even longer to be recognized as important considerations that needed to be addressed.

The crescendo of controversy surrounding large dams led to a precipitous drop in investment in the 1990s as the financial risks from protests and armed conflict became too large to ignore by Western governments who directly or indirectly set the standards. Environmental groups allied with social justice organizations effectively blocked new dams, but as with dams themselves, the pent-up pressure from the natural flow of financial investments prompted a surprising dialogue in the form of the World Commission on Dams (WCD). Created by an exasperated World Bank, with support from borrowing countries and many of the same groups that were in deep dispute with the dam industry, the commission was charged with assessing the experience of large dam projects in developing countries (explicitly not including the already developed countries), and issuing recommendations about what to do. Should dam construction continue? Should there be restrictions? Should there be some new guidance? The Commission's recommendations would not have any legal power, but based on the legitimacy of the Commission itself (which was carefully staffed with a cross-section of critics and supporters) the recommendations would have to stand or fall on their perceived merits.

When the WCD issued its report in 2000, there were some surprising recommendations (WCD 2000). "Surprising" partly because the heterogeneous commission was able to agree at all, and even more surprising because of the recommendations themselves, calling for "free, prior, and informed consent" ahead of dam projects, and careful assessment of non-dam options. Dams were acknowledged to be singularly destructive, but also, under the right conditions, uniquely beneficial. Dams were given not a "green" light, but a "yellow" signal to proceed with caution, but nonetheless, to proceed.

The WCD report acknowledged that there are many sides to the issue of dams in general and any one dam in particular. The way to deal with these conflicting interests is through a thorough process of consultation and information sharing. Only with the free, prior and informed consent of the people who would be dispossessed from their project area (and particularly if Indigenous Peoples are involved) should the dam proceed. Regardless of the potential benefits to downstream populations, the people who were being asked to move in order for the dam to be constructed, should have the ultimate decision-making authority. Cost-benefit analysis based on utilitarian principles, in other words, should not be the deciding factor. The issue of forced evictions of Indigenous Peoples from their ancestral lands thus became re-categorized from an economic question (Do the downstream benefits justify the social and economic costs?) to an issue of human and cultural rights protected by already existing UN resolutions.

From the perspective of water ethics, the WCD report was revolutionary in shifting into a new paradigm for thinking about dams and resettlement. Instead of the utilitarian logic that served as the framework for the 45,000 large dams constructed up to that time, a new logic was now proposed. The rights of people, at least Indigenous People (the moral standing of non-indigenous residents of prospective reservoir areas remains ambiguous in the WCD guidance), take precedence over economics. Cost-benefit analysis remains a useful tool for understanding economic trade-offs in dam projects, but it should no longer be applied to deciding whether to evict indigenous communities.

The WCD report, while lacking any official authority, was highly influential among development agencies (World Bank and regional and bilateral agencies), private banks, and the engineering firms that specialize in dam building (Moore et al. 2010). Prompted in part by the decline in new dam construction, the report's findings further complicated efforts to build new dams by pointing out the sorry history of less-than-advertised benefits at far higher-than-promised costs. Yet within a few years of the report's release, investment in new dams started ticking upwards, as dam builders discovered a new way to justify them: climate change. Today we are seeing a new rush to build dams, for the claimed benefits of mitigating the vagaries of droughts and floods through more water storage capacity, and generating electricity that is basically carbon-free (Fletcher 2010). The dam industry has adapted to the new conditions sparked by social and environmental concerns, and is now justifying new dams as necessary for both social and environmental benefits. Can an ethics perspective add some clarity to this murky development?

Can Dams Be Good?

Dams are uniquely destructive to river ecosystems, but they are also uniquely "natural" as a category of engineered structure. Does the river flow decrease to a trickle in the dry season? Build a dam to capture the excess wet season flows. Is there an unmet demand for electricity? Install turbines in the dam to power a generator. The very simplicity of the concept of dams has spurred their popularity among political leaders eager to demonstrate national progress, and among downstream beneficiaries keen for more reliable supplies of water and energy. The siting of dams, often in remote mountain ranges has served to keep the victims, the local populations whose homes and lands would be inundated, at a convenient distance from where the decisions are made that affect their lives. And the rivers, of course, are not invited to offer their views!

India's Prime Minister Nehru referred to dams as "the temples of modern India." Whereas traditional temples are constructed to honor God, these modern temples are built in praise of man's ingenuity in taming nature, the original gift from God. In his 1935 dedication of the Hoover Dam, the first dam on the main stem of the Colorado River, Franklin Roosevelt, once a critic of massive infrastructure projects as a gross misuse of public funds, admitted that he had been won over. "This morning I came, I saw and I was conquered, as everyone would be who sees for the first time this great feat of mankind." Roosevelt went on to elaborate:

> We know that, as an unregulated river, the Colorado added little of value to the region this dam serves. When in flood the river was a threatening torrent. In the dry months of the year it shrank to a trickling stream. … Labor makes wealth. The use of materials makes wealth. To employ workers and materials when private employment has failed is to translate into great national possessions the energy that otherwise would be wasted. Boulder Dam is a splendid symbol of that principle. The mighty waters of the Colorado were running unused to the sea. Today we translate them into a great national possession. Today marks the official completion and dedication of Boulder Dam. This is an engineering victory of the first order—another great achievement of American resourcefulness, American skill and determination.[5]

What were the values that stirred President Roosevelt to effuse about the dam he had earlier criticized? The theme of conquest is certainly at the forefront of responses; so too are social values about creating employment in the midst of the Great Depression. Harold Ickes, Roosevelt's Secretary of the Interior declared that "no better example of understanding cooperation between man and nature can be found anywhere than this imagination-stirring project … that ranks as one of the greatest engineering undertakings in the history of the world" and demonstrates, "the prudent use of … our natural resources for the greatest good of the greatest number of our people."[6]

The combination of pride at accomplishing large-scale engineering projects, while providing economic benefits for the citizenry, fueled a construction boom which left a legacy of intensive water control structures throughout the United States, a process which was also echoed in Europe, and later – and still continuing – in the developing world. Each individual project has its supporters; otherwise they would not be built, but probably without exception, those projects have critics as well. On what basis are decisions made about the design, the siting, and the scope of dam projects? Whose voices prevail when controversies ensue?

Box 2.1 Cochiti Dam

Cochiti Dam, on the main stem of the Rio Grande 50 miles north of Albuquerque, takes its name from the Pueblo of Cochiti which sits precariously under the dam's shadow. One of nine pueblo communities still remaining along the river, some 400 years after the Spanish conquest, the members of Cochiti Tribe have borne the brunt of a different sort of foreign conquest, the damming of their ancestral river. The US Army Corps of Engineers decided in the 1950s that a dam on the Rio Grande, inside the Pueblo's territory, would be the best location for controlling floods that might otherwise threaten downstream levees (also constructed by the Corps) and flood portions of the city of Albuquerque. Never mind that those levees were unnecessarily constricting the river, and if they had been set back further into the floodplain, the city and the river would have been able to coexist. But that solution would have taken up floodplain land that the city could use for development, if the river's floodwaters could be stored instead in a reservoir sitting on the Pueblo's land.

Constructing what at the time was the largest earth-filled dam in the world, on lands belonging to an indigenous community, for the purposes of reducing the threat of floods downstream which (we now know) were actually necessary for the ecological health of the river, met with little controversy in the 1950s and 1960s when the planning was taking place. Cochiti tribal members were themselves divided over the prospect of the dam, with recent World War II veterans convincing the more conservative tribal members that the development which would surely be sparked by the dam would bring modern conveniences and opportunities. Once the tribe conceded to the request from the Army Corps, construction of the world's largest earth-filled dam got underway, night and day, just a mile from what had, for the past 700 years, been a peaceful village. Here is the memory of one of the residents, Regis Pecos:

> One of the most emotional periods in our history was watching our ancestors torn from their resting places, removed during excavation. The places of worship were dynamited, destroyed, and desecrated by the construction. The traditional homelands were destroyed. When the flood gates closed and waters filled Cochiti Lake, to see the devastation to all of the agricultural land

upon which we had walked and had learned the lessons of life from our grandfathers destroyed before our eyes was like the world was coming to an end. And all we could do was watch (Pecos 2007).

The Problems and Opportunities of Dams

Why have dams become so controversial? Part of the reason is that so many bad dams have been built through autocratic processes that rode roughshod over the will of local people and the good sense of impartial observers. That part of the reason is relatively easy to deal with conceptually. The thornier issue about dams is deciding when they do represent a good solution to the problems at hand. What constitutes a good dam? The WCD report identified five functions of dams which we can also use to describe broad categories of potential benefits: (1) irrigation, (2) hydropower, (3) water supply, (4) flood control, and (5) additional purposes such as recreation, transportation, fisheries, etc. Weighing these diverse benefits against the social, environmental and, of course, economic costs, depends not only on the economic costs of those services, but how we choose to accord value to those services.

One of the innovative contributions of the WCD report was to outline a process of "comprehensive options assessment" (WCD 2000:221) which has two parts. One is to explore options for meeting a given demand, e.g. the anticipated irrigation demand for water during the dry season. A dam is one way to store the water, but an alternative might be to store the water in natural aquifers and then pump the groundwater during the dry season. The other dimension of the options assessment is to question the need for that much water in the first place. Could farmers grow other crops that are less thirsty? Perhaps agriculture is not well suited to this particular location, and should not be supported at all. This is the logic of the "soft path" (discussed in Chapter 1) applied to dams.

In the case of Cochiti Dam (Box 2.1) the goal of flood control benefits was part of a larger flood control strategy which included a system of already constructed levees downstream, to protect the city of Albuquerque and allow urban development in the floodplain. The levees in turn were part of a "command-and-control" approach to channelize the river into an artificially narrow space. An alternative to building the dam might have been to modify the land use within the floodplain so that flood-waters could be accommodated, or a hybrid alternative of building a much smaller dam upstream along with floodplain management down-stream. Choosing among competing alternatives depends on the values given to the impacts, and the range of impacts of those alternatives. The large dam at Cochiti has allowed the development of the floodplain, which is considered a benefit to developers, but a harmful impact to environmentalists. Similarly, the lack of fish ladders in the dam results in severely negative impacts to endogenous fish populations (Cowley 2003), but is perceived as a benefit to developing fisheries within the reservoir, based on introduced species.

Box 2.2 Dams and Fish in the Lower Mekong River

Fish are a critical component of diets as well as household income along the Lower Mekong River. Freshwater fish consumption averages 80g per person per day for each of the 60 million people in the basin. The economic value of these fish is estimated at US$2.5 billion. But the Mekong River is "under construction." More than 120 tributary and mainstream projects are either operational, planned, or under construction throughout the basin. Within the Lower Mekong, 11 mainstream dams are proposed, which would reduce the production of fish in this part of the river by 60–70% (Orr 2013).

Aside from the direct impacts of the dams on river-bank agriculture, floodplain ecology, and traditional lifestyles, the indirect impacts from the lost fisheries are very substantial. Within the Lower Basin, estimates of the additional pasture land required to replace fish protein with domestic livestock ranges from 7,080 to 24,188 km². Increased food prices associated with higher costs of livestock production could impact the poor and exacerbate poverty, as would the additional stress on already scarce land and water resources. Yet the very predictions of impact on the fisheries, viewed against the near certainty that many of the proposed dams will actually be built, gives rise to the self-fulfilling prophecy that since the fisheries will be severely damaged in any case, there is little reason not to move ahead with constructing the dams (Hirsch 2010:318).

The varieties of impact

The WCD report distinguished two main categories of impacts: on the environment, and on people. Both these categories include not only the direct impacts (e.g. to the river itself, and to the people who were living in the reservoir area) but also indirect impacts whose cumulative effects can be far greater than the direct impacts. Like an iceberg, the magnitude of impact from what we see superficially, is not immediately visible. Environmental impacts include the plants, animals, and soils adjacent to the dam and reservoir, as well as the aquatic ecosystems upstream and down, and particularly the fish, and the downstream floodplain interactions. Human impacts start with the socio-economic dynamics throughout the project planning cycle, displacement of people from the reservoir and dam area, social and cultural impacts on Indigenous Peoples, inundation of archaeological resources, gender and social impacts (e.g. from the influx of dam workers over a multi-year period), health impacts from the dam itself, and the health and socio-economic and cultural impacts from the resettlement process (WCD 2000:74–93).

Social vs. cultural ethics. One of the innovations of the WCD report, and the consultation process that went into the report, was to give special treatment to indigenous communities. The report recommended that in the case of Indigenous Peoples living within a proposed reservoir area, the project should go ahead only with their "free, prior, and informed consent." In other words, if the indigenous community refused to leave their ancestral lands, they should not be evicted; rather, the dam and reservoir should be situated somewhere else. This provision does not apply, in the logic of the WCD report, to non-indigenous communities. The long-established principle of eminent domain applies in their case, whereby the state can evict local populations who stand in the way of development projects.

In making this special provision for indigenous communities, the WCD report adopts a specific cultural ethic which is distinct from a social ethic. A social ethic might argue in favor of a dam that would displace local people, if the dam would provide important benefits to society as a whole. A cultural ethic, however, recognizes the rights of indigenous cultures to exist as an inalienable right, institutionalized in the 2008 UN Declaration on the Rights of Indigenous Peoples (see Chapter 7). Since anthropological research demonstrates that removing indigenous communities from their ancestral lands can lead to the extermination of the culture (e.g. Cernea 2003, Scudder 2006), a strongly held cultural ethic logically leads to opposition to a dam that would precipitate indigenous resettlement. In the case of non-indigenous communities, their cultural identity is not so specifically tied to their lands. They are not at risk of losing their cultural identity, so if they are forcibly removed, they have the capacity to regenerate their lives in a different place. The ethics of resettling non-indigenous communities from dam-affected areas involves considerations of social, environmental, and economic justice, but not specifically cultural justice.

Even "free, informed, and prior consent" is not a guarantee that cultural justice will prevail, however. In the Cochiti Dam case described above (Box 2.1), the indigenous community did give its consent, following an intensive internal deliberation about the best course of action. Yet today, in hindsight, the community regrets that choice; indeed, "regret" cannot convey the deep sense of remorse which the community continues to feel over that decision taken 50 years ago. Allowing the dam to be built and forever altering the sacred riverscape of their ancestors, would be firmly rejected by the community today for both environmental and cultural reasons. The assumptions about what constitutes ethical water development have shifted for both the Cochiti people and for the US government as well. The federal policy of assimilating Indian tribes, i.e. obliterating their culture in favor of blending into the US melting pot, has also changed. Cultural diversity has become a desirable feature of national society, and the sustainability of native American indigenous cultures is now a stated priority of the federal government, as well as of the tribes themselves.

In the eye of the beholder. The benefit side of dams depends not only on the intrinsic merits of the dam design, or the siting of the dam, but also on the way in which these direct and indirect impacts are managed. In this complicated process, there are ethical choices at every turn, starting with the very logic of building the dam in the first place. Buying into the concept of a dam as a desirable development activity depends upon buying into the larger gestalt that supports the logic of the dam, and provides a basis for placing values on the multiple benefits and costs of the dam's impacts. The dam's benefits and costs, in other words, are only partly a result of what the dam "does" and mostly are a result of how we *perceive* what the dam does. Benefits, like beauty, are to a considerable extent, in the eyes of the beholder and depend, ultimately, on our values.

In a study of how different types of water professionals in China view dam development, researchers identified 21 biophysical, socio-economic and geopolitical impacts of dams and then asked a diverse group of stakeholders to evaluate the importance of each impact (Tullos et al. 2010). The stakeholders were recruited from an international conference on the impact of dams, held in Yunnan, China, in July 2009. They were divided into three groups: (1) engineers and public officials, (2) representatives from environmental and civil-society NGOs, and (3) academics from a mix of disciplines. Each group was asked to ascribe values to each of the 21 impacts (e.g. water quality, social capital, etc.) representing whether it is a positive or negative impact, and an indication of its magnitude (from 1 to 4). The test group of stakeholders discussed the indicators to arrive at a common understanding of the "facts" that were being assumed for purposes of the study, e.g. the number of people displaced by dams, the amount of sediment trapped by the dams, and other quantifiable information. The values each group gave to the 21 different impacts was therefore reflective of their own interpretations of the impacts, and not about the quantitative facts.

The results? As might be expected, the NGOs and the academics gave strongly negative valuations about dam impacts, while the engineers and government officials gave strongly positive valuations. Dams were seen as highly negative or highly positive, depending not on the physical impacts of the dam, but on the values accorded to those impacts. For example, all respondents agreed on the "fact" that dams inundate features of cultural importance to local people. How bad is it to lose cultural heritage? According to the engineers and officials, the dam and the reservoir constitute a new cultural feature that can be a symbol for a *new* cultural identity for the local communities. According to the NGOs and academics, the local communities have lost irreplaceable heritage. Environmental accounting follows a similar dynamic. Does the dam result in the loss of valuable riparian habitat, or in the gain of a new reservoir (lake) environment?

Along with viewing dam impacts with different eyes, the three groups in this example are also viewing the dam with different minds. Presumably the engineers had less understanding about the ecological costs of blocking a river than did the NGOs or the academics. In a critique of the WCD report, Baghel and Nüsser discuss the cultural assumptions that dam builders bring to their craft. "Both advocates and opponents of large dams form coalitions in order to strengthen their position and influence in the planning and implementation phases, and to reinforce their perspective. However, the positions of these actors are derived not only from their political and economic interests, but also from the symbolic and cultural aspects of both rivers and dams" (Baghel and Nüsser 2010:234).

If we explore the underlying assumptions that both critics and proponents bring to the debates about large dams, we will come closer to an understanding of why they hold their positions, but we will not necessarily be any closer to a practical assessment of whether a particular dam proposal is a good idea or not. It is not "we" – as outside observers of the battles over dams – who can decide, but it is very much we – as policy analysts – who can offer a perspective to the protagonists that can help them winnow out their personal preconceptions from the elusive objectivity of assessing costs and benefits.

Flood Control

Floods hold a special place in the human psyche as the archetype of nature's dominance over man, immortalized in myths from Mesopotamia to China. Even today, with modern flood control measures, floods continue to be the most frequent and damaging type of disaster, accounting for 55% of disaster-related deaths globally in the decade from 1985–96, with the remainder mostly from cyclones and earthquakes (Green et al. 2000). Casualties from flooding are likely to rise in the future with climate change and the combined pressure of increasing populations and degraded lands and riparian corridors.

It is no mystery why people choose to live in or near floodplains in spite of the dangers. The many advantages of living near water outweigh the risks most of the time. Alluvial soils tend to be good for farming, while cities enjoy access to transportation routes and abundant water. In river valleys where flooding is recurrent and predictable, as in the Nile before the Aswan Dam, or along the Mekong River to the present time, the floods themselves are welcomed for their ecological services of nourishing and refreshing the land. Societies that have evolved along floodplains incorporate floods into their cultural identity. Traditional villagers in the floodplains of Bangladesh, which constitutes the majority of the country, or along the Amazon River, view the annual floods the way Scandinavians view the annual swings of winter darkness and summer sun, as an expected and reassuring cycle that defines their relationship to the natural world and to each other.

The War against Floods

From the perspective of floods as natural events, the taming of floods through flood control measures introduces a separation between man and nature which helped to justify the role of early states. This lesson in state-craft was identified by Karl Wittfogel in his study of ancient "despotic" kingdoms which developed along rivers and utilized the organizational requirements of water control to legitimize control over their subjects (Wittfogel 1957). Ancient rulers, however, viewed their control over rivers as an alliance with the river deities, as mentioned above. The metaphor of war between people and the hostile forces of nature is a later development that required a new religion, Christianity, coupled with post-Enlightenment rational materialism. In the war against nature, engineers serve as generals. This is more than a metaphor. In the United States, the government agency charged with the task of flood control is a branch of the military, the Army Corps of Engineers. These engineers implement their responsibility through a mix of offensive and defensive measures. Offensively, the Corps leads the charge with pre-emptive attacks to weaken the capacity of rivers to flood, through dams and channel straightening ("rectification"), and defensive levees to contain the inevitable floodwaters and prevent harm to people or property.

The US Army Corps of Engineers (USACE) is run by generals, who, like generals in other branches of the army, are concerned not only with fighting battles, but in developing strategies for conducting, and winning, the larger war. The Corps traces its history to a "corps" of engineers hired by General George Washington to construct forts during the War of Independence and formally established in 1802 as the Army Corps of Engineers. After building forts in New Orleans during the War of 1812, to protect the city from the British, the Corps took on the added role of building levees to protect the city from another enemy, the Mississippi River. This was the start of river works, mostly focused on dredging and canal building for transportation, as a major part of the Corps' work during the 19th Century. The formal man-date to keep the nation safe from floods came with the Flood Control Act of 1936 which delegated river flood control to the Army Corps, while the Department of Agriculture was charged with building preventative works in upstream watersheds.

From "Control" to "Management"

If you utter the term "flood control" in a meeting with USACE technical staff, you are likely to be corrected. The preferred term is "flood risk management" whose objectives are not necessarily to do away with floods, but rather to reduce the risk of flood damage. There is a long history behind this change in terminology, but the short version is that "flood control" doesn't work. River channels can be controlled with dams, levees, dredging, and channel straightening, much as ropes and chains can control an unruly prisoner. But just as physical abuse to prisoners can produce hardened criminals who lash out at the first opportunity, rivers that are "tamed" have a way of unleashing even more ferocious floods when nature provides an opportunity.

The Oder River between Germany and Poland became a poster child of the futility of flood control with the flood of 1997, exactly 50 years after the "once-in-a-century" flood of 1947 (Blackbourn 2006:352). Exceptionally heavy rain at the beginning of July in the Czech and Polish catchment areas of the Oder River was exacerbated by deforestation which sped the runoff. The highly regulated (straightened and walled) stream systems sped the passage of water down to the main river, pushing more water into a river whose channel had been narrowed by flood control levees. Partly because of this massive network of flood control levees, when the water broke through it had catastrophic consequences. Some 1,200 towns and villages were inundated and scores of lives were lost. Greater destruction of downstream cities was inadvertently spared by the levees breaching further upstream and providing relief for the raging floodwaters. A direct result of the flood was the decision to create 1,500 acres of wetlands along the river to serve as a future flood-retention basin.

A similar lesson was learned, or at least experienced, with the 2011 floods along the Missouri River in the United States. Fueled by record snowpack in the upper watershed of the Rocky Mountains, along with near record Spring rains in the Midwestern states, the river could no longer be contained into the artificial straitjacket created by years of flood control projects. Again this was a case of heavy summer rains in the upper and middle catchment swelling a river that had been disconnected from its floodplain by levees. Faced with a choice between sacrificing farmland or downstream cities, the US Army Corps took the decision to blow up the levees and sending the floodwaters into 130,000 acres (59,000ha) of farmland.[7]

The extreme precipitation events that resulted in the Oder and the Missouri floods were reminders of what flood managers have always known, but seldom talk about: flood control is a temporary strategy awaiting the next record flood that will overwhelm the defenses. Lowering the public's expectations to that of "managing" rather than "controlling" floods provides a signal to the cities, towns, and farmers along the way that floods can and do happen. More importantly, it sets the stage for a different kind of strategy which looks for opportunities for buffering the impact of floods. Some of those buffers will be natural, like wetlands which can store extra water without being damaged (since they're already wet), and natural meanders that can slow down the water, and upland forests and farms that can retain some of the water that would otherwise rush to the already swollen streams below.

The concept of managing floods also presumes an understanding that floods have beneficial attributes as well as destructive ones, and it is worth looking for opportunities to create artificial floods to replace the lost ecological functions imposed by dams. The Manantali dam on the Senegal River, for example, drastically altered not only the downstream ecology but also the farming economy which relied on the annual floods to irrigate fields in the floodplain and provide moisture for an entire growing season. Constructed in the 1980s primarily for hydropower, efforts were made in the 1990s to adjust dam releases to provide artificial floods for downstream flood-recession agriculture, while still meeting hydropower needs. While economic analysis demonstrated a win-win opportunity, politics intervened to the detriment of agricultural interests (Scudder 2006: 311). The Glen Canyon dam on the Colorado River upstream of the Grand Canyon has experimented with periodic floods released to enhance the health of the river channel. Flushing the banks of the channel is needed for vegetation and fish habitat, and to deposit silt and sand along the way.

Decentralized water storage through wetlands or agriculture can reduce the need for dams. In Japan, one of the most important ecosystem services of paddy rice agriculture is considered to be the water retention capacity of the paddies themselves. Like filling an ice cube tray by holding the tray at an angle and letting the tap water run into the spaces, rice paddies can capture the initial rainfall from sudden downpours and provide a buffer against flooding. As the captured water infiltrates into the soil, the groundwater table is replenished, and while there is standing water in the paddies, there are opportunities for raising fish and ducks (Groenfeldt 2006a). The rice paddies are providing the same kind of ecosystem services that wetlands would otherwise offer.

Releasing artificial floods from dams to restore lost ecological functions, or using rice paddies as surrogate wetlands are examples of "environment as infrastructure" (Smith and Barchiesi 2009). By going beyond the black-and-white concepts of floods as bad and flood control as good, the door is open for a new paradigm based on a mix of structural and non-structural measures. The new paradigm of working with nature to manage floods is, of course, not entirely new. In his 1954 book, *The Flood Control Controversy*, Luna Leopold advocated a two-part strategy for working with nature in flood control (Leopold and Maddock 1954): In the upper watershed, land management aimed at trapping water with vegetation on hill slopes, plus very small dams to catch rainfall-induced rivulets, to help the soil fill its potential as a sponge. In the lower, flatter reaches of the river, a combination of planning and infrastructure are needed. Leopold cites the case of the

Miami Conservancy District in Ohio, where farmland was designated as a flood overflow area, with houses and farm structures designed to survive periodic inundation.

The Dutch have been implementing a similar strategy in their "room for the river" program. As global experts in constructing dykes and levees to keep both sea and river waters off their reclaimed lands, the Dutch historical approach was based on controlling the water. This has been a good strategy for sea water, which would destroy the agricultural potential of farmland, but the Dutch have decided that it no longer makes sense to try to control river floodwaters in the same way. Farmland flooded by rivers creates only a temporary inconvenience; once the waters recede, the land can be put back into production. Wetland areas formed by periodic flooding provide wildlife habitat, and serve to recharge groundwater aquifers. There is no real need to keep fresh water off the land, nor is there any guarantee of being successful in doing so, especially given the bigger floods anticipated with future more erratic climatic conditions. A smarter strategy is to create enough room for rivers and their floodplains so that floodwaters can be accommodated temporarily, without causing undue damage to roads, bridges, houses, and other high value infrastructure. Levees are used not to control the river, but to manage small floods within the levees while allowing larger floods to overtop the levees and flow into wetlands, or fields that can serve as temporary wetlands until the floodwaters subside (de Groot and de Groot 2009).

At an international level, and especially in Europe, the new paradigm of flood management which the Room for Rivers program reflects, has already become the new convention. The European Floods Directive[8] as well as the Associated Programme on Flood Management[9] (a joint program of the Global Water Partnership and the World Meteorological Organization) have endorsed the concept of living with floods and making room for rivers using the framework of "integrated flood management." Within the United States, there are competing views about whether to design flood management infrastructure for 100-year floods or 500-year floods, but no one, not even the Army Corps, is arguing for a return to command-and-control approaches. The Association of State Floodplain Managers (ASFPM), a professional association, has called for re-imagining floods as both inevitable, and, except for the case of severe floods, as having many welcome environmental benefits (ASFPM 2008). In urban settings where high value infrastructure has been built in or adjacent to floodplains, levees are a practical necessity, but they should not be used to encourage new development in floodplains (ASFPM 2008).

While the concept of "room for rivers" has broad acceptance, deciding exactly how much room the river should get is still controversial. The current standard of building levees to withstand a 100-year flood, used by the Army Corps of Engineers, serves as encouragement to develop floodplains which are better left in a natural state. Eventually (and usually considerably before 100 years has elapsed), a flood will exceed the 100-year mark, resulting in a bigger catastrophe than if no levees had been built at all. Levees capable of holding back a 500-year flood may sound expensive, but they do not need to be very large if they are set far enough back. The aim is not to build big levees, but rather to build smarter to allow the river to handle larger volumes of water. Under the Room for Rivers program, the Dutch plan to steadily increase the capacity of the Rhine River to hold water (without flooding) from 15,000m^3 to 16,000m^3 by 2015, and to 18,000m^3 by 2050. This is being done through buying and converting agricultural land to provide room for the project.

In the United States there is usually a lot more land available that can be converted into room for rivers, and the approach is gaining some traction in both rural and urban settings. Following disastrous floods in 1993, Iowa farmers within the Mississippi floodplain were interested in a different solution to the cycle of floods and recovery. They opted to sell their lands under a federal program to convert floodplain fields into a wildlife preserve.[10] In California's Napa River Valley, famous for vineyards but also increasingly urbanized, local residents rejected a series of proposed levee projects which the US Army Corps of Engineers designed to protect against flooding. Instead the communities endorsed the concept of a living river which would not require huge and costly levees for flood management. Existing levees have been lowered, some bridges were relocated, and 900 acres of new wetlands created so floodwaters have a place to go.[11]

Ethics in Flood Management

The new paradigm of integrated flood management, or integrated flood risk management, is characterized by the integration of structural and non-structural measures, considering the whole basin (rather than a piecemeal approach) and recognizing the ecological benefits of floods. Floods are no longer seen as something to avoid at all costs, but rather something to prepare for and manage. Instead of a false sense of security, flood managers offer a plan for minimizing, but not eliminating, damage. "Integrated Flood Management recognizes the need to manage all floods and not just those floods up to some design standard of protection. Flood plans must consider what will happen when a flood more extreme than the design standard flood occurs, and must foresee how such a flood will be managed. Plans must clearly identify areas to be sacrificed for flood storage in order to protect critical areas in an extreme flood event" (WMO 2009:15).

Box 2.3 Flood "Control" in New Mexico

With such sophisticated understandings of the limits to engineered flood control and the ecological benefits of floods, one might assume that old-style flood control projects are a thing of the past. But old-style approaches are not so easily reformed. Take the example of a levee construction project along the Rio Grande in central New Mexico. In the 1950s the Army Corps of Engineers "rectified" the meandering, braided river channel and helped local communities and the City of Albuquerque construct flood control levees. A few years later the Corps of Engineers built the massive Cochiti Dam (see discussion about dams in this chapter) for flood and sediment control, further impinging on the river's ecological health and further reducing the chance of dangerous floods. However, in the wake of Hurricane Katrina in 2004, new design standards for levees were adopted by the Federal Emergency Management Agency (FEMA). Residents along the Rio Grande learned that they would no longer be eligible for flood insurance until the levees were strengthened.

Faced with the possibility of a drop in land value resulting from outdated levees, local communities successfully appealed to the Corps of Engineers for help. In 2012 federal funds were allocated to the Corps of Engineers to improve existing levees and construct some new levees along the Rio Grande near the town of Socorro, New Mexico. The use of the funds, while approved in 2012, needs to comply (for legal and political reasons) with the federal Flood Control Act of 1948. As the title implies, the focus of the 1948 Act is to control floods, not to "manage" them, much less to worry about the health of the river ecosystem. The levee improvement project implemented in the second decade of the 21st Century will reflect the flood control paradigm of the first half the 20th Century.

Part of the economic justification of the project is to protect the existing levees (by enlarging and strengthening them) even though, from an environmental perspective, some of them should not be there in the first place. Another critical part of the economic justification for the Rio Grande Levee project is to safeguard the Bosque del Apache National Wildlife Refuge (a wetland in the river's flood-plain) from inundation by floodwaters. Protecting a riparian wetland from floods, when wetlands depend on floods for their ecological functions, can make sense within the logic of the old flood control paradigm.

When the US Army Corps of Engineers justifies flood control infra-structure on the basis of protecting levees that were built too close to the river channel, and a wetland that is located in the middle of the floodplain (see Box 2.3) then one wonders if anything is really changing. Fortunately there are many more examples of significantly new approaches to managing floods, from "room for rivers" to integrated flood and risk management. The Rio Grande Levee project is an anachronism that would not have even raised eyebrows a few decades ago. The standards really are changing. But are the ethics changing as well? Or are the new standards of flood management merely a more sophisticated expression of the old ethic of controlling nature?

My sense is that the ethics of flood management are in a state of flux, much like the state of the art of flood management itself. The lesson of "Don't mess with Mother Nature" is a significant advance over the old paradigm of conquest which ruled during most of the 20th Century. As the Rio Grande Levee project demonstrates, the old paradigm is not yet dead, but it is dying. Much as I would like to claim that the evolution of ethics can be the cutting edge of change, the recent history of evolving best practice in flood management suggests to me that progress has been made through hard-won practical experience with what works and doesn't work in managing floods. Changes in water ethics are, perhaps, evolving in a similar way, as experience is gained in the practical effects of competing principles.

Protecting Rivers

While dams and levees represent deliberate modifications of rivers to benefit society, the other side of river management involves protecting rivers from the unintended consequences of that same society. Dams hold water for later use, but what happens to the river downstream? Is there adequate flow for the river to function effectively? Are the needs of downstream water users, both human and non-human, being accommodated? The downstream impacts of dams are relatively easy to assess, however, because everyone can see that the dam is there and that it will have a major impact. The more common and far more complicated impacts come from the myriad of direct and indirect uses of the river as it flows along: diversions for agriculture, industry, and city water supplies, and the pollution streams flowing back to the river through pipes (point-source pollution) or seeping in through groundwater or surface runoff (non-point source pollution).

The ethics of diverting water from the river for a particular use fall under the category of "water use ethics." This topic, to be discussed in the next chapter, concerns the fair allocation of water across competing demands, and the responsible use of that water. The ethics of river protection, to be discussed here, is concerned with how much water to leave in the river, and how much effort to invest in ensuring the water is clean (and the definition of "clean"). These issues are difficult in the best of times, but are becoming even more challenging with the added stress of climate change. Our discussion will be broken down into the following topics: (1) environmental flow (how much water to leave in the river), (2) water quality (what kind of water do we want in our river?), and (3) climate change (what should we do when there is just not enough water to go around?).

1. Environmental flow

A fundamental feature of ecological water management, in contrast to "command-and-control" approaches, is a commitment to a living river, with at least a minimally adequate environmental flow (Postel and Richter 2003). An environmental flow is the natural water regime of a river, wetland or coastal zone which maintains the ecosystem. A minimum environmental flow is the smallest amount of water required at any given time to allow the ecosystem to function (Petts 2009). But why bother keeping the ecosystem functioning? There are two very different answers that are commonly confused. One reason is that it's the economically sensible thing to do; a living river provides valuable ecosystem services: "Environmental flows provide critical contributions to both river health and ultimately to economic development, ensuring the continued availability of the many benefits that healthy river and groundwater systems bring to society" (Dyson et al. 2003). The other reason is that it's the "right" thing to do. Rivers have intrinsic rights to exist and we have an intrinsic responsibility to respect those rights. While the "rights of rivers" ethic can also apply to dams, levees, and pollution standards, it is most naturally evoked around the issue of environmental flow. Without at least a minimum flow, the river ceases to exist, until flow is restored. A polluted river is a sick river, but a dry river is a dead river!

Since the 1990s, the concept of environmental flows has been gradually incorporated into water laws from Europe to South Africa to Australia. The South African National Water Act adopted in 1998 granted water resources the status of public goods, under state control; the national government is the custodian of the water resources and its powers are exercised as a public trust. It has the responsibility for the equitable allocation and usage of water and the transfer of water between catchments. The Act establishes a "reserve" consisting of an unallocated portion of water that is not subject to competition with other water uses. It refers to both quality and quantity of water and has two segments: the basic human need reserve and the ecological reserve. The first one refers to the amount of water for drinking, food, and personal hygiene and the second one to the amount of water required to protect the aquatic ecosystems.

In Europe, the Water Framework Directive, enacted in 2001, requires that European rivers and groundwater have "good ecological status" by 2015 (though extensions will be considered). The Directive does not require any particular flow levels, but instead defines ecological status in terms of biological communities, water quality, and channel morphology. In order to meet healthy standards, rivers need a certain flow quantity and flow regime. The details are different for each river, hence the practical wisdom in setting outcome indicators of ecological status, rather than stipulating the flow inputs (Acreman and Ferguson 2010).

Australia initiated environmental flow policies during the 1990s when new water laws were enacted both nationally and at the state level mandating water resource planning and environmental flows. The water resources plans set caps on total water abstractions, regulated the annual allocation of water, and established water markets. New institutional arrangements were developed to hold and manage environmental water allocations, including programs to buy back water entitlements from water users and return the water to the environment (Le Quesne et al. 2010:47–8).

Does it make a difference why environmental flows are protected, whether for reasons of economics or ethics? Will the outcome be the same either way? When IUCN published the landmark report, *Flow*, in 2003 the rationale for environmental flows was seen primarily in economic terms: "Rivers and other aquatic ecosystems need water and other inputs like debris and sediment to stay healthy and provide benefits to people. Environmental flows are a critical contributor to the health of these ecosystems. Depriving a river or a groundwater system of these flows not only damages the entire aquatic ecosystem, it also threatens the people and communities who depend on it" (Dyson et al. 2003:3). No appeal was made to an environmental ethic, much less to rights of nature. The concept of "intrinsic value" was invoked but as "an intrinsic value to people" (Dyson et al. 2003:3) and not intrinsic to the river itself.

Without minimizing the importance of an economic ethic for keeping rivers alive, justified on the basis of ultimate benefits to human welfare, there can be little doubt that an explicitly environmental ethic based on rights of nature would add to the aggregate prioritization of environmental flow. Indeed, a religious belief in the sanctity of rivers would enhance the total valuation even further (Groenfeldt 2008).

2. Pollution standards

Water pollution is defined as contamination, and is patently undesirable. It is variously considered to constitute an economic cost (and often an external cost not factored into production functions), a human health issue, an environmental concern, and an ethical issue. It can be serious, if the pollution interferes with intended uses, benefits, or services, or the pollution might be inconsequential, not interfering with water management or use. Pollution of water bodies is normally thought of as pollution of the water itself, but pollution from trash is also an important issue which can cause direct contamination of water, or indirect contamination by obstructing normal flows and creating stagnant pools conducive to biochemical actions and the breeding of organisms (and especially mosquitos) which give rise to the spread of disease.

Ethical issues arise with the framing of pollution safeguards. What is it that we are trying to protect, and what methods will we favor in that process? For example, if human health is our concern, but not (at least not directly) the ecological health of the water body, we might opt for treating wastewater the way it is done in my home town of Santa Fe, New Mexico.

All household gray and black water is delivered, by gravity, to a single large wastewater treatment plant located far downstream from the city and the treated effluent is then disposed into the river bed where it is further cleaned by natural biological action as it makes its way downstream. It is a sanitary solution, but it deprives the upstream reaches of the river of the wastewater which, in this semi-arid climate, is much needed for environmental flow. A concern for the overall health of the river would argue for a different approach of smaller neighborhood wastewater treatment plants along the course of the river through the city, so that the treated effluent from each plant could recharge the thirsty river as it goes along.

Perhaps the most obvious ethical question relating to water pollution is the setting of water quality standards. How clean should the water be (and who decides)? Which pollutants will be monitored, and how will risks be assessed in the many instances where scientific studies have not been completed or show uncertain impacts to people and/or other species? Under what circumstances should we invoke the precautionary principle? How should we weigh the competing costs and benefits of economics vs. human health vs. environmental impacts in the case of fracking or oil drilling or Concentrated Animal Feeding Operations (CAFOs) which are almost certain to have significant water impacts?

Most pointedly, and a question that will undoubtedly grow in importance in the near future, do people have a right to clean water bodies and aquifers? Fifty years ago, in testimony before President Kennedy's Scientific Advisory Committee, Rachel Carson urged their consideration of, "a much neglected problem, that of the right of the citizen to be secure in his own home against the intrusion of poisons applied by other persons. I speak not as a lawyer but as a biologist and as a human being, but I strongly feel that this is or ought to be one of the basic human rights" (cited in Boyd 2012:4). Since then there has been a global movement to recognize the human right to a healthy environment either in national constitutions (92 countries) or some other law or international agreement (an additional 85 countries). However, some 13 countries still lack formal recognition of this right, including the United States, Canada, Australia, China, and Japan (Boyd 2012).

Laws are an important expression of ethical norms, but do not in themselves ensure law-abiding behavior. Compliance with the laws depends on monitoring and enforcement, and these measures in turn depend on the ethics reflected in the laws being broadly shared and strongly felt. Without these enabling conditions, laws regulating water pollution will be too easily circumvented to have any practical impact. The significance of Rachel Carson's work, and in particular her 1962 book on water pollution, *Silent Spring*, was in raising public awareness and thereby shifting the ethical norms about tolerating pollution. The US Congress passed the Clean Water Act ten years later, partly as a consequence of Carson's awareness-raising. That Act then became the official representation of water ethics, establishing a new level of debate about specific situations. Questions about whether a particular chemical should be regulated and at what standard could proceed on the premise that regulation of water contaminants, and sanctions against polluters is a legitimate and necessary function.

When companies, cities, or individuals violate water quality standards, what kinds of penalties should be exacted? How much effort should go into enforcement and who should perform that function: government agencies, industry self-policing, a citizen's watershed group, or some other arrangement? Is the principle of "polluter pays" an acceptable approach? On what basis should the fines and penalties be established (e.g. full cost of clean-up or a token fine to encourage voluntary compliance)? The answers to these and other questions will depend upon the relative priorities – the ethics – attached to social justice (ensure people's health is not put at risk), economic efficiency and fairness (hold polluters accountable) and ecosystem functions (keep fish and wildlife healthy).

3. Adapting to climate change

Climate change has added a new dimension to water management. "While reducing greenhouse gas emissions is all about energy, adapting to climate change will be all about water" (Rijsberman 2008). Within the conventional water management paradigm, the response to climate change is more and bigger technical fixes. The temptation is to go "back to the future" of command-and-control approaches relying on engineered solutions: build more dams to store more water, more pipelines to cross basin boundaries, and more pumping to tap ever deeper sources of groundwater.

From the perspective of an ecosystem management paradigm, however, the new need to accommodate the bigger floods and longer droughts associated with climate change (and in some regions generally drier conditions) imparts an even greater importance on healthy water ecosystems that can literally "weather" these changes. This is precisely not the time to inflict greater damage to natural processes. Environmental voices are calling for greater water conservation efforts and smarter "conjunctive use" strategies to rely on surface water during wet years and let the groundwater build up for the dry years (Nelson et al. 2007). Along with the calls for new and greener technologies, there is also an emerging consensus among environmental groups that restoring ecological health to rivers, lakes, and groundwater is essential to provide the resilience that will be needed to weather the anticipated greater swings of longer droughts and bigger floods (Seavy et al. 2009). Our best hope as humans, according to this approach, is to rely on "Nature's own infrastructure" (Smith and Barchiesi 2009). If we can keep nature functioning, we can survive the tribulations of climate change and prevent further damage to the rivers, lakes and aquifers on which our still growing population will depend.

The dilemma of finding consensus around the best response to climate change stems from the fundamental incompatibility between the conventional and ecological water management paradigms. Building more dams on already dewatered rivers (as often proposed in the conventional paradigm) will further damage the very ecosystems that the ecological paradigm is trying to restore. Proponents of an ecological approach have science, at least ecological science, on their side. There is a clear trend within the scientific community in favor of ecological solutions which lend themselves to unanticipated synergies, rather than conventional responses which often result in unexpected collateral damage. At the same time, there are political and emotional forces pushing in the opposite direction. Faced with popular pressure from anxious constituents to "do something" about anticipated water scarcity, and added pressure from engineering firms and land developers, the strategy for addressing climate change is unsettled.

A recent report by the Washington-based National Resources Defense Council, entitled *Pipedreams* concludes that many of the water infrastructure projects being considered in the western United States will actually exasperate long-term water scarcity (Fort and Nelson 2012). Rivers that no longer reach the sea, as is already the case of the two largest rivers in the American Southwest, the Colorado and the Rio Grande, have no more water to impound with new dams and pipelines. Rather than focusing on increasing water supplies through new pipelines, or even decreasing demand through new conservation measures, the evolving water crisis needs a broader assemblage of solutions that incorporate values as well as behavior, and institutions as well as infrastructure. In the words of the Global Water System Project[12] which studies the changing dynamics of water use and availability globally, "A sustainable 'water world' must reflect social and political dynamics, aspirations, beliefs, values and their impact on our own behavior, along with physical, chemical and biological components of the global water system at a range of spatial and temporal scales" (Bogardi et al. 2011).

Conclusions

The water ethics we choose, or tacitly accept by default, establish the underlying principles for addressing the fundamental conundrum of river management, that intervening with natural rivers is harmful to rivers but necessary for people. We are going to have an impact, regardless of our ethics, but what kinds of impacts will they be? What are the alternatives? How can we, and indeed, how should we, sift through the options to arrive at a policy choice?

There are two basic types of inputs needed for sound decisions about river management alternatives. The first type of input is objective data about water supply resources, projected demands, and alternative scenarios. For example, if we construct a dam at this location, we can predict the impacts on fish populations. The second type of input needed for decision-making is subjective: What priority do we place on one alternative over another? How important are fish vs. electricity? Are the fish so important that we should look for another source of power other than the hydroelectric dam? Is resettlement of the communities within the proposed reservoir area simply an economic issue, or are there moral issues of cultural rights or social justice. Are those issues irreconcilable with the dam, or can we see the possibility of a negotiated outcome acceptable to all parties and to our own standards of fairness?

We have a multitude of tools to help us identify alternatives and assess the trade-offs. Ecological science and hydrology can define the conditions that we can expect from a particular flow regime and water quality standards. Engineering studies can show how particular designs for dams and levees will affect the riparian dynamics. Economic analysis can reveal how the material costs and benefits, when combined with social and cultural analysis, can provide a solid picture of the likely impacts of alternative water management strategies.

But who can advise us about prioritizing the alternatives? Who can, or should, decide whether fish populations are more or less important than hydropower production, or whether local communities should be forcibly evicted from the proposed reservoir area? On what basis should these decisions be made? The conventional answer in water development has been economic analysis based on comparing costs and benefits. The concept of ecosystem services, and social and cultural capital has helped refine and improve economic analysis by reducing all the values, whether social, cultural, or environmental, to economic values. If the fish have a higher economic value than electricity, then don't build the dam, or else construct a very effective fish ladder, not to protect the fish per se, but to protect the value of the fish. The main problem with economic valuations, however, is that non-economic values cannot be adequately captured in monetary terms. This is the problem of incommensurability; money cannot replace the loss of your ancestral homelands, as the community of Cochiti learned after Cochiti Dam was constructed (see above). Analyzing the ethics does not supplant the need for good economic analysis, but neither does economic analysis supplant the need for ethics analysis. Ethics is all about asking "why?" in the decision-making process. Economics often assumes an answer (for profit!) but is not designed to explore the question.

The reason for analyzing ethics by sub-category (e.g. economic, environmental, social, and cultural ethics) is that new, interesting, and practical answers will emerge. Why should we restore meanders to the Kissimmee River in Florida, that was straightened, at great cost, a few decades ago? The initial answer was economic and environmental (the ecosystem services of the meandering river were not seriously considered, but became obvious as the river's health declined), but social and cultural ethics also come into view as the issue is studied further. A rural way of life, with an emphasis on fishing and hunting, is being restored along with the river (McCool 2012:40–2).

While ethics analysis offers a way of understanding the nuanced motivations behind water policies, ethics can also serve as guideposts to inform
policies. This is the distinction between descriptive ethics (objectively
describing the ethics that exist) and prescriptive ethics (subjectively proposing what the ethics ought to be). The two roles become easily mixed, since
an uncovering of the tacit values operating in, say, a levee construction project will almost certainly expose gaps between what the project is actually
doing (e.g. disconnecting ecologically valuable wetlands from the river) vs.
the stated goals of the project (e.g. safeguarding the city from flood devastation). Water ethicists can take a cue from the role of investigative journalists,
who uncover twisted motives, but are expected to produce an objective
report. Simply by exposing ethical inconsistencies (e.g. between economic
and environmental values), the water ethicist can provide a valuable service,
without sounding overtly moralistic. Strategies for influencing the prevailing
ethical norms are discussed in Chapter 8.

In the next three chapters we turn our attention to the use of water as an
ethical issue. Given that water is scarce and has opportunity costs, using
water for one purpose precludes using that same water for another purpose,
at least at the same time. While this may seem obvious, it serves as the basis
for viewing water use from an ethical perspective. Using water to grow
thirsty crops in a desert, or conversely, taking well-watered lands out of
agriculture in favor of building shopping malls, are counter-intuitive examples of ethics at work. More than a tool for criticizing bad decisions, however, ethics can be applied to the constructive task of guiding current and
future decisions. We begin the discussion by considering agricultural water
use in Chapter 3. Since the majority of freshwater use in the world goes to
the agricultural sector, there would seem to be a particularly strong rationale
for examining the values which the agricultural sector is serving. Chapter 4 is
devoted to the water supply sector (drinking water and sanitation) which has
received unprecedented attention thanks to its emphasis in the Millennium
Development Goals. Chapter 5 discusses the ethics of water use in industry
where pollution is often unavoidable ... but how much and under what
conditions?

Notes

1 See Scarborough 2003 for a discussion of the role of water engineering in ancient
  civilizations.
2 For details of the history of the Dujiang irrigation system, see the UNESCO
  World Heritage website at http://whc.unesco.org/en/list/1001/.
3 For example, the US Army Corps of Engineers is partnering with The Nature
  Conservancy to write new guidelines for managing dams in support of environmental flows as well as power generation and flood control. See http://www.
  nature.org/initiatives/freshwater/partnership for details.
4 The vision is for "a world in which environmental, social and economic security
  are guaranteed by fundamental changes in human attitudes and behaviour

towards freshwater and related ecosystems." The full text of the *Vision for Water and Nature* is available at http://www.rivernet.org/general/docs/Vision WaterNature.pdf.

5 Taken from the transcript of Roosevelt's Dedication speech at Hoover Dam, September 20, 1935, http://xroads.virginia.edu/~ma98/haven/hoover/fdr.html.

6 Transcribed from the audio, http://www.history.com/topics/hoover-dam/speeches# secretary-of-the-interior-ickes-dedicates-hoover-dam.

7 For details, see Wikipedia: http://en.wikipedia.org/wiki/2011_Missouri_River_floods.

8 For details about the EU Floods Directive, see the website of the European Commission, http://ec.europa.eu/environment/water/flood_risk/index.htm.

9 See the website for the Associated Programme on Flood Management, http://www.apfm.info.

10 Source: http://www.inhf.org/pdfs/protect/11_INHF_winter_mag_pp1-16_1-7-11_final_4-6.pdf

11 Source: Napa County website, http://www.countyofnapa.org/Pages/Department Content.aspx?id=4294971816.

12 See http://www.gwsp.org.

3 Water for Agriculture: The Ethics of Irrigation

The principle of Integrated Water Resources Management (IWRM), which has become a central tenet of global water discourse, is based on the intuitive notion that water use in one part of a common water basin will affect the water options in other parts of that basin (GWP 2000). When natural water basins are connected through trans-basin tunnels or pipelines, the effective basin is correspondingly enlarged. If we consider the exchange of "virtual water" in the form of agricultural commodities, or cars or computer chips, the freshwater resources of the entire planet are interconnected. Land and water grabs, the purchase of vast tracks of agricultural lands along with rights to use the associated water, are a particularly dramatic example of connecting water basins in one country with hungry consumers in another country (Mehta et al. 2012).

Against this backdrop of the interconnected world of water, this chapter considers the biggest user of the world's water: agriculture. More than two-thirds of the fresh water that is taken out of nature for human use, is used in agriculture. All the water used by cities, factories, mines, and rural communities comprise the other one-third of global water use.[1] Given the popular and professional perception that the world is in a water crisis, with dire predictions of ever-increasing stress from climate change along with population increase and (we hope) continued economic development, there is a lot of interest in the two-thirds of water that agriculture is using. Cities regard agricultural water as the logical source for expanding urban water supply systems (Molle and Berkoff 2009), while agricultural researchers focus on increasing irrigation productivity (Giordano et al. 2006).

The response to low economic returns from agricultural water reflects value assumptions (ethics) about how that water might be used "better" where the concept of better becomes an ethical touchstone. What do we want agriculture, and more specifically, agricultural water, to produce? More crop per drop, more money per drop, or more value in overall human well-being, or perhaps the well-being of nature?

In this chapter we will discuss a range of benefits that we could ask from agriculture, corresponding to the four categories of ethics outlined in Chapter 1: economic, environmental, social, and cultural, and spilling into additional benefit categories as well (e.g. nutritional, psychological, aesthetic, and spiritual). The potential benefits from agricultural water are not limited to the agricultural sector, since the water could be transferred to other sectors (e.g. those thirsty cities or energy development), or back to nature, where there is a growing water deficit.

Thinking about Agriculture

We all depend on agriculture for the food that we eat, and agriculture depends on water. Every plant needs to have water somehow, either from the rain or snow falling on the soil, or from irrigation canals or sprinklers or drip systems. The proportion of the world's agriculture that depends on irrigation water to meet some or all of its water needs has increased steadily during the past many decades, as new canals, dams, and pumps come on line. According to the Comprehensive Assessment of Water Management in Agriculture (Molden 2007), only 18% of the world's agricultural lands are equipped for irrigation, but this area provides 45% of total agricultural production. Irrigated agriculture, in other words, produces nearly half the world's food, a proportion that is certain to increase with new irrigation investments.

It does not take much ethical deliberation to conclude that it makes sense to use water to grow food, since it is so obvious that everyone needs food. But that's part of the dilemma. Agricultural interests, not just farmers, but the agribusinesses that dominate the food sector, have a vested interest in hiding behind the obvious need for food, to protect the status quo. Irrigated agriculture already accounts for 70% of global freshwater use. Do we "need" all that water to grow our food? Of course there is merit to the idea that water to ensure food security has to be a priority, but this is where some lateral thinking, soft-path approaches are needed.

If food security is the goal, what are some alternative strategies for meeting that goal, and what are the ethical assumptions underlying the competing strategies? Are food shortages best averted through centralized mega-scale agribusiness operations and global trade networks, or localized, agriculturally diverse small-scale farming systems, or some combination? What are the social, cultural, economic, and environmental side-effects of these competing strategies? And what are the implications for water quantity and quality impacts? Is one strategy clearly superior in terms of water productivity? Is this the criterion we should rely on in setting agricultural policies?

If we look at water as a fundamental input for agriculture, we can think in terms of "investing" water into the agricultural sector. Since we are investing 70 out of every 100 units of our scarce water into agriculture, we want to be sure that we are getting some good returns on our investments. What are those returns? What benefits are we receiving from the agriculture that is absorbing so much of our water? What are the underlying ethics that motivate the agriculture that uses that water? The standard American answer is usually "cheap and abundant food." This concept of agriculture as a type of industrial process that converts inputs of water, nutrients, seeds, and soils into a box of cereal or a hamburger is a distinctly Western, and even more distinctly, American notion. For most other countries, whether developing or fully industrialized, the process of farming and the range of side benefits in addition to food production, take on almost as much importance as the food itself. The water invested in agriculture is seen as not only an investment in food production, but an investment in rural employment generation, wildlife habitat, landscape aesthetics, cultural heritage, and eco-tourism, to name a few.

Taking a broader view of farming that encompasses rural landscapes and local cultures can lead to new possibilities about the uses of agricultural water. In this big-picture view of agriculture, the water which makes food production possible also makes all the other benefits possible. In Japan, for example, rice farmers are cultivating not only rice, but also fish that live in the paddies, and ducks that eat the fish. The socio-economic benefits of this diverse agricultural strategy range from employment to rural tourism to food security. The cultural benefits include a stronger sense of local identity and the environmental benefits include wildlife habitat and groundwater recharge (Groenfeldt 2006a).

What Kind of Agriculture?

What kind of agriculture do we, as a society, want to support with precious allocations of water. What kind of agriculture is worth 70% of the world's water? What are the benefits, and what are the opportunity costs, of the agriculture approach that we, as a global society, have inadvertently chosen? If we could go back in time and choose the kind of agriculture that would provide the best overall package of benefits, what would that agriculture look like?

These questions can relate to your home vegetable garden, to the farms near your town or city, or to the agricultural sector of your state or province, your country, or the entire globalized food system. What relationship do we wish to have with the food that we eat, and perhaps also grow? We cannot not have some kind of relationship with food; eating, along with drinking water, are non-optional behaviors. We can choose the path of least resistance and let the larger society determine what we eat and how we think about our food, or we can be very deliberate about choosing what we eat, where it came from, how it was grown, and how it has been handled between its harvest and our plate.

There is a renewed interest in food, and indirectly in agriculture, as a result of increased environmental, social, and cultural awareness. In North America and Europe, labels of organic and fair trade have become de rigueur on our coffee, while fresh produce from the local farmers' market is the preference for summer meals. For urban dwelling professionals, the incentive is about taste and nutrition, as well as social solidarity, environmental stewardship, and cultural statements (Pollan 2008). But for farmers, who are also food purchasers for whatever they don't grow themselves, the choices are very personal. Via Campesina has emerged as a collective voice for small farmers around the world to assert their rights of food and seed sovereignty.[2] The Slow Food movement fills in the spaces between, with both food producers and consumers joining to support an agricultural system that is more meaningfully integrated into daily life.[3]

Decisions about agriculture may seem to be about lifestyle choices and values, but, with 70% of water used for agriculture, those decisions are also about water. How do we want "our" water to be used within the agriculture sector? What values, and whose values, should be reflected in those choices? In Western capitalist societies, economics is the usual way of answering the question of competing values in water allocation: Whichever agricultural strategy can provide the highest net benefits is where we should invest our water. The analytical tool most commonly used is "cost-benefit" analysis, which, as the name suggests, adds up the costs and subtracts these from the benefits. Which costs and benefits to include in the analysis is a process that entails a great many value assumptions (Soderbaum 2008). In its classical form as promoted by my erstwhile employer, the World Bank, economic analysis was applied "to estimate the income-generating potential of proposed projects" (Gittinger 1982:xii). As a general rule, the more classical analysis stayed very close to measuring the costs of production inputs (fertilizer, labor, land rent, etc.) and subtracting these from the market price of the product.

With the popularity of "sustainable agriculture" in the 1980s and 1990s, the application of economic analysis also evolved. By taking into consideration the environmental, and sometimes social, impacts off-farm (e.g. indirect costs of water pollution from fertilizer and pesticide runoff, or benefits of employment opportunities in depressed regions) the costs and benefits of sustainable agriculture were described more holistically (National Research Council 1989:195–241). Additional value categories such as landscape values or farmer health impacts could also be incorporated to the extent that their benefits or costs could be quantified in monetary terms. These new social and environmental concerns were incorporated into the concepts of "ecosystem services" (Daily 1997) and "multifunctional agriculture" (OECD 2001, and see discussion below).

From an environmental perspective, the ecosystem services of small-scale farms using natural approaches to manage pests and soil fertility are certainly preferable to the environmental impacts of high-input industrial farming methods. Aside from corporate lobbyists for agribusiness companies, few would argue that there is anything wrong with small-scale farming. The controversy among serious policy-makers is whether the little farms with friendly animals comprise a practical alternative to large-scale industrial agriculture. We know that "Big Agriculture" really can and does feed the world. We do not know if small-scale eco-friendly agriculture could do the same. But we also know that there are huge environmental costs to industrial agriculture which cannot continue indefinitely. Is it wise, or ethical, to invest our scarce water in an agricultural system which is deemed by its own scientists as unsustainable? Agriculture is at a crossroads (see Box 3.1) and there is an important opportunity to reconsider the ethical principles underlying the sector.

Box 3.1 Agriculture at a Crossroads

"Agriculture at a Crossroads" is the title of a major report issued in 2009 by a who's who of international agriculture and development interests. The "International Assessment of Agricultural Knowledge, Science and Technology for Development" (IAASTD) was sponsored by seven UN-affiliated organizations: the Food and Agriculture Organization (FAO), the Global Environment Facility (GEF), United Nations Development Programme (UNDP), United Nations Environment Programme (UNEP), United Nations Educational, Scientific and Cultural Organization (UNESCO), the World Bank, and World Health Organization (WHO). The purpose of involving some 800 participants over a period of four years was to assess the role of agricultural knowledge, science, and technology "in reducing hunger and poverty, improving rural livelihoods and facilitating environmentally, socially and economically sustainable development" (IAASTD 2009:vi). Following are some excerpts:

> The general model [of Agricultural Knowledge, Science and Technology, AKST] has been to continuously innovate, reduce farm gate prices and externalize costs. This model drove the phenomenal achievements of AKST in industrial countries after World War II and the spread of the Green Revolution beginning in the 1960s. But, given the new challenges we confront today, there is increasing recognition within formal S&T organizations that the current AKST model requires revision. Business as usual is no longer an option (p.3).

> Despite increasing polarization of the debate on new technologies, especially biotechnology and transgenics, and years of well-published knowledge on differential access to technologies and appropriate institutional arrangements, formal AKST has yet to address the question of democratic technology choice. AKST as currently organized in public and private sector does little to interact with academic initiatives in basic biological, ecological and social sciences to design rules, norms and legal systems for market-oriented innovation and demand-led technology generation, access and use

appropriate for meeting development and sustainability goals (p.25).

Currently AKST actors and organizations are not sufficiently able to deal with the challenges ahead because of the focus on too narrow a set of output goals. The current knowledge infrastructure, which is oriented toward these goals, historically has largely excluded ecological, environmental, local and traditional knowledges and the social sciences (p.25).

The Ethics of Irrigation Development

All agriculture depends on water in some form, whether as precipitation from the sky or human-directed delivery of water to crops, i.e. irrigation. Even this seemingly clear distinction has exceptions, as in the case of flood recession farming, which involves the deliberate planting of crops in a river's floodplain, moistened naturally by the receding river. An irrigation "system" refers to the infrastructure – a well, canal, a sprinkler, etc. – which is used to control the water, plus the human management system which operates the infrastructure. The choice of technology, the way it is applied to the particular setting, and the management arrangements by which the system is operated and maintained, reflect the ethical principles of the people involved in its design and management.

The co-evolution of ethics and irrigation systems, and the agricultural systems supported by that irrigation, is more readily visible in historical hindsight than in contemporary context. For our purposes in tracing the ethics underlying irrigated agriculture, history can be divided into two periods: before the Green Revolution, and after. Our focus will be on the latter period because, as the term "revolution" implies, there were some very big changes that took place in how agriculture, and agricultural water management, were perceived.

The first murmurings of the Green Revolution in the 1960s had to do with the reframing of agriculture from a predominantly subsistence activity to an engine for economic growth that would drive the underdeveloped world out of poverty and the recurring danger of famine. The technologies which the Green Revolution popularized – high yielding seeds, fertilizers, pesticides, and irrigation – followed in the wake of a re-imagining of what agriculture is at two levels, the farm and the national economy. At the farm level, the farmer was told that he is operating a business. In the words of Arthur Mosher in his book, *Getting Agriculture Moving* (Mosher 1966:51), farming "is a business because each farmer's purpose is economic: to produce products either for sale or for use by his family." He goes on to acknowledge that farming is also a way of life, but ultimately it is about economics. "Even in a largely subsistence agriculture the better farmers think like other businessmen and *learning to think in this way is a part of development"* (Mosher 1966:52, emphasis added).

At the level of the national economy, agriculture was given the primary responsibility for serving as the engine of growth, and specifically industrial growth. Economic theories developed in the 1950s by Arthur Lewis and elaborated by John Fei and Gustav Ranis, among others, viewed productivity increases in agriculture as essential for creating the surplus labor needed for emerging industries (Todaro and Smith 2003:116–27). Agricultural development was the answer to economic growth, but what was the key ingredient to agricultural development? More than any other single factor, it was irrigation (Mellor 1966:272).

Investments in irrigation canals, dams, pumps, and pipelines were justified not merely on the humanitarian grounds of alleviating poverty and hunger, but on economic grounds of stimulating broad-based industrial growth. The most ethical use of water, within this paradigm, was in modern, efficient agricultural production to make this economic growth cycle possible. Escobar (1995:158) quotes Norman Borlaug, the Nobel Peace Prize laureate and father of the Green Revolution as follows: "in provoking rapid economic and social changes ... [the Green Revolution] was generating enthusiasm and new hope for a better life ... displacing an attitude of despair and apathy that permeated the entire social fabric of these countries only a few years ago."

The notion that traditional cultures suffer from attitudes of fatalism which need to be transformed into entrepreneurism was central to the discourse of agricultural modernization. The idea that traditional farmers were actively and continuously engaged in experimenting with new seeds and cultivation practices emerged only gradually while the Green Revolution was blossoming (e.g. Richards 1987). The most virulent critics, such as Vandana Shiva's *Violence of the Green Revolution* (Shiva 1991) could be readily labeled as alarmist, while detailed analyses of how traditional agriculture is actually conducted took time to develop into an alternative paradigm which could challenge conventional agricultural development strategies (see Netting 1993 and Scott 1998).

Understandings about the role of farmers and local communities in modern irrigation development also evolved very slowly to challenge the earlier confidence that traditional farmers had nothing to lose and everything to gain from irrigation schemes. This more nuanced view recognized the value of traditional technologies and social systems for both economic production as well as for community capacity-building and empowerment (e.g. Coward 1980, IIMI 1987, and Diemer and Slabbers 1992). Irrigation systems were seen as integral components of the local society and culture, comprising complex "socio-technical" systems (Uphoff 1986), which developers need to understand before suggesting improvements.

Building on the work of Edmund Leach (1961) and other anthropologists, archaeologists, and historians (notably Wittfogel 1957), Hunt and Hunt (1976) developed a theoretical framework for the interactions between the physical features and dynamics of irrigation systems and the socio-cultural systems that construct and manage them. Along with other contemporary anthropologists working directly or indirectly on irrigation systems in cultural context (e.g. Clifford Geertz, William Kelly, and William Mitchell), the socio-cultural analysis of irrigation systems became established as a recognized theme within both anthropology and among irrigation research institutes and development agencies. Practical guidance for enhancing the effectiveness of irrigation development during the 1980s and 1990s emphasized the importance of participatory planning, design, and management to ensure that the physical system (canals, pipes, etc.) made sense socially, and could be managed sustainably by local farmers and/or agency staff (IIMI 1987, Chambers et al. 1989).

Social scientists working on irrigation development during the 1990s could feel hopeful that the forces of international development finance, notably the World Bank, were committed to the notion of designing irrigation systems to accommodate the given socio-cultural circumstances. While the dominant conception of irrigation within the World Bank and other development agencies continued to focus on the economic benefits, the potential social benefits of participatory irrigation management were also acknowledged.[4]

Whether the World Bank regarded participation as a means to more effective (and less costly) management of very expensive irrigation infrastructure, or whether participation was a social end in itself, was a moot question when both goals could be achieved simultaneously.

Under the participatory approach to irrigation management (discussed in more detail in Chapter 6), farmers were to be given training so they could manage the new irrigation systems themselves, with minimal technical and financial backstopping from government agencies. Moreover, those new irrigation systems would be designed to fit the social facts on the ground, taking into account clan or village boundaries. In his preface to the book, *Putting People First*, World Bank senior social advisor, Michael Cernea, noted that "'Putting People First' is more than an ideological appeal. It means making social organization the explicit concern of development policies and programs and constructing development projects around the mode of production, cultural patterns, needs, and potential of the populations in the project area" (Cernea 1991:xiv).

The ethical principles underlying irrigation projects at the tail end of the Green Revolution, during the 1980s and 1990s, revolved around the dual goals of economic efficiency and social equity (but not environmental sustainability, which was slow to gain traction within the production-oriented irrigation community). The concept of social equity was generally interpreted to include the meaningful participation of stakeholders, and particularly women, in both the design and management of new irrigation infrastructure. Economic efficiency was interpreted as greater agricultural productivity per unit of water. Cultural rights or sovereignty was implied by the principle of building upon existing social institutions as well as pre-existing physical infrastructure (Groenfeldt 1991), but in practice, cultural concerns were rarely considered explicitly.

The ethics of community-oriented equity gave way to an ethics of individualistic "opportunity" following the World Development Report on Poverty in 2000, and the World Bank's reassessment of poverty as having three dimensions in addition to income: opportunity, empowerment, and security (World Bank 2000). The practical interpretation of this new definition, however, has shifted the emphasis from providing technologies intended to fit into the existing social structure, to more intrusive interventions legitimized as providing new opportunities and/or empowerment, typically involving entrepreneurship and the private sector. The ethics of water development become more complex when the aim is explicitly to transform traditional farmers into entrepreneurs with an emphasis on the commercial potential of irrigated agriculture.

The entry of investment firms into rural development programs, and new alliances of business interests and charitable foundations (e.g. the Rockefeller Foundation) has also introduced a profit-making goal to development assistance. Indeed, the profit motive is described not only as a means to an end (raising investment capital to promote rural economic development) but also as a cultural end in itself, to inculcate an ethic of capitalism: "Social enterprise and impact investing, by definition, proactively intend to create positive impact as well as generate profits. ... [S]ocial enterprise development offers an attractive way to accelerate the creation of shared value. Inclusive and sustainable growth promotes economic and social development and subsequently creates a more enabling business environment in which both investors and corporations may prosper" (UN Global Compact and Rockefeller Foundation 2012:4–6). Culture is viewed not as a collective good to be supported by agricultural strategies that fit into the cultural setting. Instead, local cultural systems are seen as necessary, but not necessarily desirable, contexts for generating economic growth. What is clearly desirable, and where there is a recognized ethic of how things should be, is economic growth and cultural attitudes that encourage growth.[5]

The Pesky Notion of Sustainability

Conventional agriculture went into a defensive mode when the concept of "sustainable agriculture" entered the development agenda during the 1990s. The idea of sustainability was popularized by the 1987 "Brundtland Report," *Our Common Future* (World Commission on Environment and Development 1987), as "development which meets the needs of current generations without compromising the ability of future generations to meet their own needs." When applied to agriculture, this concept raises the question of whether the agricultural practices of today can be sustained into the indefinite future. The answers to this question are highly controversial, with the basic dividing line between the forces of conventional agriculture on one hand (from Monsanto to the agricultural universities) and an informal alliance of economic, environmental, and social critics on the other, who are convinced there are better ways to put food on our tables. While the specifics of chemical inputs, soil erosion, water pollution, and even GMOs can be argued from diverse perspectives (e.g. chemical residues are bad but will dissipate, etc.), other issues, such as groundwater mining offer greater scope for alliances. Who would defend the wisdom of depleting the Ogallala Aquifer that serves as the basis for agriculture on the Great Plains? Yet nearly all the farmers with land overlying that aquifer are contributing to its early demise. At current levels of pumping, the aquifer is forecast to be effectively dry in some spots as early as 2030.[6]

Current levels of pumping will not be maintained, of course, because as the aquifer gets closer to depletion, farmers will be forced by economics, if not ethics, to use less; it will become prohibitively expensive to pump the last drops. Hopefully that specter of the near-term future will motivate farmers (and the towns and industries that also pump from the aquifer) to adopt a different approach while there is still some water left. "In the long term, it is impossible to extract more water from an aquifer than is recharged to it by seepage from precipitation or surface water bodies. Sooner or later, the pumping rate will automatically have to adjust to the availability of water. Clearly, it is wiser to strike this balance when groundwater levels are high than at low levels, to provide leeway for temporal overdraft and, therefore, supply safety, and also because the cost of pumping increases as water levels decline" (Sophocleous 2005:362).

Can agriculture that depends on water pumped up from the soon-to-be-dry Ogallala aquifer be considered sustainable? More to the point, on what ethical principles can the use of water from the Ogallala aquifer be justified? Elinor Ostrom, who won the Nobel Prize in economics in 2009, showed in her PhD research that California farmers could, under the right conditions, manage their groundwater sustainably (Ostrom 1965). Great Plains farmers can do the same thing, but they need the help of "rules of the game" which they can then follow and enforce themselves. In the case of Ogallala farmers, it is the existing rules, the water laws already in place, which are a major part of the problem. The law gives individual farmers a right to pump, effectively encouraging them to place their individual welfare above the group welfare.

Ogallala farmers have two big obstacles standing in the way of sustainable groundwater management. First is the natural challenge of being dependent on a common resource and needing a clear set of rules that they can all follow, the second is having to contend with existing laws derived from outmoded, unsustainable ethical principles. By treating groundwater as an individual property right, rather than a common property right, the legal cards are stacked against local sustainable management solutions.

Agricultural policies impact water ecosystems in many other ways besides encouraging the mining of groundwater. Agriculture as a sector is the biggest polluter of both surface and groundwater in the United States, mostly from nitrates leaching from fertilizer and animal wastes. That pollution is effectively unregulated because of the political manipulations of agricultural lobbyists who have been successful in blocking federal regulations. Thus, while there is a federal environmental standard establishing safe levels of nitrates in drinking water, the federal government does not regulate "nonpoint" sources of nitrate pollution coming from agricultural operations (Williams 2002). This loophole in the federal Clean Water Act, is effectively a subsidy to agriculture, and more specifically to industrial agriculture, since nitrate runoff is far less an issue in small-scale farming. Allowing water users to pollute without payment for clean-up is a common type of water "use" subsidy which is also found in coal mining, discussed in Chapter 5.

When water is viewed as private property and a factor of agricultural production, the "meaning" of that water lacks an environmental, social, and cultural context (see Strang 2004). As disembodied water, it becomes an abstraction and we forget where the water came from (a natural ecosystem somewhere) or where it's going (back to nature, eventually). Though economics offers the concept of "opportunity cost" for water, when it has become a mere abstraction (e.g. as the forgotten receptacle for agricultural runoff), the many opportunities that are being lost from our management choices are too easily overlooked.

A water ethic that recognizes a moral duty to protect against pollution provides an incentive to look for economically viable ways to accomplish that moral imperative. Concentrated chicken farms, for example, create massive quantities of waste that are deadly to aquatic life when it drains into nearby streams, yet that same waste can also be tapped as a source of methane gas to produce electricity. Without any legal obligation to protect nearby streams, and without an overriding interest to go into the energy business, a chicken producer may be happy to continue polluting the streams. An ethic that values the health of the streams, however, either on the part of the chicken producer, or on the part of other water stakeholders (e.g. local residents or recreational fishermen) might be enough to motivate a different approach. Without the ethical motivation, the transaction costs of investing in methane capture and electricity production might easily outweigh the opportunity cost of not making that investment. Ethics, in this example, can make the sensible course of action desirable in a way that economics alone cannot.[7]

Agroecology to the Rescue?

The term "agroecology" has been used since the 1970s to refer to the physical interconnections between cropping systems and the natural ecological as well as social context (Altieri 1985). Gradually it has taken on the role of a counterpoint to conventional agriculture, particularly as conventional approaches co-opted the term "sustainable agriculture," so that a different term was needed to refer to ecologically and socially informed agricultural development strategies. While agroecology has had little real influence on conventional agriculture thus far, it offers an important alternative paradigm which continues to offer potential for reclaiming the concept of sustainable agriculture. From an ethics perspective, agroecology is important because it gives explicit recognition to environmental and social principles. Proponents of agroecology see themselves as participants in a cultural transformation to bring society and nature back into alignment (Pretty 2002, de Schutter 2011).

Susanna Hecht (1995:2) identifies three reasons that agroecology has not had greater influence in modern agricultural development strategies, and all three reasons are rooted in cultural values: "(1) the destruction of the means of encoding, regulating, and transmitting agricultural practices; (2) the dramatic transformation of many non-western indigenous societies and the production systems on which they were based as a result of demographic collapse, slaving, and colonial and market processes; and (3) the rise of positivist science." In addition to these sweeping, historical processes which have effectively contained and co-opted indigenous agricultural knowledge there is a fourth process which has inoculated conventional agriculture against ideological challenges. The development practitioner and critic, Robert Chambers (1986) introduced the term "normal professionalism" to refer to any professional culture which thwarts discussion, much less questions, about the normative beliefs of the discipline. Agriculture as a professional discipline fits his description perfectly:

> normal professionalism … is concerned not just with research, but with action; and its actors are not just in research institutes and universities, but also in international and national organisations, most of them in specialised departments of government (administration, agriculture, animal husbandry, community development, cooperation, education, finance, fisheries, forestry, health, irrigation, justice, planning, public works, water development, and so on). Normal professionalism is a worldwide phenomenon, and has built-in stability from its link with knowledge and power, its reverence for established method, its capacity to reproduce itself, and its defences against threat. It is sustained by the core-periphery structure of knowledge and knowledge generation, by education and training, by organisational hierarchy, and by rewards and career patterns (Chambers 1986:4).

In his own professional career, Chambers tried to counter the stranglehold of normal professionalism through the application of new methodologies of field inquiry, most notably "participatory learning and action" (Chambers 2007). By bringing agricultural policy-makers into direct contact with rural farmers, and especially the poor, female, and disenfranchised segments of the rural population, Chambers hoped to promote a new paradigm of rural development which incorporated local knowledge and solutions (Chambers et al. 1989).

How do commercial agricultural values fit into the agroecology paradigm, or don't they? Can the ecosystem services and socio-cultural benefits of agroecology be incorporated into commercial markets, as the REDD program is attempting with forestry? Under the program for Reducing Emissions from Deforestation and Degradation (REDD), forest dwelling populations can receive payments in return for keeping the forest intact. Could something similar be designed to pay ecological farmers for their services? The critical threat of losing the genetic diversity of food crops (agrodiversity) could be relaxed through agroecology (Brookfield et al. 2003). As a counterpoint to the Green Revolution's emphasis on reducing the number of crop varieties to focus on just a few high yielding improved varieties, agroecology depends on genetic diversity of many different crops and multiple varieties of the same crop as insurance against pests and vagaries of weather (droughts, hail, etc.). Diversity is a form of risk management, providing a hedge against increasingly uncertain weather patterns due to climate change, while monocropping reflects a strategy of maximizing yields when all other conditions are optimal.

As farmers in rapidly developing countries pursue more commercially oriented farming strategies, an ethics perspective can help both producers and financiers (the erstwhile development professionals) make deliberate choices. Aside from the financial costs and benefits of, for example, growing flowers for export markets, what are the social, cultural, and environmental implications? What alternative crops, or mixtures of crops, might yield higher social, cultural, or environmental benefits, and almost competitive profits?

Multifunctional Agriculture

The fundamental role that food plays in our lives renders agriculture a deep and powerful force in shaping, and expressing, our cultural values. The concept of multifunctional agriculture incorporates these cultural, social, and environmental dimensions as an integral part of the agricultural valuation process. Farmers make decisions within a cultural framework about what crops to grow and what practices to use, and where and how to market the produce, etc. At the other end of the food supply chain, consumers also make choices based on social, cultural, and (increasingly) environmental considerations, and not only on simple economics. This is not to deny the dominance of economics; farmers invariably seek higher yields and bigger profits, but that is rarely their only consideration. By viewing agriculture as an opportunity to express social and cultural values, we can use agricultural policies, including irrigation policies, more deliberately as leverage for shaping the kind of society that we want to create.

The European Union was forced by circumstances to address these issues during the process of developing a Common Agricultural Policy acceptable to diverse cultures and food traditions. The European Model of Agriculture resulting from these discussions described in 2002 called for "a farming sector that serves rural communities, reflecting their rich tradition and diversity, and whose role is not only to produce food but also to guarantee the viability of the countryside as a place to live and work, and as an environment in itself" (Cardwell 2008:1). The multiple functions of agriculture include the obvious physical production and economic services such as food and fiber, as well as ecosystem services (wildlife habitat, soil enhancement and water filtration, and aesthetic landscapes) and social and cultural services such as employment, social relations, heritage, and identity (Fleskens et al. 2009). Additional benefits from agriculture include health and nutrition, food security, and of ever-increasing importance, climate sequestration through soil management (Lal 2007).

Box 3.2 Multifunctional Agriculture in Asia

Countries in the monsoon region of Asia, from Bangladesh to Japan, have a long history of collective, small-scale paddy cultivation. A traditional rural landscape was paddy fields stretching as far as the eye could see, a tranquil appearance masking a great deal of hard labor often over centuries to construct terraces and irrigation canals. The unique social requirements of cooperative labor and synchronized cropping patterns (to share water and combat pests) have resulted in strong village-level political organizations and mechanisms for cooperation at larger levels within the watershed (Bray 1986). Japan's Basic Law on Food, Agriculture, and Rural Areas of 1999 notes that agricultural lands not only "function as places for food production, living and resting, they also fulfill a variety of other roles and multifunctionality. The lush forests and rice fields that spread throughout help to preserve our land and natural environment and offer us green and beautiful landscape." What, precisely, are the functions that paddy agriculture provides?

Social values

Paddy agriculture is uniquely communal. The strong cultural value of cooperation has evolved with paddy cultivation and has endured into modern life (Yamaoka et al. 2009).

Cultural and spiritual values

Religious rituals and cultural identity are tied to the rice cycle. In Bali, the indigenous associations of rice irrigators sharing water from a common source (subak) serve as religious and social communities as well as a productive unit.

Psychological value

Paddy landscapes provide a comforting influence on the mind, providing an emotional therapy.

Landscape value

Many people, both urban and rural, enjoy the scenery of paddy fields. Korea has instituted direct payments to farmers for maintaining the agricultural landscape as both an aesthetic measure and to provide adequate floodwater storage.

Cultural heritage

Significant components of cultural heritage may include the visual landscape, the architecture of rural buildings, the irrigation channels themselves, as well as particular varieties of rice which have cultural meaning.

Social capital and decentralized governance

The skills and experience that farmers gain through the cooperative management of their irrigation system can be applied to other aspects of their lives, and also leads to psychological satisfaction.

In the context of agroecology and other forms of ecologically oriented agriculture (Altieri 1995, Pretty 2002), the logic of multifunctionality can help in identifying a range of important social and cultural "externalities" which add further weight to the agroecological approach. At the same time, the emerging science of climate change provides further evidence of negative externalities that had not been adequately accounted for as costs associated with energy-intensive industrial forms of agriculture. This is why the concept of multifunctionality is gaining proponents. It offers a framework for enlarging the community of ethical concern.

Via Campesina, an organization representing small farmers around the world, was initially skeptical about multifunctional agriculture as a luxury for the wealthy North, but has since endorsed the approach:

> We ... emphasize the need to recognize and foster the multifunctional role of agriculture in the Global South. The EU, which champions

multi-functionality to defend its system of subsidies to European agriculture, has failed to apply the same yardstick to African farming. This anomaly should go and the Global Donor Platform should clearly recognize this multi-functionality as the pivot on which African agriculture rests and not repeat the sterile argument about productivity. It is time to recognize that rural areas in Africa are the repositaries of African culture. African farming and food production systems are integral to the cultural process. Therefore it is mandatory that the EU, alongside African governments, acknowledge, respect and protect the cultural nature of rural areas in their development plans.[8]

Conclusions: The Ethics of Agricultural Water Use

The use of water to grow the food that society needs to ensure food security is a basic necessity which transcends questions of ethics, or rather, already constitutes an ethical obligation. Of course water must be allocated to agricultural production so people can have foot to eat. But how much water and what kind of production, and who will make these decisions? The inextricable links between irrigation water and the crops which that water supports suggests the logic that decisions about agriculture are also decisions about water. Furthermore, as the concept of multifunctionality reminds us, that agricultural water is producing much more than raw products. It is also generating ecosystem services, as well as social and cultural benefits. If the agricultural system is not producing these additional benefits, then we need to analyze those opportunity costs, and consider those opportunity costs as choices that have been made, perhaps implicitly, about what not to value. There is no escape from ethics!

How can we know that we are getting our full value out of the water used in agriculture? First we have to know what aspects of the agricultural water system we consider most valuable and only then will we have a frame of reference for evaluating the total returns (economic, social, cultural, and environmental) from the agricultural water. This process entails an explicitly subjective assessment about the "why" of the agriculture that is using the major share of water which everyone agrees is scarce and getting scarcer. Imagine an agricultural visioning process for an entire region or watershed, with a cross-section of participants including farmers; food-related businesses; local government representatives; technical experts in agriculture, water, and natural resources management; religious leaders; Indigenous Peoples; NGOs; and the public at large. Some questions for the group might be "What do we want our agriculture to look like 40 years from now? What do we want our agriculture to be contributing to our livelihoods, to our social welfare, to our cultural identity, and to our environment and landscape?"

These questions are already being answered by default, driven by market forces that reflect a narrow set of economic values and political pressures.

For example, an aquifer contaminated by nitrates from concentrated animal feeding operations (CAFOs), is a water problem caused by agriculture (Landen and Propen 2012). It is not directly a problem for agriculture; it is a problem for the water impacted by agriculture. But solving that water problem requires looking at the agricultural policies and behaviors that are impacting water outcomes. The familiar argument that agricultural producers can't afford the cost of containing the nitrate runoff needs to be considered in the context of the environmental costs of not containing the runoff. This is where agricultural practices and water management are connected. It is also where the ethics about water are connected to ethics about agriculture. If society places a high value on clean water (including groundwater) that ethic can move upstream so to speak, into the agricultural sources of the pollution. Negotiations with farmers can proceed along ethical lines that identify shared ethical principles ("We all want to protect our groundwater") that all parties can use as a starting point for exploring practical solutions.

Ethics can be applied to the exploration of new opportunities, as well as the solving of old problems. An ethical perspective can help identify synergies among different types of values, whether economic, environmental, social, cultural, or something else. For example, rural employment could be enhanced through conventional agriculture that emphasizes monocultures and chemical inputs. But if additional goals are added to the planning framework, e.g. a goal of protecting groundwater quality, or a goal of increasing crop genetic diversity, or the goal of enhancing habitat for beneficial birds and insects, or a goal of strengthening local cultural identity, then a different agricultural strategy might provide higher total value. Similarly, a goal of community empowerment would give priority to investing in farmer associations for their social capital benefits, and a goal of improved health and nutrition might favor agricultural solutions that minimize chemical contamination in the food and water supplies. Cultural goals of strengthening local identity and cultural heritage can easily be incorporated into agricultural planning since nearly every region has local heirloom crops which are valued for their cultural meaning. Agricultural heritage is also linked to architecture (barns) and traditional irrigation infrastructure such as traditional canals and qanats (English 1998).

The desired outcome, from a water perspective, is that the water used in agriculture should produce more total value. The outcomes that give "value," however, depend on the person doing the valuation. Finding agricultural solutions that meet the value preferences of diverse stakeholders is a challenge that can best be met through a process of negotiation and consensus building. Even top-down decision-making, while effective in the short-term, relies ultimately on finding a workable consensus. The key to sustainable water management (which I am assuming to be a generally shared goal), is to find a workable consensus among the stakeholders which is also a sustainable solution in terms of the physical resilience of the water ecosystem.

Exploring the ethics underlying the conflicting views of competing stakeholders offers a way of clarifying their values and setting the stage for more fruitful negotiations.

Notes

1 Water "used" by nature for ecosystem function, and water "used up" through pollution, are not included in these statistics.
2 See the Via Campesina website at http://www.viacampesina.org.
3 See http://www.slowfood.com.
4 For insights into the Bank's interest in participatory approaches to development, including irrigation, see *The World Bank Participation Sourcebook*, 1996 [available on-line through the IRC-WASH library, http://www.irc.nl/docsearch/title/112925].
5 The question of the relative rigidity of cultural values in the face of economic opportunities is addressed in Rao and Walton (2004).
6 Source: Dr. Kevin Mulligan, in a speech to the 21st annual Southern Plains Conference at Texas Tech University, Lubbock, Texas, April 2010, see http://lubbockonline.com/stories/041510/loc_609927860.shtml.
7 Economic logic does not lead to the desirable outcome in this case, because of a failure in environmental regulations which allows the chicken producer to impose the cost of pollution on society. In a perfect regulatory system perhaps we would not need ethics, but we would need ethics to establish effective regulations in the first place.
8 Excerpt from the Civil Society Statement to the EU-Conference on Rural Development (June 2007, Berlin), http://www.iatp.org/files/451_2_99191.pdf.

4 Ethics in Urban and Domestic Water Use

Human settlements, whether rural villages, small towns, or megacities, all face the same challenge of providing adequate supplies of water for their residents. When this basic function cannot be met, through drought or political breakdown, those communities literally fade into the dust of time. The Moghul capital city of Fatehpur Sikri in India, for example, was abandoned shortly after its elaborate construction, when it became clear that the local water sources would be insufficient to support the population (Revi 2008). Most other cities that have succumbed to water shortages, however, have done so more gradually and anonymously, waiting patiently to reveal their stories to future archaeologists.

Water supply, in other words, is not to be taken lightly. It can mean the difference between life and death both for individuals and their communities. This self-evident priority for water supply is the reason that the human right to drinking water has long been honored by cultural customs and national laws. In 2010 the right to water was incorporated as a UN-recognized human right, and not only the right to water, but also the right to sanitation (see Box 4.1). While the importance of a right to water has been intuitively obvious since the dawn of humanity, the concept of sanitation as a human right developed as a result of recent advances in medical understanding about water-borne diseases. Just as withholding water from someone dying of thirst is tantamount to murder, offering water contaminated with the cholera virus, or dysentery-inducing bacteria, or debilitating larger organisms such as Guinea worm, is also a type of murder.

Of course no one goes around offering water that is known to be contaminated. That would be criminal. But something very close to this was considered ethically acceptable prior to the 2010 UN resolution: Letting people fend for themselves to find water that is safe to drink. And since the biggest cause of life-threatening water-borne disease is human feces, the provision of safe water depends very much on effective sanitation. The pertinent language of the UN Resolution is the following, the General Assembly "*Declares* the right to safe and clean drinking water and sanitation as a human right that is essential for the full enjoyment of life and all human rights; [and] Calls upon States and international organizations to provide financial resources, capacity-building and technology transfer, through inter-national assistance and cooperation, in particular to developing countries, in order to scale up efforts to provide safe, clean, accessible and affordable drinking water and sanitation for all ..." (United Nations General Assembly 2010).

From an ethics perspective, the UN recognition of "access to safe water and sanitation" as a human right has significance for two reasons. First, it shows that ethics can and do change. Not only did the resolution formalize the prevailing view that since everyone needs water to survive, that it is effectively a human right already, but it expanded the category to include sanitation. Second, the UN Resolution underscores the linkages between safe water and human well-being in the form of social equity (everyone has the same right) and health. The goal of safe water and sanitation has the purpose not only of survival, but also better health and "the full enjoyment of life and all human rights."

Box 4.1 Water as a Human Right

The UN vote on July 28, 2010, which recognized access to clean water and sanitation as a human right, served to formalize what was already de facto international policy, as reflected in the Millennium Develop-ment Goals (MDGs). Yet it was an important step to make that de facto right explicit and put into place a standard against which national governments could be held morally, if not legally, accountable. The success of the resolution surprised even its supporters. On the day of the vote, opposition had been anticipated, but in the end, did not materialize. Maude Barlow, who was at the UN General Assembly that day, lobbying for passage of the resolution, recounts how it happened (Barlow 2012:xv).

> Bolivian UN Ambassador Pablo Solon introduced the resolution by reminding the assembly that humans are about two-thirds made of water ... "Water is life," he said. But then he laid out the tragic and growing numbers of people around the world dying from lack of access to clean water and quoted a new World Health Organi-zation study on diarrhoea showing that every three-and-a-half sec-onds in the developing world, a child dies of water-borne disease. Ambassador Solon then quietly snapped his fingers three times and held his small finger up for half a second. The General Assembly of the United Nations fell silent. Moments later, it voted overwhelmingly to recognize the human right to water and sanitation. The floor erupted in cheers.

The expansion of ethical standards from water provision to also providing sanitation and to upgrade these standards of expected behavior to the status of morally required behavior (i.e. a human right) is an exciting development reminiscent of Aldo Leopold's hope that some day our society would embrace all of nature as falling within our ethical sphere. While we haven't gotten that far, our ethics are on an expansionary trajectory. It is hardly conceivable that a future UN General Assembly would vote to remove sanitation as a human right. But are we done with the ethics of water supply? Have we become adequately ethical? This is a rhetorical question. The realization of the right to water and sanitation is still in its infancy, and an estimated three-quarters of a billion people lack access to reliably safe water and at least twice that many lack reliable sanitation. But even if we could wave a magic wand and provide those missing services, we would barely scratch the surface of the ethical dimensions of water supply.

Let's return to the schematic in Chapter 1 (Table 1.1) showing four categories of ethics: economic, environmental, social, and cultural. Where does the human right to water fit within this schema? The recognition of a human right can be considered a social ethic, since it applies to everyone equally (social equity) and is aimed at improving general health and well-being. At the same time, economic ethics come into play. Investing in clean water and sanitation can be dramatically cost-effective in developing countries, with benefit-cost ratios as high as 7:1 (OECD 2011). On the environmental side, untreated sewage is the primary source of pollution in many rivers, such as the Yamuna River in northern India (Haberman 2006). Providing sanitation in such cases would give environmental as well as health benefits. Indeed, cultural ethics offer yet another logic for sanitation improvements along the Yamuna River. As a holy river which Hindu adherents use for ritualistic bathing and drinking, the health of the river is also a religious issue.

By considering the various categories of ethics and asking the question, "How could water supply and sanitation advance the values/ethics of [economic, environmental, social, cultural] life within a particular river basin or city?", we can open a constructive Pandora's box of ideas and possibilities. The context can broaden from simply that of supplying water for conventional uses, such as domestic and business uses or irrigating gardens and public spaces, to conservation strategies for reducing the water footprint, and to creative use strategies for obtaining more value from the water that is used. From riverfront development to daylighting urban streams to installing fountains and other water features, water can be "used" aesthetically often at no additional cost in terms of lost water. Rainwater harvesting technologies can significantly add to the total urban (and rural) water supply while irrigating gardens with overflow water (Lancaster 2008). One of the messages of "water sensitive urban design" (discussed below) is that saving water, and obtaining additional value(s) from the water that is used, can be beautiful, creative, and fun.

This chapter is divided into two sections, reflecting a fundamental division in the water supply and sanitation sector, rural and urban. Rural water supply focuses on the provision of safe water and reliable sanitation to individual dispersed dwellings, hamlets, and villages. Urban water supply and sanitation focuses on towns and cities. These two domains have very different structural needs. Individual homes or hamlets are usually best served by shallow wells. Sanitation can be accomplished through pit toilets, so no water is needed, but the siting becomes important to avoid contamination of the wells. Villages typically shift from several village wells to a centralized treatment and piped distribution system which can be locally managed. Pit toilets are still a workable option. But in the larger towns and cities, indoor plumbing is the standard. This is not too difficult for water supply (though in practice it often is!), but sewerage infrastructure lags far behind. Perhaps the worst of the megacities is Jakarta, where only 2.8% of the city's 10 million people are served by sanitation sewers (Water and Sanitation Program 2011:3).

Ethics of Rural Water Supply

The emotional messages that we routinely see in the media, and especially social media, about the need for water and sanitation do not come from governments touting their responsible behavior in meeting the needs of their citizens. Rather we hear from the organizations who have adopted the mission of providing water and sanitation services to the people whose rights are not being realized. "Donate Now" is the message. Donate to our organization so that we can provide water services to communities in Africa where women spend hours each day in the search for water. Recently I received a fund-raising letter from a university student, the daughter of a friend, asking for support so she could travel to Africa on a summer program to help install wells in rural communities in Ghana. Those communities, the letter told me, do not have safe drinking water now. With my support a group of American students will construct wells and those people will have drinking water. The letter made me uneasy.

Helping the world's poorest people to realize their rights to water and sanitation seems very clearly the right thing to do, just as helping a starving person find something to eat is also the right thing to do. But the distinction between emergency aid as a stop-gap measure, and long-term development assistance to build local capacity, has been largely overlooked in the rush to meet the MDG for water. After the American students build a well in that village in Ghana, who will have access to it, and who will repair the pump when it breaks, or the walls if they collapse? Where have the villagers been getting their water up to now? Do all the villagers take water from the same source? Are there any existing wells in the village? Who uses those wells? What do the other villagers do for water, and why don't they use the existing wells?

The maxim, "The road to hell is paved with good intentions" does not imply that there is anything wrong with good intentions, but rather that intentions alone are not enough. The injustice of children dying because the water their mother spent three hours collecting is contaminated with harmful bacteria, is a natural motivation for ethically minded people to try to do something. And when the means for saving lives is so technically simple and cheap (e.g. drill a new well that taps into clean water), it opens the door for action. There are probably thousands of organizations based in the developed countries who are involved in the global effort to provide clean water and sanitation to the world's poor. These organizations range from UN organizations like UNICEF to international development agencies like the World Bank and all the national aid agencies like DFID, SIDA, USAID, JICA, NORAD, etc., and the many more private organizations who rely on donations from literally millions of contributors around the world.

From an ethics perspective there is a lot going on in this picture. There are organizations that have been created out of ethical concern for providing water and sanitation to the poor, whose fund-raising campaigns also serve as awareness-raising for water and sanitation as a moral issue. There is activity on the ground in countless communities, sometimes coordinated through local and national health and water agencies, or through national or international NGO networks. There is even a name for these activities: *Hydrophilanthropy* (Kreamer 2010), the application of water (*hydro*) to *philanthropy*, defined by my dictionary as "good will to fellow members of the human race; especially: active effort to promote human welfare."[1] This definition combines intentionality with action, which seems appropriate. We want to help; we are willing and able (at least financially) to help. What are the actions that we should support?

The Ethics of Why

Is water supply and sanitation an end in itself, or a means to some other end? Within the context of meeting the MDG of halving the number of people without access to water and sanitation by 2015, it is clearly an end (to meet that particular goal) but it is also part of a larger development agenda. The logic of having so many different but to some extent related MDG goals is that there are inherent synergies. Indeed, the MDG for safe water and sanitation is only a "target" within Goal #7 (Ensure Environmental Sustainability). One could argue that the safe water target better fits into Goal #1 (Eradicate Extreme Poverty and Hunger) or Goal #4 (Reduce Child Mortality).

The ideas of inter-linkages, synergies, and multiplier effects are built into the MDGs. Progress towards one target will help in meeting other targets and goals as well. There is a whole system of social structure, political economy, health, education, as well as finance and business, connected to seemingly simple decisions about what kind of water system to provide in any given location. Choices about how to provide water services, and what would be the "best" approach, can have powerful and far-reaching implications, which all start from the initial "why" question: Why provide clean water and sanitation? Most water supply and sanitation programs are motivated by some combination of concerns about (1) health, (2) social and gender equity, and of course, (3) economics.

1. Health

A standard justification given for water supply projects is that by providing clean water and sanitation, the health of the entire community will improve (and especially young children who are most vulnerable) by eliminating most water-borne diseases and breaking the cycle of anal-oral infections. These basic and well-documented health benefits are the main reason for including water and sanitation in the MDGs.

2. Social and gender equity

Since women have primary responsibility for obtaining domestic water in most societies, water supply schemes can benefit women directly. And since the poorest segments of society are the least able to access clean water and sanitation, whether in rural communities or urban megacities, new water supply initiatives offer an effective way of delivering benefits directly to those most in need. These social values are well recognized in rural development projects and typically are highlighted in the objectives of both rural and urban water supply projects. Ensuring that women and the poor of all classes, castes, and ethnicities will truly have access to the new water and sanitation facilities, however, requires careful analysis, design, implementation, monitoring, and follow-up.

3. Economics

Investments to provide basic rural and urban water supply and sanitation services are highly profitable to society at large, because of the health benefits and time savings. By staying healthy and not spending so much time collecting water every day, productivity increases. Children are more likely to attend school, and their parents can spend more time working (or looking for work). Water supply and sanitation is not a panacea but it is a critical enabling condition for economic productivity.

There is so little controversy about these objectives that it may be difficult to see how ethics might be involved beyond the general consensus that individual well-being of people is important and that health and social equity are inherent components of their well-being. Differences in ethical viewpoints start to emerge, however, when the question is raised of the relative importance of health and social equity vs. economic productivity. How much should the government, or outside development agencies, spend to provide clean water and how much should the water users pay for that service? Are the development goals of health and equity limited to the point where society as a whole benefits economically from the improved health and social conditions? Should we worry about providing water and sanitation services to the poorest 5% of the population, even if the service would be very expensive and the economic returns very small?

There are two main sources of ethical guidance that influence water supply investments, and neither involves professional ethicists. The primary arbiters of water supply investment decisions are the policy-makers who normally look to economics as a reference. Their actual decisions may be made politically, of course, but largely within an economic framework. Is the proposed scheme to extend urban service into poor neighborhoods worth the cost, or could the funds be more usefully spent elsewhere? What will be the economic benefits of a rural sanitation program? The unstated corollary to these questions is: Is this use of funds a responsible (ethical) choice given the competing demands for those same funds in other areas? Since the adoption of the UN resolution on the human right to water and sanitation, however, there is a second source of ethical guidance. People have a fundamental right to water and sanitation services. In theory, it is no longer a question of whether it is a good use of funds. It logically becomes a first priority. Investments in water and sanitation no longer need to fit an economic agenda because they have become part of a moral agenda.

The Ethics of "How"

The first step in approaching the ethics of water supply choices is to consider the development context and look for opportunities for synergies between the need to provide water and sanitation and other development goals. As with agriculture, the water supply sector is also "multifunctional." Water supply is intimately connected with other aspects of development, and the process, the "how," of providing water supply will influence the lives of people in ways far broader than just having water. It helps to imagine the water coming out of the tap as just one key linkage in a whole system of interconnected parts both upstream (the things that have to happen to get the water to the tap) and downstream (the social, economic, and environmental effects of the water after it comes out of the tap).

The opportunity for using water supply systems as leverage for other development agendas has long been recognized by Christian missionaries who see water and sanitation as basic needs that have to be met before religious conversion can proceed. More secular development "missionaries," promoting agendas ranging from entrepreneurialism to environmentalism to socialism, tend to be less transparent about their intentions. Indeed, the thesis of this book is that many development professionals are not even aware of the agendas they are unwittingly advancing. This is not to suggest that the water engineers designing water supply projects in African villages are unaware of their contribution to a larger development effort. Just about every project report includes a statement of objectives which connects the ground-level effort of building wells and pipelines, to a larger set of development goals. The engineers working on rural water schemes are usually proud that they are contributing to the betterment of the communities served by their water systems. But those water systems are even more important than their builders might imagine. Through the magic of multiplier effects from the water system, its influence extends to the spheres of governance, equity, economics, and environment.

An Indian NGO, Vikas, which works in parts of India where caste and class divisions are especially challenging, uses the promise of new water supply and sanitation systems as leverage to create a stronger sense of village identity and build social capital. Vikas offers to help a village to finance and construct a community water system on the condition that the community will agree to provide water to each and every household regardless of caste or economic standing. Typically this means that the wealthier (usually upper caste) families will have to subsidize the water connections for the poor low caste sections of the village. If they refuse, Vikas goes to the next village with their proposal for a comprehensive village-wide water scheme. This is an example of social ethics guiding choices about water development. Vikas insists on this policy not only as a way of ensuring water service to the poorest members of the community, but to stimulate a new set of expectations about social equity and community responsibility. By insisting that the wealthier families subsidize the water connections of the poor, a larger lesson is being taught which can raise the self-esteem of the poor and the sense of community responsibility among the wealthy.[2]

In this example, Vikas is treating the provision of clean water as both an end in itself, and as a means to the social objective of community empowerment. This twinning of objectives also makes sense from a sustainability perspective, since a cooperative community will be more likely to be able to fix broken water pipes or resolve disputes among neighbors. Strategies to incorporate additional development objectives into water supply projects reflect an ethic of economizing, or squeezing more value out of the water supply investment. Indeed, there is an inherent and potentially powerful messaging that takes place in the implementation of a water supply project. Because clean water is so important, it can serve as a very strong incentive for introducing new behaviors or even for reinforcing traditional behaviors such as community cooperation.

Water supply and sanitation programs are, in this sense, too important to waste in simply offering the water infrastructure and going away. And in any case, a quick intervention and turnover to the local community is likely to end in failure. Deciding what, if any, additional development goals to piggyback onto the water project becomes an important step that can contribute to the sustainability of the water system while also nudging the local community in a particular direction. The ethical questions then become what direction and who decides?

The issue of how to use the development opportunity of a water and sanitation program to best effect is more than simply a water question. It becomes a development question and opens up all the ethical issues that development experts have been debating for decades. What is the vision of society that should guide a particular community, or region, and what input will that community have in defining and implementing its vision? From the outside perspective (which includes the donors and foreign NGOs that are promoting water supply projects), what values and political/economic agendas will be embedded in those projects?

By adopting the position that access to clean water and sanitation is a human right, the UN is effectively telling its member governments that they are responsible for doing something, but it is up to them (not only the governments, but also the development agencies and private companies and NGOs that have decided to help with this mission) to decide how to go about meeting this challenge. On what basis will they choose between the many alternative ways of ensuring access to water and sanitation? They will be guided by a myriad of values, mostly unexamined, and often conflicting, such as the following.[3]

Community empowerment. Development programs have often focused on building institutional capacity at the community level. Some societies, notably the rice-based societies of Southeast Asia, place greater emphasis on the well-being of the community (see Bray 1986) than do Western cultures, but even in the individualistic West, the importance of the community and social capital is well recognized (see Putnam 2000). In the example of the NGO, Vikas cited above, the requirement that the entire community agree that every household will be equally serviced is not only a way of leveraging social equity, but is also intended to strengthen the community's capacity to act on behalf of the common good and in this sense, develop.

Individual empowerment. In direct contradiction to the goal of community empowerment, some development agendas explicitly seek to promote entrepreneurial behavior, including in water supply projects. For example, the approach of "self-supply" relies on local entrepreneurs (individuals, households, or small groups) to finance water service for themselves, and then sell water service to their neighbors (Danert 2012:19).

Environmental justice. Providing clean water in a situation of contaminated supplies (e.g. from oil production or mining operations) serves to substitute, however inadequately, for the loss of the customary water sources. Providing sanitation can have a conservation goal of keeping surface water clean for downstream users and/or aquatic life. Both water supply and sanitation infrastructure can also be targeted to relieve pressure on parks and protected areas, as in the case of the Ranon'ala water supply project in NE Madagascar (Bonnardeaux 2012).

Cultural restitution. Boreholes for water supply are helping the Kalahari Bushmen in Botswana to reclaim ancestral lands that are now cut off from traditional water sources due to land ownership patterns. In this case it was a national court decision that accorded the Bushmen with water rights, a ruling based largely on the precedent of the UN in recognizing the human right to water (Barlow 2012:xvi).

Technical efficiency. Some water supply projects focus on a technical "fix" to supply water without trying to affect anything else. An unusual example of this is the LIFELINK project of Grundfos, a Danish pump company, which is trying to make its pumps useful to pastoralist communities in Kenya. Under the project, the company drills a well and installs a solar-powered pump which is activated by a prepaid card. The pastoralists use their mobile phones (which they already have) to add money to their card through their bank accounts (which they also have) so they can purchase water at the pump. While the company sets its rates high enough to recover its costs, the government can choose to subsidize the cost to the users. The only noticeable effect on the status quo has been that the men have taken over the job of collecting water because they are intrigued by the flashy technology involved.[4]

Decentralization. Rural water supply programs can be an opportunity for building the capacity of local agencies, whether governmental or NGOs. Improvements to water supply service in Burkina Faso, for example, is carried out by local authorities, reflecting an ethic (and also a national policy) to decentralize responsibility and promote local capacity-building. In the Ferghana Valley project in Uzbekistan, a similar agenda of decentralization, participation and local capacity-building is being pursued but for different reasons. This approach is deemed the most effective way of managing the drinking water system. Social capacity-building is being done primarily for economic reasons, not social ones. This distinction can sometimes make a practical difference in the level of commitment to participatory approaches. In Sri Lanka the implementing agencies in a rural water program had an initial objective of working through community-based organizations but later backed away from this approach, and opted for an agency-run approach (James 2011).

Environmental ethics. One of the motivations for constructing centralized water supply schemes is that local water sources may be contaminated by human or industrial waste. If environmental restoration is a clear ethical priority, however, cleaning up local water sources can provide a decentralized water supply, while relieving stress on the non-local sources of supply that would otherwise need to be tapped. An example comes from my own city of Santa Fe, New Mexico. Shallow groundwater, the historical source of drinking water, is a renewable resource, recharged by the local river (when it is not dammed further upstream). However, this shallow aquifer is potentially contaminated by past urban and industrial waste (e.g. leaking petrol storage tanks and chemicals from former factories). Rather than remediating the sources of possible pollution, the water utility taps into a deeper, cleaner, but non-renewable aquifer which is steadily declining as a result of pumping. The capacity to tap into new water supply sources is an understandable priority for an expanding city, but, in the absence of a countervailing environmental ethic, can lead to mismanagement of existing sources.

The Ethics of What

After the goals of a water supply or sanitation project are clarified (the Why) along with the strategy for meeting those goals (the How) there remains the issue of doing the work, and deciding what that work will consist of. The weak links in this process, typically, are at the very beginning of project development, including strategy development and deciding what steps need to be taken in order to implement the strategy (Smith 1988). Rural water supply projects are particularly prone to cutting corners in thinking through the implications of good intentions to provide safe water. Water provision seems like such an obvious need, and is presented this way in fund-raising publicity for charitable organizations, that analysis of community ethnicity, social structure, and power relations can seem to be a needless distraction from actual project implementation: drilling wells, installing pumps, and training local people to use them. This was why I hesitated when I read the letter from my friend's daughter who was going to Ghana for a summer program to help rural communities. Was the sponsoring organization committed to what I considered the necessary preliminary analysis of understanding the problem, before launching the solution?

There are lots of things to consider. "Look before you leap" is advice meant to protect not only you, the one who is leaping, but also the people whose lives you are about to leap into. There is a well-established discipline of rural development that has attracted some of the best minds of social science over the past half century. The designers of new water supply projects have a lot of homework to do to avoid the mistakes and take advantage of the rich lessons of development practice. In particular, the discipline of rural development has refined participatory approaches that strike a careful balance between respecting local socio-cultural traditions and self-determination, while offering new opportunities, e.g. in the form of improved water and sanitation systems. That balance can be easily upset when new water supplies are controlled by government agencies rather than by the local communities themselves. Citing the case of a community in Soweto, South Africa that received water services accessible only through a prepaid meter, Clark (2012:186) proposes "taking a *water sovereignty* approach to *water security*" (emphasis in the original). Water is more secure, in his view, when it is controlled by the local community.

Professional diligence in applying rural development knowledge and professional best practice comprises a dimension of water ethics that might be termed "methodological ethics." What kinds of knowledge will be selected by the sponsoring organization as being relevant to the challenge of providing clean water and sanitation? How much effort will go into assessing the current practices and understanding the community from the inside (what anthropologists call the "emic" perspective)? We know from the history of agricultural development that, typically, more inputs from specialists in ethnobotany, soil science, ecology, and social science would have been a good idea. The hubris of projects trying to replace indigenous farming practices, rather than build upon them, has resulted in a lot of collateral damage, ecologically, socially, and culturally. Are we making the same mistakes with rural water supply schemes? After all, every society already has a water supply "system" of some kind. Everyone gets water somehow or they wouldn't be alive. Similarly, every society has customary rules about waste management, whether defecation or trash disposal. Making the effort to understand the existing system, including the values and ethics underlying the system, is an important first step in designing water supply assistance.

Ethics in Urban Water Use

Urban water supply is more than just a bigger version of rural water supply. Whereas rural water supply and sanitation is almost exclusively about providing water and sanitation for households (or a central water point for a small village), urban water supply places more emphasis on the city as collective space. Water is used not only for domestic and office needs and light manufacturing, but also for creating a pleasing urban environment with irrigated landscaping, parks, and occasionally fountains. Moreover, the streams, ponds, and rivers, which the city has grown up around also become integrated into the urban waterscape whether deliberately (e.g. riverside parks) or by default. The issue of how urban water is governed, including the contentious issue of privatization, is discussed in Chapter 6 (The Ethics of Water Governance). Here we consider the topic of where the water supply comes from and how it is used within the urban context.

Sustainability of Water Supply Sources

Cities need to be concerned about the security and sustainability of their water sources, even if the sustainability of the city comes at the expense of the sustainability of the resource, from the perspective of self-interest, at the very least. This position, which seems to be commonplace, is similar to utilitarian logic at the individual level (Brown and Schmidt 2010:79–85). When I lived in Tucson, Arizona in the late 1970s, the city's water supply came from purchasing surrounding agricultural lands having groundwater rights, and then over-pumping that groundwater, which contributed to the drying of the local Santa Cruz River (Glennon 2002). Today Tucson's water supply no longer depends on the aquifers; it is gradually transitioning from this supply source to surface water imported via canals from the Colorado River 336 miles (540km) away and involving cumulative vertical lifts of more than 2,400 feet (730m).[5] Given that the Colorado River no longer reaches its once biologically diverse delta, this new source of water is hardly more sustainable than the depleted aquifer it is replacing.

The picture of a city depleting not only its local aquifers, but also the aquifers and rivers of neighboring regions, raises questions about the full spectrum of water ethics, from economic to environmental, social, and cultural. As cities grow, both the cities themselves, and their agricultural hinterlands, bring increasing stress to the affected water ecosystems, and thereby on the customary users of those ecosystems. In Arizona, as in the western United States generally, the problem of rapidly increasing urban water demand has been addressed by finding new sources of supply. For the Arizona cities of Tucson and Phoenix, importing water long distances from the Colorado River helped to solve not only the economic problem of finding affordable water, but the social and cultural problems as well. Even the local environmental problem of declining aquifer levels was remediated by replacing that local supply source with imported Colorado River water.

How is it feasible to import water from the distant Colorado River? Subsidies from the federal government are a big part of the answer. The canals and pumping stations that transport water from the Colorado River to the cities of Tucson and Phoenix are mostly paid for by the federal government, i.e. by society as a whole. Those same subsidized canals also provide water for subsidized cotton production along the way (Hanemann 2002). The economic ethics of bringing water so far at such expense smacks of a type of water hubris common in the water history of the western United States (McCool 2012). But the economic costs are only part of the total costs. Environmentally the capture of so much water[6] from the already depleted Colorado River further weakens the aquatic habitat and the river's channel-forming capacity (National Research Council 1991, Morrison et al. 1996).

From the perspective of social and cultural ethics, however, raiding the Colorado River has brought benefits. Farmers, who should be cultivating less intensive crops in any case (or none at all!) are able to continue in agriculture thanks to this new supply of water which has reversed the trend of cities purchasing farms to capture their groundwater rights. Now cities are "resting" the aquifer by substituting subsidized Colorado River water. The intense competition over groundwater between farmers and cities (Molle and Berkoff 2009) has now been replaced by cooperation, as both sectors enjoy the luxury of ample water, at least temporarily. Similarly, the Gila River Indian Tribe whose customary irrigation sources had been usurped by the growing city of Phoenix nearly a century ago, have been able to return to farming. Though their revitalized agriculture bears little resemblance to their traditional practices, their renewed ability to pursue agriculture is revitalizing their cultural identity in important ways (Lewis and Hestand 2006).

When the source of urban supply is a distant river in failing health, can the cities themselves be sustainable? And when the urban use of water supported by that fragile support line continues to favor irrigated lawns and swimming pools, how resilient is the overall water system, both the natural river source and the cities themselves? A strategy that relies on augmenting the supply to meet demand is usually the preferred option initially as cities face water stress, but demand management offers a more promising path to both economic and environmental sustainability. Cities throughout the arid southwestern United States are recognizing the need for water conservation. The city of Las Vegas, Nevada has become a surprising poster child for water conservation through replacing lawns with gravel, promoting indoor conservation, and utilizing gray water (Cooley et al. 2007).

Ethics of Water Conservation

The logic behind water conservation programs in arid cities like Las Vegas, Nevada is straightforward. They do not wish to share the fate of Fatehpur Sikri in India (see above) and become an archaeological heritage site for future tourists! Conservation is just one of the strategies being used by Las Vegas to attain water security. A parallel strategy is to purchase and retire agricultural groundwater rights 300 miles away and construct a pipeline to deliver the water to Las Vegas, a proposal which has sparked considerable controversy (Food and Water Watch 2012). The ethical debate is an old one: Should water be used to support the vibrant economy of a city, or should it be used to support a rural way of life, agricultural production, and the associated ecosystem services?

Urban water conservation strategies are particularly appealing because they offer the potential for meeting the objectives of urban and rural residents simultaneously. If demand is relaxed sufficiently, the problem of water scarcity is solved, at least for the moment. But relaxing demand through water conservation does not necessarily solve the deeper issue of prioritization, a problem which will certainly return with a drought, or gradually as the population increases. What is the purpose of water conservation? Is it aimed at preserving business as usual? Or does water conservation reflect a new commitment to a new ethic about water?

In Tucson, the city has also taken steps to promote water harvesting and water reuse to reduce its overall water footprint (Kiser et al. 2011). That is not particularly unusual, but a pilot program called "Conserve to Enhance" went one step further. The program started in 2010 with the aim of returning saved water to the local Santa Cruz River, which was normally dry from over-use. The program quickly encountered the practical difficulties of converting water conservation credits (e.g. from installing front-loading washers or low-flow showers) into actual water which could be delivered into the river. These logistical challenges inspired a more symbolic program. Participants in the program commit to a set of water conservation elements, which results in net savings on their water bill. That money is then donated to local watershed restoration efforts, and not necessarily within the same watershed. "Conserve to Enhance" awareness campaigns in Tucson and in other locations where the program is being implemented, establish the conceptual connection between the act of conserving water and the donations to watershed health (Nadeau et al. 2012). The program is a roundabout way of raising funds for environmental causes, based on an honor system, motivated by an environmental ethic.

Making Better Use of Urban Water

Reducing a city's water footprint represents an economic ethic of minimizing waste, but it does not necessarily address the question of how the water is being used, only how much water is used. Replacing a water-wasting lawn with gravel and keeping just a small piece of green lawn would save water, but might not have much aesthetic appeal. Landscaping with desert-adapted plants and rocks could result in identical water savings and a more inspiring viewscape. This is the idea behind the concept of "water sensitive urban design" being developed in Australia. The goal is to save water without sacrificing aesthetics. It involves "working with communities to ensure the planning, design, construction and retrofitting of urbanised landscapes are more sensitive to the natural water cycle" (see http://www.wsud.org). The liberation of clever design is that quality of life can actually improve while saving water, through capturing urban storm water in urban lakes and water parks, and at the household level, using rooftop water and/or gray water for landscape irrigation and toilet flushing, and upgrading to water-saving appliances.

Another way of making better use of water in an urban context is to incorporate natural rivers, streams, lakes, springs, or in arid regions, dry drainage courses, into the fabric of the cityscape. In Seoul, South Korea, the Cheonggyecheon waterway restoration project saw the replacement of a large freeway with a restored river channel and the welcome return of waterway flora and fauna to the city (Revkin 2009). In Los Angeles, water ethics are taking visible expression through "daylighting" the Los Angeles river that had become buried by urban development. Highways, buildings, and parking lots had been constructed over the river, and the channel, where it existed at all, was lined in concrete. Over the past decade, the river has been slowly coming back to life, and is now recognized by the city as its "landmark resource."[7]

Restoring urban streams and rivers has become a leading strategy for urban renewal, but it can also serve an equally important role in renewing people's connection to nature. Indeed, urban renewal and "human-nature" renewal can be integrated and synergistic. Nearly every city has one or more rivers, which is usually the reason the cities exist at all. Restoration of the urban riparian corridors inevitably involves restoring historic buildings and central spaces, along with re-naturalizing the ecology of the river itself. The result might be artificial, but with flowing water it can still feel natural. The "River Walk" in San Antonio, Texas, features a river running through the heart of the city which is fully regulated by pumps and pipelines, but the aesthetic feel is authentic enough to attract people, businesses, and especially cafes and restaurants. These new green open spaces are helping to drive local economic activity in the city (Binney et al. 2010:18) and have many additional "multifunctional" benefits for city residents.

The impetus to invest in urban river restoration comes from ethics that place a value on the river itself, along with human enjoyment of the river. While economists can often find quantifiable benefits through "willingness to pay" calculations, the vision to pursue river restoration, whether in Los Angeles or Seoul, is motivated by much more than economics. In both cases there was a shared vision not only of what the river could look like in the future, but why it would be a good idea for that vision to become reality. Clarifying the values of the river's stakeholders, including the business community and local residents, can help define a consensus vision which appeals to everyone.

Conclusions about Water Supply Ethics

While the analysis of water ethics calls for disaggregating different types of ethics (social, economic, environmental), ethics do not work inside the silos of our categories. The real world is much messier and more interesting. The environmental priority of re-naturalizing a river channel – whether in Santa Fe, Seoul, or Los Angeles, does not exist in isolation from the related social motivation of the human enjoyment of the new river channel, or the economic interest of enhancing tourism appeal, or the promise of other intangible benefits such as educational learning, psychological solace, spiritual insights, or aesthetic inspiration. This is the reason that restoration projects which may be highly controversial at the time they are adopted, typically find new and enthusiastic converts after the fact, as the multiplier effects of interacting benefits are gradually realized and appreciated (Grossman 2002:1–8).

The designation of water as a human right reminds us that water is not optional. It is not like education, or even health services, both of which add dramatically to quality of life. Water is different. It does not add to life; it gives life, and in this very real sense, water is life. The thousands of organizations working to provide cleaner water and safer sanitation attest to a vibrant ethic of helping others who are less fortunate. That is admirable both as an ethic and as a basis for action.

Who promotes which ethics reflects to a rather alarming degree the institutional ethics of the sponsoring agency, rather than any on-the-ground realities. To predict whether a water supply project will emphasize community capacity-building or individual entrepreneurialism, one only needs to know which organization is sponsoring the project. The local socio-cultural context and historical traditions are rarely considered as anything more than potential constraining or enabling factors in implementing an approach reflecting the ethics of the sponsoring agency. This situation is most evident in developing countries where there is a power disparity between local institutions and their international benefactors, but very similar power dynamics can be seen in the so-called developed countries as well. The ethics of the sponsoring agency are bundled into the technical assistance package.

Deliberate analysis of ethics can contribute to designing water and sanitation efforts that do justice to the good intentions of the donors. We want to save the lives of children and enhance the health and happiness of poor, isolated communities. Clean water and sanitation are fundamental to health and happiness. That part is straightforward, but then what? Sustainable solutions to the challenge of clean water and sanitation will depend upon an understanding of the social, economic, environmental, and cultural context. How will these dynamics be addressed? Ethical intentions such as gender equity or ecological integrity are only words and concepts that need to be operationalized through actions. What kinds of actions, and at what level of intensity? There will be competing ethical viewpoints about the hows and whys of implementing a project in particular ways. Which ethics, and *whose* ethics, will prevail?

The lessons from the world of urban water supply projects and policies are similar. There will always be competing values and ethical assumptions which will manifest as controversies. Should Las Vegas be allowed to de-water a rural valley 300 miles away in order to continue its runaway urban growth? The controversies around competing values can, I believe, also serve as a basis for building cooperation. The incessant thirst of large cities is frightening not only to their rural neighbors but also to the urban residents themselves. Where will their water come from when the next drought strikes? Perhaps cities can start trying to earn the respect of the farmers by adopting radical water conservation through state-of-the-art water sensitive designs for collecting rainwater, reusing gray water, and recycling at least some of the water back to drinking water, as Singapore has already institutionalized (Barnett 2011).

But even more important than making peace between the cities and the farmers, is peace between people and the water ecosystems on which we – our cities as well as our food supplies – ultimately depend. We can't live without nature, and if we could, we probably wouldn't want to. Not only poets and artists, but also psychologists can attest that we are happiest when we feel connected to the natural world (Roszak 1992) and when our built environments, whether buildings or cities, incorporate "biophilic" design principles (Kellert 2012). While the world has had cities for more than 5,000 years, it is only in the past few years that city dwellers became a global majority. The water supply systems that service the needs of this urban majority can, with creative designs and clear ethical principles, help us to reconnect with the natural world and inspire our efforts to use nature's water respectfully. Rural water supply systems offer much easier ways to integrate the functions of water and sanitation provision with an awareness of water ecosystems. With an awareness of the importance of keeping that connection alive (environmental and cultural values), we can meet our economic goals, honor our social values (the right to water and sanitation), and perhaps live happily ever after!

Notes

1 Merriam-Webster online dictionary (2012).
2 Source: "Empowering rural communities through water and sanitation: the mantra program," Solutions for Water website, http://www.solutionsforwater.org/solutions/empowering-rural-communities-through-water-and-sanitation-the-mantra-program.
3 This list of ethics is drawn partly from the set of about 1,500 "water solutions" submitted to the 6th World Water Forum and posted on the Forum website, http://www.solutionsforwater.org.
4 WBCSD Case Study (n.d.) "Grundfos LIFELINK – Sustainable & transparent drinking water solutions for the developing world," http://www.grundfoslifelink.com/pdf/GRUNDFOS_LIFELINK_CASE_WBCSD-12.pdf.
5 Data from the Central Arizona Project website, http://www.cap-az.com/.
6 The actual amount of Colorado River water delivered to the cities of Phoenix and Tucson varies each year, but the contracted allocation of Central Arizona Project water for Municipal and Industrial use in 2009 was 621,000 acre feet (0.766 km^3). For current information see the Arizona Department of Water Resources website, http://www.azwater.gov/AzDWR/.
7 See the "Los Angeles River Revitalization" website, http://www.lariver.org.

5 Water for Industry: What is Responsible Use?

Nearly every manufactured good or industrial process requires water for at least some phases of the production process: the extraction of the raw materials, processing of intermediate products (e.g. steel), manufacturing, transport, its use and maintenance, and finally its disposal or reuse. The ethics of using water for such purposes can be assessed at two basic levels. The first level is the issue of how much water is used in the production process and opportunities for reducing overall water use and impacts. These are the issues captured in the concept of "water footprint" which is discussed below. The second level addresses the products themselves, how they are used after being produced and purchased, and their "ethical utility" in terms of the four categories of ethics used throughout this book: economic, environmental, social, and cultural. The concept of "ethical utility" is discussed below in the conclusions to this chapter.

An other way that companies have an impact on water, aside from the water footprint of making the product, or the water use of the customers using those products, is through the behavior of the companies as companies. Companies can "mind their own business" and go no further than basic water footprint analysis to eliminate waste, or they can choose to engage with local communities, NGOs, or other companies in actively promoting sustainable water use beyond their company walls. For example, a company might sponsor a river festival, or a long-term water quality monitoring program, or help in stream restoration. The policy level comprises another domain where companies, either individually or collectively, have a great deal to offer the cause of water sustainability.

The "Water Footprint" Concept

The concept of "water footprint" offers a shorthand way of thinking about, and measuring, the water used in making a product, or in operating a factory. The footprint refers to the net "cost" in terms of water, after subtracting water that is reused, recycled, or reclaimed during or after the manufacturing process (Hoekstra et al. 2011, Hoekstra 2013). While the water footprint is a tool that can be applied to a range of goals, the basic orientation of the footprint concept is economic and environmental. The tool helps companies, municipalities, organizations, or individual households to measure current water use (including indirect uses) and then to identify opportunities for reducing that use.

The basic ethical goal of the water footprint concept is economic and environmental sustainability. A smaller water footprint is desirable because it implies higher water productivity (economic water ethic) and removes less water from nature (environmental water ethic). Society is better off because there is more water that can be used for other purposes, including collective goods (e.g. river recreation, fishing, etc.). Companies adopting the water footprint methodology may do so for a variety of ethical goals ranging from economic cost savings to environmental values (saving water) or even social and cultural purposes (e.g. reducing pollution loads which have social and cultural impacts).

Water footprint analysis as a sustainability strategy is inherently limited without a policy component. If Company X reduces its water footprint and diverts less water from the river, what is to prevent Company Y from capturing that additional water? This is the same issue confronted in urban water conservation programs which can inadvertently stimulate more water consumption by others, unless there is a policy in place to return the saved water to the environment. Since companies, like cities, have a natural tendency to grow, their overall water footprints will eventually get bigger, even if their water use becomes more efficient. Aggregate industrial demand for water will continue to grow and will inevitably clash with the growing demands from the other use sectors, namely agriculture and urban/domestic use.

This competition for water, between sectors as well as within sectors, is the basic reason that industry has become a leading force in water policy discussions at all levels, and particularly at the global level. With water supplies already stressed, climate change adding new stress, and water ecosystems already on the verge of collapse from contamination and over-use, far-sighted CEOs are understandably concerned. The World Economic Forum launched a major new initiative in 2010 " ... to forge a groundbreaking concept – the creation of a global public-private-civil society partnership with access to international best practices and best practitioners, designed to support those governments who wished to undertake water resource reforms, in order to secure sustainable and equitable economic growth" (Water Resources Group 2012:7).

The United Nations, meanwhile, has established a Global Compact as a platform for companies to join forces under the UN umbrella to tackle issues of sustainable development, including water. The CEO Water Mandate is taking a very operational approach: "Its structure covers six key areas and is designed to assist companies in developing a comprehensive approach to water management. The six areas are: Direct Operations; Supply Chain and Watershed Management; Collective Action; Public Policy; Community Engagement; and Transparency" (Global Compact 2011:3).

If the motivation for industry to get involved in water is to mitigate the water crisis, what is industry's strategy for accomplishing this goal? On one hand, industry is raising the alarm that something needs to be done, and that governments should be doing it, e.g. investing in more water infrastructure and adopting better policies to promote water conservation. But the private sector is also offering to take action within its own sphere, to reduce industrial water use and invest in water treatment and recycling. Part of industry's appeal to national governments is to put clear and uniform regulations in place requiring industry-wide compliance at the national level – and through the World Economic Forum and World Trade Organization at the international level – so that all companies have an equal incentive to adopt water-saving practices.

When Neville Isdell was CEO of the Coca-Cola Company, he distinguished three domains of corporate commitment to the water sector: First was the company's water "footprint" and the technical challenges and opportunities all the way through the supply and delivery chains, to find water-saving solutions. Second was the company's "blueprint" for influencing water policies beyond the company walls, from local to global. The third domain was the "handprint" of engaging with communities to enhance the sustainability of their water supplies, irrespective of direct returns to Coke (Isdell 2009). All three domains of action stemmed from a very deliberate corporate culture of sustainability, and in particular sustainable water. The company aims to become water neutral by 2020, i.e. "to safely return to nature and to communities an amount of water equivalent to what we use in all our beverages and their production by 2020" (Coca-Cola 2011:2).

The Coca-Cola Company has adopted an unusually aggressive stance on water sustainability, which includes community outreach around minimizing their water risk, and in the process conserving water which Coca-Cola can add to its water goal of net neutrality by 2020. Their chief competitor, PepsiCo, has also addressed a broad range of water conservation efforts, including funding rural water supply and sanitation programs. In recognition of this work, PepsiCo received the Stockholm Industry Water Award in 2012.

Industrial Water Ethics without Boundaries?

Implied in the concept of a water footprint is that there is a clear boundary of the factory, company, or city whose footprint is being measured. The model is that of an industrial process where water is an input, or as economists say, a "production factor." Add up the water used in the production process and you have the footprint. This works if you are simply trying to put your own house in order, and you define your house as that particular factory, company, or city. But who is looking after the space between those individual houses – the rivers, lakes, and aquifers that contain the water used by a particular factory?

Water conservation and sustainable management beyond the boundaries of companies' direct water use has become the next frontier of corporate concern as they evaluate future water risk. With climate change causing greater swings of droughts and floods, increasing threats to water quality from new uses and from inexorable leaching of contaminants from old waste dumps, and water competition from growing cities on one hand and thirsty farms (and agribusinesses) on the other, corporate managers are giving new focus to managing not just water, but the risks to that water.

The growing realization of critical water risks outside the boundaries of a company's footprint has led corporations to look upstream to the watersheds and river basins they depend on, and even more broadly to regional, national and international policies about how water should be managed. A participant at an international water conference is just as likely to be from a private company that uses water, as from a research institute that studies water use or a government agency that sets water policies. It is in everyone's interest to cooperate and share ideas about managing a resource that is a public good and a shared responsibility.

Box 5.1 Corporate Water Initiatives

Three important business initiatives that have emerged recently point to the diversity of approaches being taken even within the unified domain of water sustainability. Each of these initiatives shares a vision of sustainable water management through the corporate sector.

1. *The World Business Council for Sustainable Development* emerged out of the original "Rio" sustainable development meetings in 1992, and now has more than 200 corporate members from all business sectors. Their collective purpose is to "share best practices on sustainable development issues and to develop innovative tools that change the status quo."[1] The water strategy being developed by the WBCSD is aimed "to help businesses and key stakeholders identify the water tools and initiatives that will best meet their specific needs, and to preserve the sustainability of our water resources" (WBCSD 2012:3). The water management framework adopted by the WBCSD stays very close to the internal interests of companies. Engagement is called for with stakeholders, but not explicitly with water policy-makers.

2. *The CEO Water Mandate*, in contrast, takes corporate water management and water footprinting as a starting point for engaging in water policy and governance beyond the company walls. The CEOs who sign the mandate commit their companies to, among other things, "Build closer ties with civil society organizations, especially at the regional and local levels [and] work with national, regional and local governments and public authorities to address water sustainability

issues and policies ... [and to] exercise 'business statesmanship' by being advocates for water sustainability in global and local policy discussions" (Global Compact, 2011:8–9).

3. *The Alliance for Water Stewardship*[2] brings together companies, research institutes, and environmental organizations to develop mutually agreed standards for water stewardship, which companies or any other entity (e.g. a city) would be asked to adopt on a voluntary basis. The purpose is "positive outcomes in terms of (a) more equitable governance, (b) sustainable water flow regimes, (c) good water quality, and (d) protected, managed and restored areas. Social (e.g. culture- or health-related), environmental (e.g. species- or habitat-related) and economic (e.g. financial- or livelihood-related) impacts relating to these outcomes will benefit stakeholders from different sectors."[3] The Alliance's strategy is to develop partnerships both locally and internationally, which in turn will create peer pressure to comply with the voluntary standards. This "soft law" approach is seen as a pragmatic alternative to rules and regulations.

Water Ethics in Manufacturing

Water management associated with the industrial manufacturing processes, include efficiency, conservation, reuse, and treatment or filtration of the water that has been used. Every company has a water footprint to some degree, but there is a great diversity of responses to those footprints. Most companies, of course, do nothing, many do something, and a very few have, for various reasons, made water a key element of their sustainability strategies. By investing time and resources into finding ways to use less water to produce the same products, and to return good quality water back to the environment, manufacturing industries are acting "responsibly" and ethically. For example, the Intel Corporation uses a small fraction of the water it previously needed to manufacture computer chips, as a result of R&D efforts in the manufacturing process (Sarni 2011:201–4).

The company's water footprint provides a convenient starting point for embarking on a sustainable water agenda. More progressive companies interpret their footprint to also include the water footprints of their suppliers and sometimes even their customers. Unilever, for example, is reducing the amount of water used in manufacturing its products, and is reformulating its clothes washing powder to require less water for rinsing. A second domain where companies sometimes get involved is in the management of water within the watersheds or regions where they are stakeholders. Examples include local businesses sponsoring a river clean-up day, as well as PepsiCo's $8m gift in 2011 to Water.org for rural water supply projects in India.[4] A third domain of water action by private companies is in trying to influence government water policies whether at local, regional, national, or global levels. Often, of course, companies seek a business advantage by lobbying for policy changes that relax environmental regulations (e.g. the American Coal Council). Conversely, however, corporations are also promoting a more active role for government to set stronger policies and invest in more infrastructure to avert water shortages for everyone, including businesses.

Ethics play a role in the priority companies give to their water work, and the kinds of water policies and programs they choose to support. But the most important variable, and, in my view, the most interesting aspect to explore, is a company's motivation for getting involved in water at all. If corporations are thought of as people (which is how American law treats them), then, "What are they thinking?" and why are they thinking about water? What are the corporate values (ethics) being expressed through their water behavior? We will explore that behavior in three domains of water action: (1) reducing the water footprint, (2) water management beyond the footprint, and (3) influencing water policies.

1. Reducing the water footprint

Every year the city of Stockholm hosts "World Water Week" which has become the premier venue for water policy-makers, researchers, NGOs, and businesses to simultaneously boast about their accomplishments and learn from their colleagues. In the 2010 conference I attended a session on business ethics where one of the speakers was the Sustainability Officer from the Swedish clothing company, Indiska. The company produces women's clothing designed in Sweden, but made with fabric sourced primarily in India and Turkey. The speaker explained how Indiska was partnering with several other Swedish clothing companies, including H&M, in a new initiative to help their textile suppliers in Rasjasthan, India to drastically reduce water pollution from the dyeing process. Although local water regulations did not require it, Indiska was investing in water treatment equipment and training for the textile factories that produced its fabrics. As part of the contract with those suppliers, Indiska was setting up water quality standards that the factories had to meet, to ensure that the textiles used in Indiska clothing was not contributing to water pollution in Rajasthan. The company's goal, she explained was not only to protect, but to improve local water quality by encouraging local governments to enforce the weak regulations that were already on the books, and by providing training to local textile workers regardless of whether they worked for an Indiska supplier. This was an example, the speaker said proudly, of Indiska's commitment to making the world a better place.

In the Q&A that followed the presentation, an American business consultant in the audience asked why Indiska was doing something that obviously added an expense to the final product, which ultimately would be paid by the customer. Listening to my perplexed compatriot's question, I felt I already knew the answer. The Indiska speaker would explain that the environmentally sound manufacturing process used in Indiska clothing would add value to the final product, and customers would happily pay more for it. This is the standard philosophy behind green labeling: Give the customers the opportunity to support their environmental values through their purchase of the product. But that was not the logic the speaker used in her response. The reason Indiska is doing this, she explained, is simply that it's the right thing to do. When Indiska began in the 19th Century, the textiles were made in Sweden and the pollution involved in manufacturing was also in Sweden. Today Indiska imports all its textiles from other countries, in order to keep costs manageable, but not in order to pollute those countries in the process. The company believes that Indiska should support the same environmental standards in other countries that it would need to comply with in Sweden. Since the company is family owned, it is free to set its own policies without regard to shareholders, but in this case, she added, there would probably not be any objection. In her view, what Indiska was doing was simply an acknowledgment of the company's responsibility to the people and communities supplying their textiles.

Indiska's pilot program has since grown into the Swedish Textile Water Initiative[5] and includes more than 30 companies along with advisors from the Stockholm International Water Institute (http://www.siwi.org). Their plan of action is to focus " ... on topics such as production technique, water treatment, sludge management, and policy engagement, which will serve as platforms for a learning process and the development of guidelines for sustainable water use ... and we have the ambition, in future projects, to address [other] ... issues which include: farming, transportation, cleaning and recycling."[6]

A company's goal of reducing its water footprint is not necessarily motivated by environmental or social ethics; old-fashioned economic interests often provide sufficient cause. By reducing water use, a company's water bills are usually lowered, along with the cost of treating the wastewater. (However, it may also be the case that using less water actually increases manufacturing costs if other inputs have to be substituted.) Beyond the potential win-win of lower water costs plus the environmental benefits of removing less water from nature, the business case for further reductions in the water footprint becomes more complex. In the case of Indiska, the motivation is a sense of corporate responsibility to society. Treating the wastewater of Indian textile factories is seen as a social benefit to the local people through protecting their domestic water supplies. The same action (treating factory wastewater) could also be motivated by environmental ethics of protecting downstream water quality for the benefit of the riparian ecosystems.

A different kind of company, Unilever, has also adopted a clean water strategy, which in this case is being presented to customers as part of the corporate identity. The company is embarking on very tangible programs aimed at reducing water use through new products and awareness-raising among current (and potential) customers. Here is an excerpt from the company website:

> Our footprint analysis work showed that around 44% of Unilever's domestic water footprint in water scarce countries is associated with our personal care products (soap, shower gels and shampoos). A further 38% comes from the laundry process – a significant proportion from washing laundry by hand.
>
> Our future strategy for water will therefore be led by the Personal Care and Laundry categories. The main approach will be to design innovative products and tools which help consumers reduce water when doing the laundry, showering and washing hair, combined with behaviour change programmes to help shift to a new habit.[7]

As a publicly traded company, Unilever needs to answer to its shareholders and would certainly be reined in if it put environmental ethics far ahead of profits. But Unilever, and many other companies both large and small that have positioned themselves as "green" businesses have made commitments to their shareholders and to the world, that they will reduce their water impacts regardless (up to a point) of the economics involved. If only national governments would be so bold in making commitments to reducing CO_2 emissions!

While there are more and more examples of companies setting goals for substantially reducing their water footprints, there are a great many more companies who are not jumping on the bandwagon of water reductions. What determines whether a company embraces water issues in a serious way, or sits back as an observer while water stress increases and water ecosystems continue their decline? And when they do embrace water issues, to what degree is this motivated by self-serving marketing to attract brand loyalty and to what extent is there an element of genuine altruism, of trying to help people and the planet? Perhaps the complacent companies are "free-riders," convinced that their more active competitors will solve the water problems for the benefit of all, so there is no need to get involved. But I suspect that the answers have more to do with deep-seated values and cultural or psychological assumptions that interfere with accurately assessing the risks of inaction or the opportunities for action.

2. Beyond the footprint: community engagement

When companies engage in water activities beyond their boundaries, their mix of motivations more clearly includes ethics of social and/or environmental responsibility in addition to hard-nosed economic reasoning about managing risk. This can be a powerful motivation for a company to engage with local communities and environmental groups to protect water resources at a basin level. Since all stakeholders within the basin share a common interest in the sustainability of the water resource, steps to improve that sustainability can be seen as reasonable investments to enhance a company's long-term water security. The Coca-Cola Company explains its reasons for working in local watersheds this way:

> Clean, safe, accessible water is essential to the health and economic prosperity of the communities we serve, and the ecosystems upon which we all rely. It is also critical for our business. Water is the main ingredient in our beverages. It is central to our manufacturing process and necessary for growing the agricultural products we use.[8]

An interesting component of water security that has big implications is "replenishment." If a basis for secure water is a stable balance sheet, then replenishing the water that is removed from the system (not just diverted and put back, but removed and shipped somewhere else as bottles of Coke or Perrier, for example) becomes an important concept. This is how Coke approaches replenishment:

> In addition to reducing our water use ration and recycling wastewater, we are also working to replenish an amount of water equivalent to what we use in our finished products. Our facilities around the world are developing strategies and targets to balance their water use by replenishing how much they use, with a focus on local needs and specific source vulnerabilities ... We estimate 23 percent of the water used in our finished beverages ... was replenished through projects we conducted between 2005 and 2010 ... Around the world, our bottling partners are engaging in community water projects as a way to achieve their replenish targets and build connections with local residents, governments and NGOs. To date, we have engaged in 320 community water projects in 86 countries ... The projects we engage in have at least one of four objectives: to improve access to water and sanitation; to protect watersheds; to provide water for productive use; and/or to educate and raise awareness about water issues. In many cases, projects provide additional benefits, such as improving local livelihoods, helping communities adapt to climate change, improving water quality and enhancing biodiversity.[9]

Engaging with communities and watersheds beyond the company borders is not limited to trying to replenish lost water. With the publicity surrounding the UN Millennium Development Goal for halving the number of people without access to safe drinking water and sanitation by 2015, many companies have looked for ways to contribute to this effort. For most companies (unless they have a business interest in providing water infrastructure) the motivation is philanthropic. Both Coca-Cola and PepsiCo underwrite rural development activities in Africa aimed at providing safe water and sanitation to underserved rural areas. Coca-Cola partners with the United States Agency for International Development (USAID) and the United Nations Development Programme; PepsiCo works through intermediary NGOs and Columbia University's Earth Institute, among others.

If multi-million dollar programs sponsored by major global corporations constitute one extreme, local companies promoting water stewardship within a local watershed or river basin are at the other end of the spectrum. Particularly in the United States, where the governance of rivers large and small is not normally considered a state function (as discussed in the next chapter on water governance), local businesses play a crucial role in supporting citizen initiatives on river conservation. Hundreds of local watershed associations and river councils depend on the financial support of these businesses that feel a responsibility to the community and watershed where they live.

Box 5.2 Local Business Support for the Santa Fe River

When the Santa Fe River in New Mexico was declared "America's most endangered river" in 2007 (an annual designation by a national river advocacy NGO), the news took the local community by surprise. The logic for the designation was that the river was dammed for urban water supply, effectively dewatering the entire small river and leaving a dry ditch running through the historic city of Santa Fe. (The Santa Fe River's flow policies are discussed in Chapter 2.) When a Vice President of the local Santa Fe Natural Tobacco Company[10] heard the news on national radio while driving to work, he sensed an opportunity for community engagement. The company contacted the Santa Fe Watershed Association (where I was serving as Executive Director) and established a three-year program of direct grant support to the Association (at $50,000 per year, about 25% of the Association's budget) as well as paid time for company employees to participate in Watershed Association river clean-ups and tree planting.

Why was a tobacco company interested in supporting the sustainable management of the local river? While the company's offices were, in fact, dependent on the water resources of the Santa Fe River and its aquifer, water security was not the motivating factor. Based on the many conversations I had with company executives (the Vice President, his boss the CEO, and the company communications director) I perceive three overlapping motives: First, as a tobacco company they wanted to enhance their image by doing something positive and non-controversial for the community. Second, the three-year program to help restore the endangered river provided a convenient way to strengthen the already strong sense of cameraderie among company employees. But a third and key motivation was the ethical sense that a river should flow "naturally." The company prides itself on its natural and organic tobaccos, and the same natural ethic was extended to the river.

The potential motivations for a local company to engage with the community on water stewardship will be unique to the type of company, its culture, and the personal views of the company managers. With growing awareness about climate change and a sense of water insecurity, fear is likely to become an increasingly important motivation for companies to engage with other stakeholders in the watershed. When the glass is viewed as already half empty and in danger of becoming all the way empty, companies will be drawn to act. But positive values can also be strong motivators (thankfully!) and a sense of fairness can extend to the natural world more readily, perhaps, than we often think possible.

3. Policy engagement

One promising attribute of private companies, as contrasted with "faceless" government agencies or "moralistic" environmental NGOs, is that the private sector is a world of personalities, cultivating distinctive corporate cultures internally (to employees and shareholders) and offering distinctive brands to tempt their customers. Business managers know that while the market has rules that must be obeyed, there can be creative solutions to those rules; indeed, business success often depends on offering alternatives that are not just more efficient, but more fun and emotionally rewarding. Can the same creativity be applied to finding water solutions that challenge convention and transcend the gray drudgery of bureaucratic accounting?

If there is indeed a realistic potential for corporate engagement in water policy, however, that potential remains unrealized. Corporate efforts to affect water policies are far better known for seeking exemptions to environmental standards rather than promoting stricter ones. Coal companies in the United States have waged political battle against oversight by the Environmental Protection Agency, arguing that clean water standards should be drastically scaled back (see discussion below about the water ethics of the mining sector). At the same time, other companies are requesting national governments to develop a stronger regulatory framework to protect water resources from wanton exploitation that would have negative consequences for everyone.

In a communique from 20 CEOs issued at the Rio+20 meetings in June 2012, the signatories state, "We wish to urge you [heads of government attending the Rio Summit] to take decisive action … on one of the world's greatest challenges – water." The communique goes on to say, " … We will not make meaningful progress towards global water security without much greater action by Governments to create an enabling environment in the form of proactive funding and supportive policies in the coming years and decades ... [including] ... Integrating water policies with other key sustainable development issues, most notably energy, agriculture/food, and climate change. This should be done in order to bring freshwater withdrawals back in line with natural renewal."[11]

One of the specific ways that the private sector is getting involved in water policies, at least indirectly, is through developing voluntary water stewardship standards. Under the auspices of the Alliance for Water Stewardship (also discussed above), standards of good practice are being developed for key industries. By moving an entire industry along the path to sustainable water practices, the hope is that these standards will eventually get institutionalized in new regulations overseen by national government agencies. This approach is a form of policy engagement, but directed at the level of the company's own operations, i.e. its water footprint. Can the business sector also take a leading edge role in promoting environmentally sustainable policies at the river basin, state, national, or global levels?

Extractive Industries

In a packed auditorium at the University of Charleston, West Virginia, Bobby Kennedy, Jr., founder of the NGO, Waterkeepers, and nephew of America's former president, faced off in a debate with Don Blankenship, CEO of Massey Energy, the largest coal employer in central Appalachia. The date was January 21, 2010, and the topic was "Mountaintop Removal." Should companies like Massey be allowed to blast away the tops of mountains to expose the coal deep inside, and contaminate the streams and downstream rivers in the process? Massey had pioneered this new mining method which was far cheaper than conventional underground mining, as it employed only a fraction of the former workforce. Other companies quickly adopted the method, with the result that huge swaths of the Appalachian Mountains were being pulverized into toxic dust. Small villages were abandoned and families who had worked in the coal mines for generations were without work, even as coal production increased.

Bobby Kennedy accused Blankenship of "literally liquidating this state for cash, using these giant machines and detonating 2500 tons of ammonium nitrate every day – the equivalent of a Hiroshima bomb every week – to cut down the Appalachian mountains" for coal. He denounced out-of-state coal companies for "destroying the environment, leaving barren landscapes, poisoning the water and permanently impoverishing communities."[12] Blankenship cited the contribution of the coal industry in the regional and national economy:

The health and well-being of people greatly depends on the quality of life they're able to have; that quality of life is greatly dependent on electricity – affordable electricity. Affordable electricity in this world is greatly dependent on cheap and abundant electricity, which in turn depends on coal. There's no country that mines coal more safely and more environmentally soundly or consciously than this country does, and no company within this country that does that better than Massey. Again, when you criticize what we do as an industry, Massey or the coal industry, you're criticizing the people that are teaching your Sunday schools, that are coaching your Little League, the people that are in the communities of West Virginia, and to characterize those people as … wanting to destroy their own environment makes no sense at all.

The idea that you're going to stop all surface mining in West Virginia over water like this [shows a bottle of apparently clear water which violates EPA standards] … while you're competing with Chinese slave labor and people that don't even have to get a permit, is atrocious; it's just not going to happen. You have to make choices in life, and these surface mines recover a lot of reserves and a lot of energy that could not otherwise be recovered. They don't have any meaningful pollution although the media would have you believe that.

Not only the media, but environmental NGOs, documentary film producers, and the US Environmental Protection Agency have accumulated overwhelming evidence of significant water pollution that severely harms human health and all other life that depends on local water sources.[13] While the environmental and social ethics of Bobby Kennedy and Don Blankenship could not be further apart, similar moral dilemmas abound, albeit in more nuanced ways, throughout the industrial sector. Water ecosystems are routinely sacrificed for economic progress. Dams, mines, and industrial pollution impact rivers and lakes in ways that are clearly harmful to those water bodies. If we hold strong environmental values, but also want to indulge in the conveniences of modern life, what should we do? What does it mean to "balance" economic growth with the environment?

The term "management" is generally used to refer to the art of balancing the seemingly conflicting demands of the economy and the environment, and in this sense, the mining sector offers the starkest challenges. Just as you can't cook an omelet without breaking eggs, you can't have a mine without digging into the earth. Something is going to get destroyed, or at least transformed, regardless of how advanced our environmental values might be. Mining in particular, and the industrial use of water more generally, imply another concept that goes beyond management. That concept is "sacrifice" which my dictionary defines as "destruction or surrender of something for the sake of something else."[14]

In mining through mountaintop removal, instead of removing the coal from the mountains, the mountains are removed from the coal. It is far more destructive than underground mining, and it is even more destructive than conventional strip-mining. "Instead of excavating the contour of a ridge side, as strip miners did throughout the '60s and '70s, now entire mountaintops are blasted off, and almost everything that isn't coal is pushed down into the valleys below. As a result, the Environmental Protection Agency (EPA) estimates that at least seven hundred miles of healthy streams have been buried by mountaintop removal ... and hundreds more have been damaged ... Creeks run orange with sulfuric acid and heavy metals. Wildlife populations have been summarily dispersed. Entire ecosystems have been dismantled" (Reece 2005:5).

How is it that sacrificing mountains and the associated forests, wildlife, and water, along with the impacts on human health, is judged to be a reasonable sacrifice? The outrage sparked by mountaintop removal points to a clash in both environmental and social values. The mining companies view coal as a resource that economic logic compels them to extract regardless of the costs to human or environmental health. What is particularly moving about the Appalachian context is that local residents are largely in agreement with this view. While some local people oppose mountaintop removal, a majority appear to support it, agreeing with the view that even the dwindling number of jobs needs to be protected.

The issue of mountaintop removal highlights a complicating feature of environmental ethics which has to do with sources of information, the analysis and interpretation of information, and the ability or willingness to imagine alternatives. While he was CEO of Massey Energy, Don Blankenship became the leading spokesman for the Appalachian coal industry and was insistent, at least publicly, that there was no plausible alternative to coal-based energy. The environmental costs were painted as "not meaningful" partly because the pollution impacts were denied and partly because the health impacts were deemed acceptable, given the economic benefits. Does this position reflect an underlying ethic that profitability of the industry is actually more important than the health of local residents, or is that position a willful betrayal of more humanistic ethics which are being denied along with the inconvenient truths of scientific data?

The US coal industry has adopted a strongly defensive position about the role of coal as an energy source into the future and at the same time justifying current mining practices, including mountaintop removal. The American Coal Council along with the West Virginia Coal Association present a public face that the methods the coal industry is following are both environmentally and socially responsible (Ledford 2012). No changes in current industry policies are possible, we are told, because of the already tight economics of coal mining. But in any case, no changes in industry policies are necessary. The workers are safe and well paid, the mountains destroyed for coal become more useful when they are flat, streams that are buried in toxic mine tailings are inconsequential, and the water is still safe enough to drink even if it does not meet federal water quality standards. The policy reforms that the US coal industry would like to see are not in their own policies but in the government regulations about mine safety, and water and air quality, and particularly CO_2 standards. Relaxing those regulations, they argue, would allow the mining industry to become even more competitive and thereby contribute more effectively to the American economy.

The official lobbying position of the US coal industry in trying to lower or eliminate environmental standards is dramatically at odds with green business associations who tout the "triple bottom line" of economic profits, social benefits, and a healthy environment. Is the coal industry's position an expression of truly held beliefs that the local economic benefits of coal mining outweigh the impacts on stream and river health (not to mention the global environmental impacts through climate change)? If so, the underlying ethical assumptions would include a strong sense of individual self-interest taking precedence over the common good, and a view of nature as having purely economic value in service of those individual interests. Or perhaps some members of the coal industry do hold more environmental values which they willfully disregard because the temptation for personal gain is just too high to resist (Ariely 2012).

Regardless of the true beliefs and ethical assumptions of the coal industry, the question that Bobby Kennedy asked during his debate with Don Blankenship remains: Why have the rural communities, who appear to be such clear victims of the coal industry, not fought back? Why do they support the very mines that are making their children sick? The answer from the coal industry would be that the local residents don't complain because they are actually benefiting from coal and the human and environmental impacts which seem so outrageous to outsiders are actually not so bad. The other possibility is that the local residents are traumatized by their political powerlessness and are unable to imagine a different and better life, so they defend the status quo.

In either case, the ethical assumptions people hold about their social and environmental responsibilities make a difference. If they are indeed happy with the way things are, it would be due in part to values that see nature as a resource to exploit. While local residents would still feel the physical effects of air and water pollution in this scenario, they would not feel psychological trauma at witnessing the destruction of their mountains and rivers. On the other hand, if they are indeed grieving at the loss of nature around them (as would be predicted by the theory of biophilia, see Kellert and Wilson 1995), then they would presumably experience a double impact of physical and emotional loss, and might be more likely to take action.

Water-Friendly Mining?

Mountaintop coal mining is not the only extractive industry with a serious water impact. Just about every form of mining poses severe risks to water ecosystems, human health, and the social and cultural integrity of local communities. What to do? Not mining is not a realistic option everywhere, though in particular situations, not mining is clearly going to be the best alternative. But who will decide, and on what basis? Limiting mines to someone else's back yard (most often marginalized populations who either cannot or choose not to say "No") would not be very fair. The practical dilemma, really, comes down to open and transparent ways of deciding where to mine, and strong enough institutional frameworks to ensure that the least harmful methods will be used.

Since mining will inevitably impact water availability and quality, the initial predictions about those impacts become critical to the local communities, whose water sources are directly at risk. A recent study on actual levels of water pollution from 25 mines around the world suggests that project plans generally underestimate the magnitude of water impacts (Brown 2010). In some cases, the estimates are four times too low and in none of the cases was the actual impact lower than anticipated. While part of the problem lies in unreliable data, a bigger part of the problem can be attributed to "bias in mine water quality predictions made by organizations paid for by the mine operator" (Brown 2010:88).

Some impacts are inevitable but other impacts could be avoided through better land use policies and adopting state-of-the-art mining practices. Unraveling the inevitable from the avoidable is a highly controversial process which highlights dramatically conflicting value positions about the rights of indigenous communities, economic development, and social and environmental values. Ethical assumptions about water and water ecosystems are embedded in these broader interconnected controversies. Nonetheless, it may be helpful to try to isolate the ethical assumptions and trace how perceptions about water may reflect the larger controversy in a more manageable form. If we can make progress on understanding how different sides of a mining controversy look at the water implications of the mine, we may find unexpected common ground on some of the non-water issues as well.

Conclusions on Water Ethics and Industry

Ethics comes into play in many overlapping ways within the industrial sector. The most intuitively obvious connection between water ethics and industry is in conserving the amount of water used both in direct operations and through the supply chain. The water footprint concept offers a systematic way of accounting for this water use and helping identify where water savings can be most effective. The water footprint, however, does not come with built-in ethics; these are added, consciously or unconsciously, by the company using the methodology. What is the goal of reducing the water footprint? Are the goals only economic, lowering upfront costs and long-term risk? Does the company have an articulated goal of reducing pollution to safeguard water ecosystems? What about social and cultural goals? In the case of Indiska's involvement with textile suppliers in India, the company's concern with reducing the water pollution of those suppliers reflects both environmental and social ethics. Investing in training and equipment to avoid pollution to surface water and groundwater used by countless people downstream for domestic water supply is social ethics in action.

A very different set of ethics is reflected in the case of Massey Energy's mountaintop removal mining. Environmental ethics were not ignored, but were very deliberately discounted, and even lobbied against in an active campaign to discredit the logic of having environmental regulations at all. Social and cultural ethics were treated similarly. The company's claim that the welfare of local residents was improved because of the (dwindling) employment opportunities in the mining operations reflects a social position which cannot meaningfully be termed an "ethic." Cultural ethics refers to the value placed on the traditional culture of the region. The Big Coal River Valley, where Massey Energy's operations were focused, had also been the focus of a seven-year (1992–99) Coal River Folklife Project[15] part of the US Library of Congress "American Memory" program to "document the American experience."[16] The obliteration of the folk culture of the Big Coal River Valley through the contamination of the air, land, and water, and the eviction of the majority of residents, was a reflection, inter alia, of the non-recognition of any cultural ethic other than the culture of coal mining.

Both the Indiska case and the Massey Energy cases outlined thus far have described only the industrial processes leading to the final product: clothes and coal respectively. The water ethics identified were in relation to the process of producing the textiles and mining the coal. But what about the use of the products thus produced? What is their "ethical utility?" What ultimate benefits will these products, or any products, provide to society? This question is implicit in prioritizing water allocations across sectors (e.g. agriculture vs. energy vs. manufacturing). The question can also be addressed at the level of specific products, whether food crops or industrial output. Will the corn grown with precious irrigation water be converted into high fructose corn syrup and ingested as a soft drink contributing to diabetes and expensive health care? Will the coal produced through so much environmental, social, and cultural suffering be used in a power plant and contribute to global warming while producing electricity to run air conditioners in poorly designed homes which should not require cooling at all?

There is no end to the potential ramifications of the manufacturing process, and it is probably outside the useful parameters of water ethics to attempt to analyze third- and fourth-order consequences. Where ethics analysis is most useful is at the start of those causal chains, in blasting the mountains that destroy the streams below while exposing the coal inside the mountains, or in the Indian textile factories where the cloth is dyed and the residue flows into local watercourses. These initial stages of production offer opportunities for establishing the values whose impact will be multiplied through successive stages of production.

Why are ethics about water so important for companies to address? Why not just observe the relevant laws and let the government set the standards? The accumulating evidence of degraded water ecosystems suggests that governmental regulations will not save us from ourselves. The regulations are inadequate, are the subject of disputes between different government agencies responding to different interest groups, and are often not enforced anyway. Companies who merely operate within the law (e.g. in deciding how much to invest in pollution controls) are part of the problem as much as renegade companies that very deliberately subvert the law (e.g. Massey Energy's practice of accumulating thousands of infringements knowing they would never be fined significantly).

The industrial sector is playing a critical role in the water crisis, as both villain and hero. In the role of villain, some industries are deliberately polluting streams and aquifers (e.g. through surface coal mining) knowing they are causing irreparable damage to human and ecosystem health. The more common villain behavior, on the other hand, is passive aggression through "sins of omission": Not taking steps to curtail pollution or to avoid dewatering rivers or to adopt water-saving equipment. From an ethics perspective, operating inside the law is not sufficient. Ethics is about setting standards (or taking the time to uncover tacit ethical standards), and making reasonable efforts to meet those standards. The Alliance for Water Stewardship is doing exactly this in a systematic and inclusive way, inviting representatives of different industries to suggest what realistic standards might look like for their particular businesses. This approach offers real hope, but it will be a slow process. A more dramatic but complementary approach is being pursued through the CEO Water Mandate, through appealing to industry leaders to raise the alarm about the water crisis and lobby the industries they represent, engage with local and national policy-makers, and participate in global efforts through the United Nations and the World Economic Forum, among others.

Solving the water crisis requires active involvement of industry. With the increasing corporatization of the global economy (Korten 1995), the balance of power over water management continues to shift toward industry in most regions.[17] How industry thinks about water management, therefore, becomes critical to any lasting solutions. Fortunately, business schools have been teaching ethics for a long time, and the concept of ethics as something deeper and more important than merely complying with legal requirements has already been inculcated into the minds, if not the souls, of corporate managers. While the application of ethics as taught in business schools is generally confined to financial transactions and human resources management, the same basic concepts could be extended to natural resources management as well.

What is preventing more businesses from adopting an ethical approach to water management? A major obstacle, in my view, is the way the corporate world, encouraged by the mainstream water profession, has framed sustainable water management as being largely about "risk management." The logic goes like this: Water is scarce, and it is becoming scarcer from increased demand and less secure supplies. If you are a forward-looking company, you need to minimize your water use (footprint) and try to secure your water sources through physical and institutional actions (watershed protection, groundwater management, and community engagement so your neighbors will look kindly on your company when the drought comes). Within this frame, your only real responsibility is to continue making a profit, and the environmental restoration you do in the watershed, or the donation you give to your town's water conservation initiative has the purpose of securing your financial bottom line.

Corporate Social Responsibility (CSR) and Green Business models have challenged this money-is-everything view of business for the past 20 years or more, yet the water profession seems reluctant to hold industry to these higher social and environmental standards. The CEO Water Mandate discussed above is a reminder that at least some large corporations are already committed to helping solve the water crisis beyond their corporate boundaries. Their operative model is not the one-dimensional bottom line of profits, but the three-dimensional model of sustainable societies and ecosystems along with profits.

When this broad three-dimensional business model frames the goals, then values and ethics become a natural part of the solution. Relocating a proposed gravel mine from a fragile watershed to a less erosive location becomes an easy choice for a gravel company, for example, if the watershed environment (including the trout stream below) is included in the ethical frame of the company's objectives. The gravel mine will need to go somewhere, and will have an environmental impact in the new location also, but that impact can be minimized when the choice of location is guided by all three categories of business objectives (environment, social, and profit).

Industry is both the greatest threat to sustainable water management, and its greatest hope. The business community has invested significantly in coming to terms with sustainability principles and applying these principles to water use. Most importantly, business leaders are already familiar with the concept of values and ethics. The notion that business decisions can legitimately be based on social, cultural, or environmental ethics is not shocking to the CEOs who have signed the CEO Water Mandate. They understand that business decisions are always based on values, albeit usually economic ones. Greater clarity about the ethics that industry wishes to advance, along with public accountability for those ethical positions, will help spark new thinking about water options. Businesses that have achieved success through innovation are sorely needed to apply their creativity in meeting not only business goals but ethics goals as well.

Notes

1 From the WBCSD website, http://www.wbcsd.org/about/overview.aspx.
2 See http://www.allianceforwaterstewardship.org.
3 See http://www.allianceforwaterstewardship.org/about-aws.html#faq2.

4 See 2011 press release for details, http://www.pepsico.com/PressRelease/PepsiCo-Foundation-Expands-Commitment-to-Waterorg-with-8-Million-Contribution-to10 272011.html.

5 See http://www.STWI.se.

6 See http://www.STWI.se.

7 From http://www.unilever.com/sustainable-living/water/why/index.aspx.

8 Source: Water Stewardship section from Coca-Cola's 2010/11 Sustainability Report, http://www.thecoca-colacompany.com/sustainabilityreport/in-our-company/water-stewardship.html.

9 Ibid.

10 The Santa Fe Natural Tobacco Co, though initially locally owned, is now a division of Philip Morris, Inc. but continues to maintain its corporate offices in Santa Fe.

11 CEO Water Mandate Communique, June 2012. http://ceowatermandate.org/files/CEO__Water_Mandate_Communique_June_20.pdf.

12 Quotations are taken from a blog post by R. Perk at http://www.dailykos.com. URL is http://www.dailykos.com/story/2010/01/22/828854/-Bobby-vs-Blankenship-The-Debate-Over-Mountaintop-Removal-Coal-Mining.

13 For details about mountaintop coal mining from an environmental perspective, see the website of the Natural Resources Defense Council, http://www.nrdc.org/energy/coal/mtr/.

14 Merriam-Webster online edition, 2012.

15 See the website, *Tending the Commons: Folklife and Landscape in Southern West Virginia*, http://memory.loc.gov/ammem/collections/tending/.

16 Quotation taken from the American Memory website, http://memory.loc.gov/ammem/about/index.html.

17 A notable exception to the increasing power of corporations over water use and governance is the European Union, where the Water Framework Directive and other related water directives have established an effective capacity for integrated water planning and management.

6   The Ethics of Water Governance

The term, *governance*, is sprinkled liberally amidst water policy discourse to a degree not found in other topics. We do not hear so much, for example, about agricultural governance, or health governance, or educational governance. Why water governance? What is different about water that we feel a need to refer not only to the way it is managed, but to how it is governed?

Management has to do with directing, controlling, and guiding. The word derives from the Latin, *manus*, meaning hand. We humans have been controlling things with our hands for a very long time, and it is our hands, as much as a our brains, that define us as a biological species. Governance is one step up from management. The word derives from the Latin *gubernare*, "to direct or steer," i.e. to direct the managers. The implication is that management needs direction. If left to their own devices, managers might do an excellent job of managing their particular domain, but in a way that harms the greater good. This is why governance is so critical to the water sector. The water profession is full of very capable managers working inside their particular domains of water management – of city water supplies or irrigation systems or building flood control levees – but too often working at cross-purposes to the interests of the water sector as a whole. The reason the world is facing a water crisis is not because of bad management, so much as bad governance.

But who "governs" the water sector? Now we come to a deeper and more systemic problem. Often there is no single person or agency or even coalition of agencies responsible for water governance. That's why we have such a hazy concept of what water governance means; it too often *is* a hazy concept! The confused status of water governance is not because the topic has been ignored. Some very smart people have devoted their careers to unraveling water governance.

The 2009 Nobel laureate in economics, Elinor Ostrom, studied groundwater governance in California for her dissertation work (Ostrom 1965) and the development of her later theories on how people make decisions about shared resources was very much oriented around water governance issues (Ostrom 1990, 1992). The focus of Ostrom and other political scientists and institutional economists who studied water governance emphasized the institutional rules and organizational arrangements for responsive and sustainable governance systems. The role of values and ethics, in their models, was seen as affecting benefits and costs, and thereby affecting actual behavior indirectly. But the role of values and ethics in establishing the governance paradigm in the first place, of setting not just the "rules of the game" but choosing what game to play and how to think about the game, is not well elaborated in institutional economics.

The issue of ethics comes into play at the initial stage of conceptualizing water governance and identifying its boundaries. The fact that there is no specific institution responsible for water, or that a country has no overall management plan (or conversely, that it does) is evidence of how water is conceptualized. When the European Union introduced the Water Framework Directive in 2000, which covers issues from environmental flow to pollution standards to river basin councils, it was responding to a shared understanding about the integrated qualities of water (Steyaert and Ollivier 2007). In the United States there has been an ongoing discussion as to whether a national water strategy would be a good idea to try to develop, and so far the answer has been that it's not! (Gleick and Christian-Smith 2012).

In a sense, the Americans are saying that water is too complicated to deal with in an orchestrated way, and in any case, water is a resource that is only useful when it's being used, so we will let the states, cities, businesses, and individual people make their own decisions about how best to use the water. Water is viewed as private property, much as Odysseus viewed his slaves in Leopold's essay. A water governance system that dares not infringe on private property rights is still a governance system, just as libertarianism is a form of political governance. To make sense of the governance system, we need to know something about the shared values – ethics – of the people who choose, or acquiesce, to be governed by that system.

Values in Water Governance

Values and ethics pervade water governance both through decisions about the governance regime itself (values about governance in general which are applied to water governance as well as other forms of governance), and through decisions about how water should be used (values about water). An example of a governance value applied to water is "democracy" or "participation by water users." Notions of democratic governance are central tenets of modern Western political systems, and it is hardly surprising that these same notions are applied to the governance of water. What is more surprising is when the concept of democratic representation is *not* applied to water governance, as in the case of most rivers in the United States. These are managed by a hodgepodge of federal and state agencies, with no systematic input from the citizenry.

Assumptions about how water should be used (ethics) set the goals for a governance regime. When economic values are the dominant consideration then we should not be surprised to find water laws favoring economic applications of water at the expense of ecosystem health. When a broader set of interests is represented within water governance institutions, the governance goals for water are more likely to reflect those broad interests. In the case of coal-dependent communities whose local streams are getting buried by mine tailings, the mining companies are effectively in control of water governance. If a stakeholder council were established with community involvement, protecting the water quality of the streams would be more likely to be incorporated as a governance goal.

It is at this macro domain of water governance where ethics can make a very profound difference. Do we want to manage water to satisfy direct human demands, or do we see the environmental needs of nature as having a higher priority? Do we want our water governance system to favor individual rights or community responsibilities? The economic demands of this generation, or the needs of future generations? Do we want the decisions about water to be made by professional experts, or local citizens? This level of question does not lend itself to rational choice theory. Rational arguments can be made for either position; selecting one over the other is ultimately an expression of the values and ethics which the decision-makers carry inside themselves.

Looking at water governance goals through the lens of ethics offers a way of understanding, and in a sense, explaining, why things are the way they are – why a particular sort of governance regime, or particular management actions – have come about. This is not to say, however, that it's all about ethics and nothing else is important. Indeed, one reason that the subject of ethics has been so seldom applied in explaining water behavior is that there are competing explanations about why water policies are the way they are. Political power is the most popular of these competing explanations. According to this model, vested interests exert power to bend water policies in their favor. Sound familiar? This is what is often accepted as a sufficient, if cynical, explanation: power, money, and politics. But this simplistic explanation ignores the complicit conspirators in this picture: Us, the silent stakeholders who allow other people's ethics to set our water agenda.

One of my favorite bumper stickers says, "If you're not outraged, you're not paying attention!" The same applies to water governance, but I would add a phrase: You're not paying attention *to the ethics*. When we leave water governance to the experts, we often fail to realize that their expertise is how to manage water and rivers, but not in the "why" of managing water. The "why" questions need to be asked, debated, and resolved by civil society, all of us together. We as citizens should be careful about whom we are delegating our governance functions to. We should "pay attention" and be outraged when egregious breaches of ethical standards are committed.

But first we have to know what our ethical standards are, and for that we need to do some ethical inquiry.

Looking for the ethics does not have to mean that we ignore the politics. In the case of coal mining and water governance in the Appalachian Mountains discussed in the previous chapter, a political power analysis would focus on how the coal company, Massey Energy, manipulated local and national governance institutions. Through a combination of campaign contributions, bribery, threats, legal suits against the EPA, and other measures, the coal company maintained its ability to blow up mountains in spite of causing huge environmental and health costs locally. This certainly seems to be a case of political (and economic) power at work. But the prevailing ethics among the impacted communities, that accorded greater value to private property rights than to the rights of nature, provided the enabling conditions for Massey's political and economic pressure to be so effective. A strongly held water ethic about protecting the sacred mountain streams might have resulted in stronger resistance to those pressures, and perhaps a different outcome.

Levels of Water Governance

Water governance regimes – and the ethics that go with those regimes – exist at every level, from the very local to national and global. The global level of water governance came into its own at the Mar del Plata conference in 1977, and has since grown into a major industry replete with specialized institutes, think tanks, and consultant pools (Conca 2006). Some of the more important international water initiatives are the Global Water Partnership[1] and World Water Council,[2] and a profusion of UN-affiliated institutes focusing on particular aspects of water development[3] (Varady et al. 2009). It is the global level where ethics are most clearly articulated, through conferences, declarations, conventions and sometimes even UN resolutions, such as the Right to Water (Pahl-Wostl et al. 2008). These documents are carefully crafted to attract the support of multiple parties.

An example is the World Water Vision, which was developed by the World Water Commission (established by the World Water Council) as input to the 2000 World Water Forum in The Hague. The visioning process was subdivided into three sub-visions focusing on the key domains of water use (Nature, Food, and People), with each sub-vision group organizing stakeholder meetings around the world, to ensure the inclusion of representative views. The document that emerged, the World Water Vision, while authored by two water experts (William Cosgrove and Frank Rijsberman) had to be crafted diplomatically to earn the support both of the World Water Commission, and of the many stakeholders who had been involved in the process. At the World Water Forum in March 2000, a declaration based on the vision document was adopted at a ministerial conference.[4] Since ministers at international meetings cannot sway too far from the views of the governments they represent, the resulting Ministerial Declaration carried a legitimacy which transformed the Vision document into a de facto global consensus on water governance.

Box 6.1 The World Water Vision 2000 (excerpts)

Our Vision is a world in which all people have access to safe and sufficient water resources to meet their needs, including food, in ways that maintain the integrity of freshwater ecosystems ... The world's freshwater resources will be managed in an integrated manner at all levels, from the individual to the international, to serve the interests of humankind and planet earth – effectively, efficiently, and equitably.

- The three primary objectives of integrated water resource management are to:

- Empower women, men, and communities to decide on their level of access to safe water and hygienic living conditions and on the types of water-using economic activities they desire – and to organise to achieve them.

- Produce more food and create more sustainable livelihoods per unit of water applied (more crops and jobs per drop), and ensure access for all to the food required for healthy and productive lives.

- Manage human water use to conserve the quantity and quality of freshwater and terrestrial ecosystems that provide services to humans and all living things.

Source: Cosgrove and Rijsberman, 2000:1–2

A perusal of international water documents reveals a remarkable congruence of "value orientations." There are controversies and minority views, of course, but there are also clearly transcendent themes, such as the "polluter pays" principle, or that water is an "economic good," or the importance of broad-based stakeholder involvement. These value orientations are expressions of global water ethics, which are important for setting benchmarks against which governance at lower levels is compared and judged.

The triennial World Water Forum, organized by the World Water Council in collaboration with the host countries, has become the largest and most important global water event, attracting not only the official delegates but also spawning a regularly scheduled alternative forum as well, organized by NGOs. Yet for all the visibility of international conferences and declarations, there is no real enforcement of international water ethics. There is only the power of peer pressure, which is itself strengthened through the activities of global meetings, conferences, and information networks (Conca 2006).

It is within individual countries where water policies have legal backing. Nonetheless, international consensus can influence those domestic policies through setting standards of good practice, or establishing transboundary commissions to address specific international issues (e.g. the Mekong River Basin), promoting various forms of water diplomacy (Islam and Susskind 2013) and perhaps most effectively, by providing networking opportunities for the water professionals working at the country level. Even the UN's recognition of access to water and sanitation as a human right does not carry any sanctions with it. National governments are free to decide what "water as a human right" means for them. The ethic is global, but implementing it has to be done at the national level.

Within the national level of water governance lie three interesting and under-appreciated levels of water ethics: (1) watersheds and river basins, (2) state and local governments, and (3) water-related projects. At each of these levels there are distinct constellations of governance forces that both reflect and express ethical assumptions about water.

1. Watersheds and river basins

Stakeholders within a watershed, river basin, or aquifer are forced by circumstances to come to terms with one another, and with their common interest in the physical water resource. Even in the western United States, where water rights have the status of private property, the neighbors cannot be ignored for long; water connects us all! Most small watersheds do not cross national boundaries, but they usually cross some administrative lines, e.g. municipalities, districts, or states. Large river basins and aquifers very commonly cross national borders, adding to the challenge of establishing a common, or at least integrated, governance approach. One important advantage of international rivers, however, is that the concept of cultural values and ethics motivating the management and governance of the river is easier for all stakeholders to recognize.

2. State and local governments

In many countries, including the United States, Canada, and India, the primary level of water governance is at the state or provincial level, and in almost all countries, local governmental bodies also play important roles in water decisions. For example, water supply and (less commonly) wastewater treatment systems are normally governed at the municipal or even village level. The community level, in particular, is often ignored in analyses of water governance, even through there is probably more conflict about water at this level (i.e. within communities) than at larger governance levels (Ravnborg et al. 2012).

3. Project-level governance

Because water infrastructure is so expensive, it is often financed through special projects with special handling in terms of the planning and design of the project components. The way in which the projects are governed also communicates and influences expectations for the way water itself is governed. When aid-funded water supply projects are developed in consultation with the village elite rather than following a more complex participatory process with the whole community, the message conveyed is that water development will, and should, mirror the prevailing socio-economic inequities (van Koppen et al. 2012). Water projects that are designed very deliberately to serve disadvantaged segments of the community (as in the case of the Indian NGO, Vikas, discussed in Chapter 4) seek to promote an ethic of social equity and fairness. This is not to imply that other projects are "unethical" but rather that the avoidance of elite capture of project benefits depends on supportive ethics built into project governance. If equity is an ethic, it needs to start at the very initial step of identifying the problem(s) that the project will try to address (Smith 1988).

Domains of Water Governance

Viewing water governance – which is already a rather abstract topic – through the lens of another abstraction, that of "ethics," is a challenging mental exercise, but an important exercise to pursue. Governance is one abstraction removed from what we might call the "practical" operational level of management. Managers do things; "governors" direct the managers to do the right things, a discernment that entails choices based, in part, on ethics. The governor needs to make judgments about outcomes (the goals) and how to get there (the process). In this chapter we will consider three domains of water governance where goals and process are inextricably linked: (1) irrigation, (2) water supply, and (3) the water environment. The general goals of these domains are straightforward: crop production, public health, and sustainable water ecosystems. The challenge for water governance pertains to the best governance process for achieving these goals. In all three domains, the same two issues stand out. First is setting the boundaries or frame for water governance. Does the irrigation governance system start from the irrigated fields, or from where the canal takes off from the river, or does it also include the watershed upstream? The second issue is stakeholder participation. How should the various stakeholders participate in decisions about water allocations, pollution standards, etc?

Irrigation Governance

Governance has been an important part of irrigation since the dawn of irrigation-based civilizations (Wittfogel 1957) and has remained just as important in the modern era. The early despotic regimes – from prehistory through colonial times – were more interested in food production and collecting taxes than inculcating community-based social capital, and their governance regimes reflected ethics that might be termed "state-centric." The ethical principle undergirding irrigation governance was to strengthen the economic power of the state.[5] During the heyday of the Green Revolution, the ethics of irrigation governance retained an explicit goal of strengthening national economies, along with food security. As irrigation management became a recognized field of professional focus, however, the expectations for irrigated agriculture as a sector also expanded. Not only could irrigated agriculture ensure food security and grow the economy, but the efficiencies of production could be increased by improving management software (people, institutions, and information) as well as hardware (canals, pumps, etc.).

Investing in irrigation infrastructure was a strategy readily understood by national irrigation agencies and international financial institutions like the World Bank. But investing in training and institutional capacity-building was a new concept within the rather conservative irrigation profession. Training farmers to run cooperatives and collect irrigation service fees? Was this really part of irrigation management?

With support from the Ford and Rockefeller Foundations, the World Bank, Asian Development Bank, and key bilateral aid agencies, the International Water Management Institute (IWMI) was established in 1984 to apply basic management principles to the irrigation sector. Irrigation investments were absorbing a huge portion of national budgets in many Asian countries, and the whole sector had become soft in favoring expensive new construction over maintenance of existing canals. Construction kickbacks and various forms of corruption were endemic, which compounded the management challenges (Wade 1982).

What exactly were the irrigation problems that investments in management were supposed to solve? Was it corruption, poorly designed infrastructure, badly trained technical staff, or political interference? It was all these things and more. For social scientists and activists, one of the biggest wasted resources that management needed to address was people. The farming communities who were the supposed beneficiaries of the new technologies were expected to implement the decisions of outside agents – poorly trained agricultural and irrigation field staff. The value of farmers' local knowledge and organizational capacity was largely dismissed as obsolete.

This misreading of local capacities happened in both small traditional irrigation systems and in new large-scale irrigation projects. In areas where traditional irrigation networks had been functioning for decades and even centuries, new irrigation projects often bulldozed away the old infrastructure and constructed bigger, more modern diversions and canals, placing the new system under the control of the government irrigation department. The investments of both social and physical capital, visible in such iconic landscapes as the Ifugao rice terraces in the Philippines, were being ignored or even destroyed, to make way for modern canal networks.

In projects that introduced irrigation into previously unirrigated areas, both the land and the demographics were altered. The new irrigation systems transformed local economies. Immigrants moved in for wage labor opportunities, or in planned settlements such as the Muda scheme in Malaysia, the Mahaweli in Sri Lanka, and the Indira Gandhi Nahar project in India (Stanbury 1987). The more common situation was that of large existing canal networks in South and Southeast Asia, originally constructed during colonial times, which were rehabilitated and enlarged through new development projects in the 1970s and 1980s. Along with expanding the colonial era canal networks, government irrigation and agriculture departments expanded their staff as well, creating large, entrenched bureaucracies.

The governance model that accompanied irrigation development continued the pattern of top-down control established during the colonial era. But as the newly (and often hastily) built irrigation infrastructure started to age in the 1990s, even as new systems continued to be built throughout Asia, the costs of maintenance quickly mounted. Economic analysis demonstrated the wisdom of encouraging farmers to play a more direct role in managing the irrigation infrastructure, particularly at the very local levels, while the application of management principles underscored the value of user participation in management decisions.

Democratic irrigation governance was not necessarily desired by autocratic Asian governments, yet effective management participation by farmers offered significant cost savings. Donor agencies, most notably the World Bank, were particularly swayed by this argument, but how much farmer involvement was optimal? How much investment in farmers' institutional capacity could be justified economically? This question became a very practical concern in designing new irrigation development projects. Should the projects be designed to be operated by farmer organizations, or by Irrigation Department staff? The answer depended on the goals – and ethics – of irrigation governance. Is increased agricultural production the exclusive objective, or is organizational capacity-building also an objective. Are rural organizations such as farmer irrigation associations objectives in themselves, as a type of social capital development, or are those organizations merely a means to economic objectives?

Developing a Social Water Ethic in the Philippines

From the early 1980s, the poster child for farmer organizations replacing government irrigation departments in managing small irrigation systems was the Philippines. Spurred by the need to cut costs and increase irrigation fees, the National Irrigation Administration (NIA) took the decision to divest itself of management responsibility for the many small, isolated irrigation

systems under its control. These had originally been constructed and operated by the villagers themselves until NIA had absorbed them following
World War II. For political reasons, however, NIA could not simply cut the
umbilical cord and tell the 50 to 300 farmers within a single small irrigation
system that they were now on their own.

A careful transition process was developed, based on (1) community
organizers to work with the local communities for up to several years, (2) a
package of physical upgrades to the irrigation system to be determined by
the community, (3) establishing a formal water users association (WUA) to
replace NIA staff in managing the upgraded irrigation system, and (4) training
programs for the farmers involved in the water user association. Within the
National Irrigation Administration there was another set of training activities
aimed at "reorienting the bureaucracy" (Korten and Siy 1989). The NIA staff
had to learn how to develop a constructive working relationship with the
new organizations.

For the initial years of the NIA program, the focus was on small,
community-based irrigation systems serving several hundred farmers, but
the next stage was to apply the same approach of management transfer
to much larger, modern irrigation networks, the so-called National
Irrigation Systems. Here the aim was to establish multiple water user associations within a single large system, with each association covering the
area irrigated by a secondary canal, roughly similar to the size of an entire
community-based system. NIA retained management responsibility for
the main irrigation canals and for coordinating among the WUA-managed
subdivisions.

From an ethics perspective, the decentralized management structure was
not particularly revolutionary in itself, but it launched a process that truly
was a paradigm shift. The initial goals of NIA to reduce its costs by transferring certain management functions to local farmer control, also resulted
in shifting the concepts, values, and ethical assumptions about the rationale
for particular governance forms. The rationale for adopting a participatory
approach was re-cast as a combination of cost savings plus community
capacity-building.

The view of participatory farmer-controlled irrigation management as
having dual goals, economic and institutional, and the Philippine model of
using community organizers, diffused to other countries in South and Southeast
Asia through the medium of donor-financed irrigation projects. Within a
decade of the Philippine model taking shape, new irrigation projects routinely included a "participation" component aimed at strengthening the
capacity of water user organizations at the bottom tier of canal networks.
These organizations were seen as a means to achieving more effective management of irrigation water. When groups of 20 to 50 farmers took control
over the maintenance of shared canals and the allocation of water among
themselves, they would perform valuable functions at no cost to the
irrigation agency.

Box 6.2 Giving Priority to Village Institutions in Pakistan

The blending of institutional and economic objectives which the Philippine model exhibited begged the question of how much priority should be given to institutional capacity-building and why. If some capacity-building is good, would more be better? At the same time that NIA was starting to apply its participatory model to larger national irrigation systems, an explicitly social model was being developed in the northern regions of Pakistan. Shoaib Sultan Khan, the general manager of the Aga Khan Rural Support Programme (AKRSP) operating in the Hindu Kush mountain regions of Gilgit and Hunza, had a vision for enhancing economic productivity through strengthening community institutions.

As a charitable organization, the focus of the AKRSP was not irrigation per se, but village development through whatever productive enterprise the villagers opted to invest in. The two objectives of physical infrastructure and building self-sustaining local institutions were seen as critically intertwined. The AKRSP strategy was to use the promise of material assistance as a stimulus to the village community to mobilize its own resources for construction, and in so doing, strengthen the institutional capacity of the villagers. An AKRSP social organizer established initial contact with villagers through a first "dialogue" followed by two further dialogues. The organizer explained that the AKRSP would fund one project of the villagers' choosing, subject to a certain budget ceiling (about US$10,000 in 1986), and on the condition that the villagers could come to a consensus as to what the project will be and how the work will be accomplished.

The village had to decide what project was of highest priority; it could be a road, a bridge, a community building, or (in 60% of the cases) an expansion of their local irrigation canal network, usually by constructing an additional intake and canal. Since the villagers were required to provide their own labor for the irrigation works (AKRSP helped arrange for technical assistance, paid through the villagers' loan), the bias was for small canals which could be more easily constructed and maintained. A village organization had to be formed as a condition of the grant. The terms of partnership negotiated with the village organization included regular savings to build up equity capital, weekly meetings, participation in extension training programs, and collective land development. AKRSP credit could also finance future projects if the village organization mobilized 15% collateral from its membership, so the initial project served as an entry point for new projects as well (Fazlur-Rahman 2007).

The Evolving Ethics of Irrigation Governance

The Philippines became the international "go-to" destination for study tours about decentralizing irrigation management to farmer organizations. The take-away message from these study tours was that farmers can successfully replace irrigation agency staff in many functions. However, a period of organizational hand-holding and training is needed for the farmer leaders, and the government agencies need to revamp their internal culture. But the critical importance of "reorienting" the culture of the irrigation agency and the key role played by trained and motivated community organizers, tended to be under-appreciated by most study tour visitors. Their focus was on the results more than the process (Raby 2000).

Investing so much in hiring and supervising community organizers, providing training to both agency staff and farmer leaders, and restructuring the irrigation agency, seemed like a very expensive undertaking for the seemingly small benefit of better irrigation management at the bottom ends of the canal network. Was all that work really necessary? The natural hesitation of irrigation agencies to invest in organizational development work was echoed by donor agency economists interested in reducing costs while retaining most of the benefits of participation. But what precisely were the benefits? Higher rates of collecting the irrigation fees? More efficient water deliveries to the crops? Or should the social benefits also be factored in: a feeling of ownership and satisfaction, less conflict, more cooperation, etc.? Without clarity about the goals of participatory irrigation management, there was no basis for how much to invest in the process.

The Mexican Model: Large-Scale Irrigation Associations

In 1992, faced with a budgetary crisis, Mexico adopted a new water law which called for transferring the management of 18 large irrigation districts (ranging in size from 5,000 to 30,000ha) to farmer organizations. Mexico's National Water Commission (Comission Nacional del Agua, CNA) would retain overall authority over the dams and main canals feeding the new *sociedads*, and would provide some technical and financial assistance, but the aim was to cut government costs, so the subsidies would be small. Each *sociedad* would be further divided into units called modules (*modulos*) ranging from 1,000 to 5,000ha and roughly 100 to 1,000 farmers (Palacios 2000). Along with management responsibility, buildings and maintenance equipment were also transferred. The Commission National del Agua (National Water Commission) effectively delegated a major portion of its portfolio to local societies.

There were two major contrasts with the Philippine model. First was the scale of the management transfer. The new organizations were far larger than any of the water user groups found in Asia. Second was the process. No community organizers were used. Instead, staff from the CNA held a series of meetings with each irrigation district to explain the law and the new arrangements. The farmers did not have a choice; the government was pulling out of management below the main canal and were offering to help the farmers set up a new management system. Farmers could accept the help or not, but they would in any case be on their own!

The World Bank lost little time in proclaiming the Mexican model to be the wave of the future. Community organizers were not needed under this model though institutional capacity-building for the new organizations was provided in the form of training in accounting and business management, but not in technical irrigation management. The new organizations hired technical expertise with the irrigation service fees collected from the members. In practice, some of the engineers formerly employed by CNA took jobs with the new organizations, but they now worked directly for the farmers, and no longer for the government.

Mexico replaced the Philippines as the preferred destination for learning about irrigation management transfer (Groenfeldt and Svendsen 2000). Study tours from Pakistan, Turkey, India, Indonesia, Vietnam, China, and even the Philippines visited Mexico to see for themselves how it was done, and to hear testimonials from farmers in the field.

The Mexican experience inspired similar irrigation reforms in Turkey (Svendsen and Nott 2000) and the state of Andhra Pradesh, India (Oblitas and Peter 1999). The program in Andhra Pradesh explicitly embraced social goals of community empowerment and social justice, e.g. by reserving leadership seats for women and underprivileged castes. The strong social ethics reflected in the Andhra Pradesh program are very similar to those of the Philippines, but the process for pursuing those social ethics were different: a top-down approach in Andhra Pradesh and a bottom-up approach in the Philippines. Rather surprisingly, both programs have had reasonable success in meeting social goals (Shivamohan and Scott 2005, Raby 2000). This seems to suggest that clear ethical intentions can have impact through different processes.

Participatory Irrigation as Governance Convention

In a review of irrigation management transfer experience worldwide, Garces-Restrepo et al. (2007) identify five "expectations" motivating management transfer: (1) cost savings to the irrigation agency, (2) increased agricultural productivity, (3) farmers will be more willing to pay irrigation fees, (4) more efficient irrigation management with fewer complaints, and (5) expedited collective action in marketing of agricultural inputs and produce. What is interesting in this list is what is not mentioned: the sense of collective pride and identity, an enhanced ability to organize collective representation for the community's welfare, be it a new school or hospital or road, or a seat at the table when regional water policies are being considered. Another possible factor is risk reduction. Irrigation management controlled by the community is more resilient to governmental crises, and presumably to climate change as well.

The intangible benefits of locally managed participatory governance are important counters to an emerging trend of private sector involvement in providing irrigated agriculture services. Proprietary drip irrigation technologies, hybrid seeds, and exclusive marketing channels for exporting high value crops are some of the perks being offered to water user associations. In the absence of other suitable farmer organizations, the irrigation groups are attractive partners for private agribusiness, and these partnerships are being encouraged by donors such as the World Bank, Asian Development Bank, and others.[6] While it is in one sense gratifying that water user associations are being courted by agribusinesses, it is important for all parties to be fully aware of their own interests and ethics.

Conclusions on Irrigation Governance

When changes are made to irrigation governance arrangements, and even when changes are not made, ethics are being expressed, knowingly or not. Are water user associations being promoted as a means of cost savings for the government irrigation agency, or as a means of social development, or to enhance the resilience of the system, or because the direct management control by farmers will lead to more effective water deliveries, or better monitoring for leaks, or lower overall water use? There are many possible advantages to participatory management arrangements, and clarifying what they are can help guide investments in organizational capacity-building.

Participation of water users in the management of the irrigation systems they depend upon became a convention of development projects in the 1990s and 2000s because there were so many potential benefits that might derive from participation. Molle (2008) cites participation as a "nirvana concept" that confuses fuzzy thinking with actual practice. No one is against participation, but whether it becomes a serious objective or a vague hope depends very much on the ethics held by the people designing, funding, and implementing the program. I suggest that careful attention to the ethics that motivate diverse actors to promote participatory approaches can serve as an antidote to the confusion. When each actor (including the farmers) can articulate why s/he believes that farmers' management participation is desirable, it becomes easier to devise a realistic strategy for enabling that participation.

This discussion of governance has focused on participation as a feature of irrigation governance which reflects social ethics about democracy, social capital, justice and equity, or economic ethics about efficiency and productivity, or cultural ethics about local self-determination. While "participation" is often viewed as an ethic in itself, it is more usefully conceptualized as a gloss for these other more specific ethics. By disaggregating the constituent ethics as finely as possible, we gain better insights into what a given project or program or team of consultants, is trying to do.

Other dimensions of irrigated agriculture could also be examined through this kind of "ethics analysis" to identify (a) what are the ethics being implicitly promoted and (b) what other ethics could potentially be advanced. The concept of multifunctional agriculture discussed in Chapter 3 provides a useful checklist of categories to consider for ethical content. Broad participation of diverse stakeholders in irrigation governance can help ensure that a broad set of potential benefits from irrigation are considered. In this way, participation is both an end in itself (to advance a social ethic) and a means for realizing a broader range of benefits and ethics.

Governance Ethics in Urban and Rural Water Supply

The art of connecting people to water in urban settings, especially in the booming cities of the developing world that have become magnets for the rural poor, is challenging in many ways. There is the challenge of finding adequate water supplies, of course, but then there are the further challenges of building the infrastructure to connect rapidly growing but often unplanned, informal neighborhoods. Now add the challenges of finding the investment to cover those expenses, recovering water fees from millions of water users to cover operating and maintenance costs, and managing the whole arrangement when bribery and informal payoffs are standard practice, and it's a wonder that so many urban dwellers actually do have access to even irregular supplies of water.

The urgent need for water, coupled with the fragile access that urban people, especially the poor, have to urban sources of water, makes urban water supply ripe for political manipulation. In rural areas, even a poor family can usually find a source of water somewhere, though the quality is problematic. In an urban context, individual families have a different set of options. Normally they will have to purchase water from a water utility, if there is one, or from neighborhood water collectives, if these exist, or from private water sellers, who fill the gaps, but at a high price. The question of whether private firms or public agencies operate water distribution networks is not only a contractual or management issue; it is also a governance issue.

Private or Public Water Services?

How best to serve the burgeoning population of urban poor in developing countries has become a flashpoint in water planning, and indeed in urban planning and management more generally. Is it better to rely on corrupt, inefficient public sector water utilities to deliver services that everyone needs for their survival? Or should the private sector be invited in to take over these functions at a profit, in the hope that the profit motive will stimulate more effective water service? The answers to these questions have multiple layers of ethical assumptions which need to be "unpacked" and considered, before any good answers can be proposed. The infamous case of failed privatization in Cochabamba, Bolivia, in 2000, provides an enduring example of what can go wrong, and proves not that privatization is always bad, but that there are no simple solutions.

Box 6.3 Learning from Cochabamba[7]

A city of 200,000 in 1976, Cochabamba's population soared to more than half a million by 2001 and the city was running out of water. The aquifer surrounding the city was drastically overtapped for irrigation and community wells serving the expanding peri-urban neighborhoods. The public water company, SEMAPA (*Servicio Municipal de Agua Potable y Alcantarillado*) (Municipal service for drinking water and sanitation) was run through political patronage and catered to the wealthier neighborhoods. In the poor barrios, fewer than half the households had water hookups and indoor plumbing. Independent private water companies filled some of this gap and contributed to the declining aquifer, competing with SEMAPA which also relied on more and deeper wells as its primary water source.

In 1998, the city launched a major ($300 million) project to construct a dam and pipeline (including a 12-mile tunnel) to import water to the city from the Misicuni River. At the same time, a major structural adjustment loan to Bolivia included a World Bank-inspired condition that SEMAPA be privatized. The privatization package that ensued included provision of water and sanitation services, as well as the Misicuni Dam and pipeline project. The sole bidder for this contract was a subsidiary of Bechtel, the giant US-based engineering and construction firm. The terms of the contract, approved by the municipal and national governments, gave Bechtel an exclusive 40-year lease on all water within the region of Cochabamba, including not only the aquifer, but even the rainwater. Private water companies were forced to close or to pay Bechtel for the water they pumped; homeowners were not permitted to harvest water that fell on their own roofs. (Note: Many cities in the western United States, including Denver, had almost identical provisions at the time.)

When the Bechtel subsidiary started raising rates by about 50%, a consumer revolt began to simmer. It started with the farmers outside the city who lost ownership of their irrigation water, and it spread quickly to the poor whose water bills were rivaling their monthly food budgets. Ultimately the popular protests and the tragic killing of one of the protesters resulted in enough pressure that Bechtel executives were forced out of the city and the Mayor adeptly shifted sides, annulling the contract and re-instating SEMAPA. In an ironic twist, the protests in Cochabamba paralleled anti-privatization protests going on in the streets of Washington, DC during exactly the same time, to coincide with the annual meetings of the World Bank and the IMF. The main leader of the Cochabamba protests, Oscar Olivera, was able to fly to Washington to join those protests, and to deliver a message directly to the World Bank.

Unpacking the ethics of the Cochabamba water story begins with the "before-privatization" situation. SEMAPA, like most public water utilities, held a virtual monopoly over the water sector of the city. Competition existed only beyond the fringes of its service area where water customers could mobilize around collective water wells, but these had to be dug deeper and deeper as the water table fell. The contract with Bechtel put an end to these collective wells as ownership of the water switched from common to private property. Here are two ethical principles embedded in the Bechtel contract: (1) private ownership is desirable; common ownership is not; and (2) centralized control is preferable to decentralized, local management.

The story of Cochabamba's unhappy experience with water privatization has entered the water policy history books as a clear failure for privatization, and a clear win for common people (e.g. see the account by Maude Barlow and Tony Clarke (2002) in the book, *Blue Gold*). When privatization is perceived ideologically, it constitutes a cultural value, or an "ethic" in and of itself, which proponents support ("Unleash the power of the private sector!") and critics condemn ("Water for people, not for profit!"). But privatization can also be favored as an expedient means to a more important end, e.g. addressing corruption in the public sector, or instating more effective management controls. In these contexts, privatization is a tool and not a goal. Even the definition of "privatization" is not clear-cut, since there are many traditional, local forms of privatization which are very different from the global companies buying up local water supplies.

Whether the privatization trend reflects the interests of donor countries to send more business to their compatriots, or whether their promotion of the private sector stems from good intentions for expanding water access for the poor, has become a matter of contention (Bakker 2010). There is a fairly strong consensus, however, that the policies favoring private takeovers of large urban water systems were very much overdone by the World Bank and the regional banks in the 1990s. While Cochabamba was an exceptional case, evidence quickly mounted during the late 1990s and early 2000s that giving water supply contracts to the private sector was no panacea for serving the poor, much less for assuring financial, institutional, or environmental sustainability.

While the private sector has proved not to be a panacea for effective water provision that reaches poor households, experience with the public sector is no better. Rather, the specific context matters more than the type of ownership, and particularly the regulatory framework, level of corruption, and the competence of the institutions involved, whether public or private (Bakker et al. 2008:1893–4). The fear of privatization of water popularized by Maude Barlow (Barlow and Clarke 2002) has helped to place the private water companies on notice that their actions are being watched. But in practice, the cases of pure private ownership are the exception. More common are "hybrid systems" sharing elements of both private and public sectors (McGranahan and Satterthwaite 2006:13). Another option for water supply and sanitation services is community systems managed by the users (see Box 6.4). Community approaches, while requiring intensive human inputs, offer the benefits of building organizational capacity as well as providing water/sanitation services (Bakker 2010:176–9).

Box 6.4 Community-Managed Sanitation in Karachi, Pakistan

The Orangi Pilot Project Research and Training Institute (OPP-RTI) began its support for community-managed sanitation in Orangi, an agglomeration of informal settlements in Karachi. As of 2005, Orangi had a total population of 1.2 million. OPP-RTI's low-cost sanitation program supports sanitary latrines in the house, underground sewers in the lane, and neighborhood collector sewers, then linking to the main sewers and treatment plants of the official water and sanitation agencies. OPP-RTI provides communities with maps and plans, estimates of labor and materials, tools, training for carrying out the work and supervision. Communities have to raise and manage the finances. In Orangi, 95,496 houses have built neighborhood sanitation systems, investing the equivalent of US$1.5 million. This accomplishment would have cost seven times as much if handled by the government. The OPP-RTI methodology consists of the following steps:

- holding meetings to mobilize people living in one lane to form an organization to build their underground lane sewer;
- once the lane organization is formed, it elects, selects or nominates a lane manager who applies to OPP-RTI for technical assistance and managerial guidance;
- an OPP-RTI survey team surveys the lane and establishes benchmarks;
- a map is prepared with a detailed design and the identification of the disposal point;
- the lane manager and committee collect money from the lane inhabitants and organize the work.

(Adapted from Satterthwaite et al. 2005:7)

Where an ethics perspective adds to the discussion of public vs. private governance of urban water supply and sanitation is in clarifying the governance goals. Are cost savings the exclusive goal? If so, it should be straightforward to assess the cost proposals from alternative bidders and compare these with the public sector option. Is the goal to expand service to poor neighborhoods? Is there also a social goal of community development and capacity-building? Now the choice might be to invest human resources in mobilizing local neighborhoods to create community water and sanitation groups. The specific context can suggest whether the conditions are favorable to effective private sector involvement (e.g. a strong regulatory framework) or to the formation of local organizations, but the ethics need to be clarified first to determine what types of governance arrangements are desired.

Setting Governance Boundaries

The topic of "urban water supply" implies a boundary around what is relevant to the governance of that water supply and what is not relevant. Normally the topic of water supply includes the functions of acquiring water (e.g. from wells, dams, or river diversions), treating the water to drinking water standards, distributing that water through a network of pipes to individual homes or public water points, and then recapturing the wastewater through sewers, treating the wastewater to some acceptable standards, and releasing that water back to nature, reusing it (e.g. for irrigation), or retreating it back to drinking water standards and cycling it back through the system. The edges of urban water supply deal with the natural environment (the source of the water supply and the destination for wastewater), and in between that supply of water is swirling through the urban space. Where do we wish to draw our ethical water boundary, within which our water governing will take place?

Will our concern extend to the actual sources of the water that our city will be using, perhaps in mountain springs hundreds of kilometers away? Or should we start at the point where the water enters the canal or pipeline destined for the city water treatment plant? Are we concerned about the impact of our city's water use on downstream stakeholders, whether farmers or other cities, or does our ethical responsibility end where our effluent water leaves the wastewater treatment plant, or where our storm drains enter the river? And what should we expect from the water supply swirling through the city-scape? What ethics of "urban water stewardship" should we adopt? How concerned should we be with leaking pipes and water wasteage; is this a moral issue? And how interested should we be in bringing the water out of the pipes into public view – as fountains, canals, or other water features – to enhance the aesthetic experience of urban residents? This is not normally considered in the purview of urban water supply governance, but perhaps it should be.

There has been a steady movement in water circles to push management boundaries further upstream and downstream and sideways as well. Integrated Water Resources Management (IWRM) has been all about getting a larger perspective of water use and considering the interactions among competing uses as well as potentials for growing the pie. One sector's waste water can become another sector's supply, as when urban effluent is reused for agriculture. Rather than drawing fixed boundaries around each water sub-sector, perhaps we should draw the boundaries with dashed lines and look for interactions and potential synergies.

Integrated Urban Water Resources Management (IUWM)

IWRM was invented to deal with the problem that whatever boundaries we try to create between, say, urban water supply and irrigation, or drinking water and wastewater, those boundaries are easily crossed. Within the boundaries of an urban region, there are specific issues to contend with which justify a new acronym, IUWM, "Integrated Urban Water Resources Management." The essential features of IUWM can be summarized as follows (adapted from Bahri 2012: 12). The approach:

- recognizes alternative water sources;
- differentiates the qualities and potential uses of water sources;
- views water storage, distribution, treatment, recycling, and disposal as part of the same resource management cycle;
- seeks to protect, conserve, and exploit water at its source;
- accounts for non-urban users that are dependent on the same water source;
- aligns formal institutions (organizations, legislation, and policies) and informal practices (norms and conventions) that govern water in and for cities;
- recognizes the relationships among water resources, land use, and energy;
- simultaneously pursues economic efficiency, social equity, and environmental sustainability;
- encourages participation by all stakeholders.

Several different ethical motivations can be imagined for adopting an IUWM approach ranging from economic efficiency to social justice or better environmental management. It is the potential environmental benefits, however, that stand out. In the conventional framework of water supply, the two major ethical themes are economic efficiency (control costs) and social welfare (try to provide water to everyone). Champions for the urban water environment may exist in the form of environmental groups, but under IUWM, an environmental ethic is incorporated into the internal *raison d'être* of governance. What could integration mean in a practical case?

In my city of Santa Fe, New Mexico, the water utility, which is a branch of the municipal government, has a well-defined "frame" within which its governance authority lies. While that frame includes elements of water supply and water conservation, the ecological health of local water ecosystems is not included. Environmental restoration of the local river can be justified for social goals of creating pleasant urban space, but not for purely environmental reasons. Indeed, "river restoration" activities conducted by the City government are handled through the Parks and Recreation Department rather than the Water Division (which falls under the Public Utilities Department). Planting trees along the riparian corridor, and constructing a bicycle path along the river, are viewed as social amenities for the public, and not compensation to the environment. There is no municipal environment department with a mandate to address ecosystem functions for their own sake. Storm water, for example, could make an important contribution to river flows, if managed to promote infiltration, e.g. by reducing the amount of urban hardscape. However, storm water management is explicitly not within the purview of the water utility, and instead falls under the "Streets and Drainage" division of the Public Works Department. While there are good economic reasons to provide drainage for streets, there is also a good environmental reason to utilize that drained water for the benefit of the environment. That unmet opportunity is easy to ignore without an integrative framework such as IUWM.

Urban Water Ethics Without Borders?

When water is defined as a commodity to serve the domestic needs of urban residents, the prevailing governance ethic is to "leave it to the experts." Other potential values of water, as an amenity in the urban landscape, or for recreation or psychological well-being, or as a habitat for wildlife, are viewed as outside the scope of what water experts need to be concerned with. This narrowly bounded concept of water supply governance is self-reinforcing. When the governance problem is reduced to a task that a single agency, e.g. a water utility, can handle within the normal competency of water professionals, it is in the utility's interest to keep the agency's mandate narrowly defined.

By enlarging our concepts, assumptions, and expectations of urban water governance, however, we discover a world of values-based choices involving financing arrangements, institutional capacity-building, community organizing, technical training, public outreach and education about water, private sector partnerships, NGO capacity-building, technical alternatives, etc., not to mention water quality and the ecological health of the water ecosystem. Water governance, in this broader definition, quickly faces the "triple bottom line" issues of economic, environmental, and social considerations, to which we have also added cultural considerations discussed in the following section, and also in the next chapter.

Governing the Water Environment

Concern about the sustainability of the water environment has always been included in the concept of IWRM, but the actual environmental outcomes have been disappointing (Biswas 2004, Jones et al. 2006). "Integrating" the environment in the goals of water management does not guarantee that the environmental dimensions will receive priority, but only that they will be considered. Indeed, this is probably the right way to handle environmental variables within a management context where decisions about one set of things (the environment) need to be "integrated" with other priorities: economics, politics, social variables, etc. Whether environment should enjoy a special status that will trump competing interests does not need to be hardwired into the IWRM concept. Rather, the issue of how to balance ostensibly competing interests is the rightful domain of "governance."

How can the interests of the environment find expression in governance, when nature has no voice (at least within the paradigm of Western science)? One answer is that human interests overlap in important ways with the interests of silent nature, and those humans can articulate those interests. *Ecosystem services* is the term that economists (mostly) use to refer to this overlap. However, the concept of ecosystem services does not capture ecosystem services that people do not benefit from. To value nature for itself, over and above the value to people, requires another concept.

Brown and Schmidt (2010) propose "an ethic of compassionate retreat" as the concept that we can use to protect nature from ourselves. The governance frame that we need for accommodating the interests of rivers must be large enough to include the behavioral pressures that society exerts on those rivers: "If the good of achieving material wealth for humans requires increased water supplies, the problems that arise as a consequence of increased water use rarely cause managers to question the overarching goal of increasing human wealth" (Brown and Schmidt 2010:273). That's because this is asking too much from managers. They are just doing their job of managing. It is at the larger level of water governance that the ethic of caring for nature needs to be addressed.

Where can we find the environmental ethics that can guide water governance toward sustainability? One approach is to involve people in the governance process who already possess an environmental ethic. By involving a wide range of stakeholders, including environmental organizations and Indigenous Peoples, the interests of nature can be reflected by proxy (Postel and Richter 2003, Jones et al. 2006). The IWRM paradigm has been central in highlighting the environmental dimension as important, and justifying stakeholder participation. However, there are ethical prerequisites to effective participation just as there are to environmental effectiveness.

Critiques of IWRM note the problem of unequal power, which leads to unequal participation of different stakeholders (Saravanan et al. 2009, Berry and Mollard 2010). A second problem is the communicative competence of those stakeholders not only for reasons of power, but also education, culture, etc. A third issue concerns the institutions governing IWRM which often lack critical capacities of leadership, staffing, information, or political legitimacy, and a fourth problem is the enabling environment of policies and programs, particularly at the national level. While these obstacles can be overcome, it requires a strong commitment to participation as an ethical principle. Even watersheds and river basins have been critiqued as imperfect units because water is not completely contained within a basin (Warner et al. 2008). Deep groundwater aquifers circulate below and across surface ridge-lines, evaporation and precipitation move water above and across these boundaries, and virtual water (e.g. through agriculture) can travel by land, sea, or air to anywhere on the planet.

Community Engagement at the Watershed Level

John Wesley Powell, the American explorer and student of Western land-scapes, proposed that governance of this semi-arid land should be on the basis of watershed boundaries, rather than abstract survey lines (deBuys 2001) His reasoning was that water, and not land, would be the limiting resource in the Western states, so the administrative units of local govern-ment should be aligned with the boundaries of watersheds. Powell's advice was ignored completely. Not only do we have state and country borders that have nothing to do with drainage lines, but the governance of the rivers themselves is driven by those administrative boundaries, rather than vice-versa.

The lack of correspondence between the administrative units for govern-ing people, land, and water, and the natural drainage basins (watersheds) poses challenges for water governance everywhere, but particularly so in the western United States. A few states, including Washington, Oregon, and California, have tried to retrofit state-sponsored watershed-level organiza-tions onto the existing arrangements. In most other states, voluntary organizations have emerged. There are many hundreds of river or watershed organizations, at varying levels of sophistication (Sabatier et al. 2005). These groups have no official standing in government, but in the absence of any other watershed-wide entity, the watershed organizations help fill a gov-ernance void. Their effectiveness depends on the receptivity of local govern-ance actors, including the public sector (e.g. municipal and county water agencies) and among private landowners, water rights holders, and businesses. It is the art of persuasion rather than the exercise of power.

Box 6.5 Santa Fe Watershed Association[8] (United States)

The Santa Fe Watershed Association (SFWA) was founded in 1999 through the initiative of a local watershed consultant who became alarmed at the ecological demise of the Santa Fe River. Not only was the river dammed upstream of the city, leaving the urban river channel totally dry during most of the year, but the channel was being drasti-cally incised by rapid storm runoff from the streets and rooftops of the

growing city. The other obvious threat was that of fire in the mountainous upper watershed where dense stands of pine and fir trees had
been artificially protected from fire by past forest policies. The upper
catchment of the Santa Fe River, managed by the US Forest Service,
was in imminent danger of a catastrophic wildfire fueled by the unnaturally
dense vegetation.

The fledgling watershed association had the aim of "restoring the
Santa Fe River to a living river, [and] restoring the heart to our community." Armed with a grant from the EPA, the association engaged
the community in a participatory process to develop a "Watershed
Restoration Action Plan," providing a whole-watershed perspective on
the river, even though the EPA grant's terms of reference stipulated a
much narrower report focusing on water quality.

The Association next became involved in a series of restoration
activities conducted in partnership with local government, e.g. designing a new park along the river, initiating regular planning meetings, and
conducting educational programs. With a membership never more
than 300 people, the Association could not claim to be representative
of the roughly 70,000 residents of the watershed, but did claim to
reflect the long-term interests of the community and of the river itself.
By participating in local government discussions about the river, and
through outreach and educational activities within the community, the
Association sought to influence water governance informally.

What are the ethics that have motivated the SFWA and its supporters in
the community? There is a widespread sense that restoring the river would
bring significant benefits to the city. That stewardship ethic has both a social/
community dimension (a healthy river is good for the community) and an
environmental dimension (we have a responsibility to nature). The people
who came together to form the watershed association built into its mandate
these intertwined values:

> We strive to find common ground among the different points of view
> regarding uses of the river. We advocate surface and groundwater man-
> agement that balances human use with natural resource protection. We
> encourage government and civic leaders to place high priority on sus-
> taining seasonal stream flow in the river, yielding hydrologic, recrea-
> tional, aesthetic, and environmental value to the community. We are
> committed to safeguarding the long-term integrity of the river and the
> entire watershed.[9]

In contrast to the SFWA, a small urban organization having a predominantly environmental focus, the Avari River Parliament in Rajasthan,

India has an ambitious agenda of social, cultural, environmental, and economic goals. The common features of both organizations are watershed-level governance and the central (but not exclusive) focus on environmental remediation. In the Avari River case, restoring the environment was the key to all the other benefits. In the Santa Fe case, there is also an explicit connection between restoring the river and meeting social goals, but this endeavor lacks the same urgency. Santa Fe association members do not depend on the health of their watershed for their livelihoods. In the Avari River case, they clearly do.

Box 6.6 Revitalizing the Avari River Watershed (India)

In the semi-arid Arwali Hills of Central Rajasthan, villages had long resigned themselves to uncertain rain-fed farming supplemented by deep wells tapping unreliable groundwater. In 1985, a local NGO, Tarun Bharat Sangh (TBS) initiated a program to address the region's poverty through the use of traditional water harvesting. The founder of TBS, Rajendra Singh, was an Ayurvedic doctor who felt that the same principles of instilling health through rebalancing the body, could be applied to the land itself (Padre 2000:14). TBS encouraged local villages to construct water retention structures (johad) in suitable locations to capture rainwater runoff from the local hills and recharge the aquifer.[10] While TBS would provide the equipment and construction materials, the labor had to be provided by the village. Discussing the terms, and deciding on the location and design of the structures, required multiple meetings of the gram sabha (village council), a process which served to revitalize these flagging institutions.

In the first ten years of the program nearly 2,500 johads were constructed across some 500 villages (Agarwal and Narain 1999). Villagers noticed that the Arvari River, the primary river in the region, no longer dried up so soon after the summer monsoon rains. By 1995, the river flow continued year-round, and has been flowing ever since. This became known as the Arvari Miracle but it also prompted new problems. In 1996 the state fisheries department issued a license to an outside contractor to catch the fish that now swam in the river, prompting the villagers to protest that the fish belonged to them and not to the government. Their protest resulted in a cancelled contract, and the realization that the river they had worked so hard to bring back to life, now needed to be governed by them as well. At a meeting called by TBS for the 72 gram sabhas of the Avari River catchment, the Avari River Parliament was created (in January 1999), comprising 110 representatives from the 72 villages. The new organization adopted a set of rules that would be morally (but not legally) binding on the member villages (Glendenning 2009:172).

The rules included a ban on water-intensive crops (e.g. rice, cotton, and sugarcane), control over water withdrawals from storage ponds, bans on deep wells (tubewells), commercial fishing, and rock quarrying, and regulations for forest protection. The rules are revisited and adjusted at biannual meetings. Glendenning (2009:173–5) notes that the rule against tubewells, in particular, is not observed in practice, presumably because groundwater levels have remained stable. Her prediction is that when the water table drops, as it certainly will with an increasing number of wells, the Avari River Parliament will be spurred to take more effective measures. The existing form of the parliament provides a potential that can be operationalized when the time comes.

Rajendra Singh's organization, TBS, has established a national network, Jal Biradari, to apply the lessons of the Avari River villages to other Indian rivers. Reviving the physical ecology of the watershed, through managing the rainfall runoff, is the first step in the approach, but it is not the goal. The goal is social, with the recognition that the health of nature and local communities is intertwined. "A river is not just water. It is the people who live on its banks, the flora and fauna in and around it," says Vikrant Sharma an activist working with Rajendra Singh.[11] The governance goal of the Avari River Parliament, or of future river parliaments elsewhere, is to guide the practical management of water within the catchment to contribute to the health of the land, the people, and the river. The Jal Biradari website puts it this way:[12]

> Jal Biradari strongly feels that decentralized water management is the solution for India ... These small local interventions have a very positive impact both on nature and communities while too often giant steps are destructive to nature and people. Jal Biradari believes that water is a common natural resource rather than the property of one individual or company. It is the basis of life and common future of the country. So community has equal rights in the management & use of the water resource.

River Basin Institutions

The same logic of stakeholder participation that applies to small rivers and watersheds also applies to large rivers and river basins. The challenging organizational logistics of interacting along a river basin extending hundreds of kilometers and involving millions of stakeholders, requires a different level of effort and often governmental involvement. There are many good models for formal stakeholder arrangements that can represent the diverse interests of basin residents (GWP and INBO 2009). These range from river basin commissions such as the Rhine River Commission or Australia's Murray Darling River Commission, to basin councils having little or no executive authority, but serving the functions of convening stakeholders.

There is general consensus that water does need to be governed at the natural scale of a river basin, whether through a single, unitary organization or overlapping entities (Molle et al. 2007). The primary ethical issue is that of voice and representation. Whose voices are heard and how are the interests of disadvantaged groups (social ethics) and nature (environmental ethics) represented? In particular, who speaks for nature? How is the organization structured to invite the participation of the various stakeholder groups? How does the basin level organization relate to sub-groups at the watershed or tributary level, and how does it relate to the local governments within its boundaries?

Without a deliberate ethical approach, governance of large river basins can easily fall into a default mode of top-down expert-driven decisions, precisely because there are so many technical issues to deal with. To counter this natural tendency, the concept of a "negotiated approach" seeks to build-in support for local decision-making. "Local, micro-watershed levels should be a priority for decision-making. Only where absolutely necessary should decisions be taken at higher and higher administrative levels. This allows local actors to develop context-specific basin management strategies and to influence regional and national decisions, with the ultimate end of developing a bottom-up process of policy development and management" (Both ENDS and Gomukh 2005:4).

The difficulties of organizing at the scale of a river basin adds to the importance of strong value-based commitment to participatory governance in the first place. It will always be easier to avoid the sometimes bothersome challenges of placating divergent interests and engaging in detailed discussions among stakeholders. The same type of temptation applies to the inclusion of environmental voices in the mix of stakeholders. A commitment to the process of hearing from social and environmental advocates is itself an ethical choice. Basin management, like democracy, is a messy process.

Conclusions

In this chapter we have examined three distinct domains of water governance, irrigation, urban water supply, and water basins. In each of these domains the process of governance is as important as the end result. Participation of irrigation users in managing the water and infrastructure of their system is important for social as well as economic reasons. Users' management involvement can also play a role in urban water supply, but the bigger issue is the accountability and responsiveness of utility managers to social justice (providing water and sanitation to everyone) and to the environment (extending the governance frame to include environmental goals). Governance of water basins, whether small watersheds or large river basins, has ready-made boundaries within which integrated water management can unfold. The Avari River case demonstrates how tightly integrated are the ethics of environment, society, culture, and economics into a quadruple bottom line.

If water basins are the natural unit for integrating what could otherwise become competing goals (e.g. economy vs. environment), then governance is the natural level for creating harmonious solutions. It is at the governance level that the "big picture" of water management policies and practices can be ordered to align with the goals of society. This presumes that the goals of society, at least with regard to water, are fairly clear, and if they are not clear, the first priority of governance has to be to determine what the goals are, what the values and ethics are which governance should aspire to advance (Groenfeldt and Schmidt 2013). Governance needs a broad framework, clear goals (ethics) and a bounded geography (e.g. a river basin, though it could also be a project, or a city, state, or nation).

The importance of goals grounded in clear ethics is seen in every case discussed in this chapter, and I would suggest, in every case not discussed as well. Is participatory governance of irrigation systems a top priority for a World Bank-funded project, or a weak priority? What about agroecology as an alternative to industrial farming? A whole stream of investment decisions depend on the answers, but what determines what the answer will be? Ethics. Not in the sense of good ethics or bad ethics, but in the sense of what values will the project try to support. Social values through supporting the organizational capacity of the farmers? Cultural values by promoting heritage food crops? Environmental values by encouraging organic and agro-ecological cultivation practices? Economic values is not a question for the World Bank, but how will the economic goals/ethics interact with the social and environmental and cultural goals/ethics?

These detailed decisions about the design of an irrigation development project can best be answered at a higher level of governance, where the organizational entity (the World Bank) sets goals for its operations. Similarly, a decision about whether to use permeable paving in constructing a city parking lot should not be made by the construction manager, but by the city agency "governing" water. If there is no such agency, the governance function will need to be created, and if it is not created, the need for the function does not disappear; it becomes an unmet need, and a potential employment opportunity for someone in the future!

A perspective of water ethics can shine a light into the dark corners of the assumptions underlying water governance. Is the river basin suffering from "scarcity" or from over-use? Why is so much water going to one particular use (e.g. golf courses) rather than another use (e.g. environmental flow)? Analyzing the ethics of water governance goals will call into question the current definition of the governance "problem" of maintaining quality of life in the face of increasingly scarce water. Evaluating the underlying assumptions and following the ethics to their logical implications can reveal new options for coexistence with the natural world, and with each other.

Notes

1 See http://www.gwp.org.
2 See http://www.worldwatercouncil.org.
3 http://www.unwater.org is the umbrella website for UN organizations working on water in some way.
4 The "Ministerial Declaration of The Hague on Water Security in the 21st Century" is available on the World Water Council website, http://www.worldwatercouncil. org/fileadmin/wwc/Library/Official_Declarations/The_Hague_Declaration.pdf.
5 This state-centered ethic is well described in the classical Indian treatise written by Kautilya, *The Arthasthastra*.
6 My information about donor encouragement of private sector partnerships with water user associations derives from a recent consulting assignment in India, with the Asian Development Bank (January–March 2011), and informal discussions with staff of the World Bank office in New Delhi.
7 This account is based on a detailed story in *New Yorker Magazine* (Finnegan 2002), and a retrospective account by an on-the-scene reporter at the time (Schultz 2008).
8 This account of the Santa Fe Watershed Association is based on the author's personal experience as Executive Director of the Association from early 2006 to the end of 2009.
9 Excerpt from the 2005 brochure of the Santa Fe Watershed Association.
10 The structures were usually concave earthen dams across a drainage line, with the resulting pond covering a large area of between 2 to 50 hectares of land (2ha = 5 acres, or about the area of five football fields).
11 Quoted in *The Hindu*, May 23, 2012, http://www.thehindu.com/life-and-style/ society/article3449172.ece.
12 See http://www.tarunbharatsangh.org/programs/jalbiradari/about.htm.

7   Indigenous Water Ethics

The water ethics of Indigenous Peoples carry particular weight in considering how ethics motivate water policies and practices. In a very real moral sense, we (the non-indigenous world) owe something to the Indigenous Peoples whose cultures have vanished, and to the Indigenous Peoples whose people and cultures are still here, still functioning, and in many but not all cases, still vibrant. What we owe them was hinted at in the World Commission on Dams report which called for "Requiring the free, prior and informed consent of indigenous and tribal peoples [because this] empowers them at the negotiating table" (WCD 2000:216). Indigenous Peoples are especially liable to be pressured into accepting terms whose implications they do not understand, because of the cultural gulf separating their world from ours.

This special consideration in helping indigenous communities understand, for example, what it will mean if the dam is constructed, and then respecting their right to decide "Yes" or "No" is part of what we "owe" them, but that is only the first step. The second step of what is gradually evolving as an expectation of good practice, is not only helping them understand us and our water policies, but accepting a reciprocal responsibility to learn their views about water, their water ethics. Chief Justice Lance S.G. Finch of the British Columbia Court of Appeal calls this "the duty to learn" (Finch 2012).[1] "How can we make space within the legal landscape for Indigenous legal orders? The answer depends, at least in part, on an inversion of the question: a crucial part of this process must be to find space for ourselves, as strangers and newcomers, within the Indigenous legal orders themselves." It is in this sense that we have an obligation, a duty, to learn how Indigenous Peoples view water and water ecosystems. In order to understand how water policies can support the cultural ethics of Indigenous Peoples, we need to have some understanding of what those ethical principles might be.

Indigenous Peoples have much to teach us about water ethics, not only because they still retain much of their traditional ecological knowledge, though this is extremely important (Suzuki and Knudtson 1992). The other reason that we have so much to learn from the experience and cultures of Indigenous Peoples stems from their position *vis-à-vis* the dominant societies that define their cultural boundaries. As minority cultures, Indigenous

Peoples are only too aware of their cultural differences, continuously reminded of the role that their cultural and spiritual assumptions, beliefs, values, and ethics play in their perception of and decisions about the natural world, including water. By trying to understand what life looks and feels like to Indigenous Peoples, we can learn something about what it means to bring ethics into the realm of conscious choice. Indigenous Peoples do this on a daily basis.

The clash of cultural values can be seen very readily in choices about the physical design of water systems. In the Mahaweli irrigation project in Sri Lanka, a state-of-the-art USAID-funded main canal was designed with steeply sloped concrete sides, making impossible customary uses such as bathing, laundry, or watering domestic animals. In the Bali Irrigation Improvement Project in Indonesia, funded by the Asian Development Bank, "improvements" were proposed to the traditional notched logs that divide the flow of a small canal into several smaller field channels, with the amount of water in each channel proportional to the size of the area to be irrigated. The project design called for concrete "junction boxes" with the larger canal going in and several small channels coming out. Either system could perform the physical task of dividing a single larger flow into calibrated smaller flows, but the easy transparency of the traditional Balinese solution also provided a way for farmers to visually monitor the proper functioning of the water division (Horst 1996).

Both these examples raise a question that is so fundamental to an irrigation project that it is too rarely asked: What is an irrigation canal? Is it a large open channel engineered for optimally conveying water from here to there? Or is it designed to provide a myriad of water benefits to the people living along its path, as well as conveying water to the network of smaller canals downstream? And what is a division structure? Is it a way to divide the flow from the larger canal into specific amounts of flow into two or more smaller canals? Or is it also a way of supporting farmers' organizational capacities through setting and monitoring which farmers will receive what proportion of the flow? In Bali the division structures also have a spiritual purpose; farmers perform pujas at the division weir for the spirits that protect the water and the crops (Lansing 1996). The water management functions of conveying the irrigation water in canals, and dividing it into the agreed-upon shares for different fields, are expressions of cultural categories or "frames" which signal information about what kind of activity is going on. Is it economic business (the canal as conveyor or water) or domestic business (the canal as supplier of household water and washing) or spiritual business (the canal as a pathway for the water goddess to move into the fields)?

For indigenous cultures, the irrigation canal connotes all these meanings and perhaps more. The meta-frame, the big picture concept, is one of relationship. As humans, we are related to, and have responsibilities for, the water that has been diverted from the river and is flowing to our fields. The water, in turn, and the spirits of the river and of the canal water, have responsibilities to us, and to the young plants in the fields that the water is on its way to nourish. In traditional indigenous worldviews (as well as in the Western science of ecology!) the world is interconnected; it is not divided into the silos of river management, irrigation management, and agricultural management, or even into the silos of agriculture and religion.

The water ethics that we can learn from, that offer a different "take" on our relationship to the natural world, are found within the normative cultures of Indigenous Peoples everywhere. This is not to deny that individual indigenous persons and even tribal governments (in the United States context) may subscribe to the same values as Western economists. We will discuss, below, the case of the Hopi tribal government's contract with Peabody Coal to strip-mine sacred tribal lands and impact sacred and scarce water supplies. But the actions of a tribal government do not necessarily represent the views of the tribal members. Indeed, the internal tribal opposition to the position of the tribal government can be seen as evidence that traditional cultural values are still very much alive (Groenfeldt 2006b).

The reason that the normative Indigenous cultural worldviews are so important to a discussion of water ethics is that they bring a different "frame" to the question of "What is water?" Western science concluded long ago that we already know what water is; it is an inert mineral resource which provides a range of benefits which we are busy managing and governing according to a well-worked-out frame of Integrated Water Resources Management! But that is not how most (and perhaps all) indigenous cultures view water. Water, to the indigenous world, is alive and conscious. And even more than being alive, water is part of our extended family of "all our relations."

Box 7.1 Is Water Alive?

At the 2006 World Water Forum in Mexico City, I co-organized a session about indigenous perspectives on water, along with Tom Goldtooth, the founder and president of Indigenous Environmental Network (http://www.ienearth.org). The title of our session was, *Is Water Alive? Indigenous Understandings of Water* (Martinez Austria and von Hofwegan 2006:7). The title was meant to convey two simultaneously obvious and opposite meanings. Within the frame of indigenous cultures, water, whether water bodies or water as a substance, is universally held to be in some sense "alive" with spiritual and life-generating properties and consciousness. Within the frame of Western scientific rationalism, on the other hand, water is universally held to be an inert substance, necessary for life, but not having life itself. The outcome of the session was the following:[2]

> *The indigenous communities are linked to their local waters in a symbio-tic relationship; indigenous culture and spirituality depends upon the health of the water and watershed, while the environmental health of the water depends on the spiritual practices of the indigenous communities.*
>
> *Indigenous peoples actively manage their water through spiritual prac-tices (ceremonies and rituals), as well as the more familiar physical practices (e.g., diverting water for irrigation). What outsiders may see as under-utilized water resources are already being managed and "used" through spiritual practices. The deep respect manifested through indi-genous spiritual is needed for sustainable management of water bodies. The degradation of the American Great Lakes and the Navajo aquifer are lessons in the dangers of ignoring indigenous peoples spiritual respect for water.*

Key Messages:

- Concept of a "social basin" that unites all the stakeholders who share a water source and have a common interest in protecting it;
- Religious ritual and spiritual practice is tied to the water source/water body on which the community depends;
- The health of water bodies is protected through spiritual practices, both directly and indirectly;
- Understanding water takes a long time. Indigenous peoples have been learning about their local waters for many generations. Their knowledge needs to be applied to local water management.

Orientations for Action:

- Include the social dimension (local communities) in the concept of watersheds and water basins;
- Include cultural knowledge and spiritual practices of local indigen-ous communities as an integral part of the watershed/basin;
- Respect the spiritual and cultural knowledge of indigenous peoples, including their understanding of their local waters and watersheds. Accept these local understandings as being equally valid as out-siders' paradigms about water management. The two sets of para-digms need not be in conflict; with mutual respect, each can benefit from the other.

Differences in cultural norms take on tangible reality when it comes to rights of water access (Boelens et al. 2007). Whose cultural understanding about water will be incorporated into the new irrigation network? How will the water flows be allocated and by whose authority will this be done? Customary understandings about access to irrigation water, or about ownership of canals and the authority to make repairs or alterations to those canals can be a source of conflict between indigenous communities and state water agencies (van Koppen 2007). Indigenous cultural values also come into play in setting up community drinking water systems. Will the new wells be under the control of the traditional chief? Or does the provision of new wells provide an opportunity to overturn that authority in favor of a democratic water supply association?

Conflicts over water sources which are considered sacred to local Indigenous Peoples have become routine, and can be seen as a clash between traditional vs. global worldviews (Mander and Tauli-Corpuz 2006). The battle lines can be difficult to distinguish, however, as there are often conflicts within the indigenous community between factions supporting strict interpretation of traditional values vs. those embracing the economic opportunities of the proposed development. In the case of Cochiti Dam discussed in Chapter 2, the question of whether to allow the dam to be built or not nearly destroyed the ability of the indigenous community of Cochiti to survive politically as a village. Ultimately the forces of modernity prevailed, and the dam was built, but the social scars continue to be felt internally.

Challenges of Bridging Divergent Water Cultures

The culturally based assumptions about water which Indigenous Peoples typically share, at least in terms of their cultural norms, present several unique water challenges: (1) indigenous cultural and spiritual understandings about water are often misunderstood or simply ignored by the dominant societies; (2) indigenous communities are rarely included meaningfully in water policy and planning processes; (3) customary access and rights to water are seldom recognized by the state authorities that now control indigenous areas, and (4) water bodies that are critical to cultural and physical well-being are being polluted, dewatered, or dammed. Each of these special challenges is elucidated below, along with some suggestions for how these challenges might become reworked into opportunities not only for indigenous communities, but for all of us.

1. Cultural distinctiveness

One of the defining features of Indigenous Peoples is that they are culturally distinct. They have their own way of doing things, and their own reasons for doing them, and their identity as a social group is tied to their shared cultural identity. This is not to claim that all members of the group have the same culturally mandated views and values. As the anthropologist, Mary Douglas, has observed, there is significant diversity within every cultural group (Douglas 2004). The relative importance of the diversity within cultures vs. the diversity across cultures has served as fodder for countless academic debates, but ultimately it is not for the outside experts alone to decide whether a group is culturally distinct. The members of the group in question also hold a right to determine for themselves whether they wish to be considered a distinct cultural group. This right has been recognized in UN Resolutions and most recently in the Declaration on the Rights of Indigenous Peoples (DRIP).[3]

Box 7.2 UN Recognition of Indigenous Peoples' Rights to Water

The most important declaration for supporting indigenous rights to manage water and water ecosystems is the 2007 UN Declaration on the Rights of Indigenous Peoples (DRIP) which has become an important standard in legal claims. The Declaration makes only two references to water. Article 25 states that "Indigenous peoples have the right to maintain and strengthen their distinctive spiritual relationship with their traditionally owned or otherwise occupied and used lands, territories, waters and coastal seas and other resources and to uphold their responsibilities to future generations in this regard."

Article 32 addresses the delicate issue of control over natural resources and makes three points (United Nations 2008):

1. Indigenous peoples have the right to determine and develop priorities and strategies for the development or use of their lands or territories and other resources.
2. States shall consult and cooperate in good faith with the indigenous peoples concerned through their own representative institutions in order to obtain their free and informed consent prior to the approval of any project affecting their lands or territories and other resources, particularly in connection with the development, utilization or exploitation of mineral, water or other resources.
3. States shall provide effective mechanisms for just and fair redress for any such activities, and appropriate measures shall be taken to mitigate adverse environmental, economic, social, cultural or spiritual impact.

When a member of an indigenous group identifies the river flowing through the group's territory as "sacred" what precisely does this mean? As with the claim to cultural indigeneity, the individual's assertion that the river is sacred has to be taken at face value. Who can prove it wrong? Yet we know from the analysis of specific cases that different members of the same group may hold very different and conflicting views about whether the river really is sacred, and what that really means. For example, Hindu adherents of the sacredness of the Yamuna River in India agree that the river is sacred, but disagree on the implications in terms of whether the river poses a health risk, and even whether pollution is a problem or not (Haberman 2006). Among the Hopi tribe in the southwestern United States, there is general consensus that the landform of Black Mesa is sacred, but there is contentious debate within the tribe as to whether a surface coal mine is a cultural abomination, or an economic benefit (Groenfeldt 2006b).

Indigenous Peoples of Australia, notes Jackson (2006), place value on their relationship to the landscape, as well as to one another. Those relationships imply both rights (the right to be acknowledged as a relative) and responsibilities (to protect the land, water, and associated plants and animals). This aggregate set of relationships and responsibilities is part of daily life experience, and it also constitutes a spiritual experience. There does not need to be a church (i.e. a specific place) nor a church service (i.e. a certain time) for Indigenous Peoples to practice their religion.[4] The ethics that motivate Indigenous Peoples in their use and governance of water, are rooted in this sense of kinship with and responsibility for nature, as a sacred duty and an ongoing spiritual experience and practice.

When the Taos Pueblo in New Mexico requested that their sacred Blue Lake, the source of the stream that flows through their village, be returned to them, they knew success was unlikely. The entire upper watershed of Taos Creek, including Blue Lake, had been absorbed years earlier into the administration of the National Forest Service. From the government's perspective, the legitimate religious rights of Taos Pueblo were already being met by allowing access to the lake for ceremonial purposes (which involved applying for a special permit from the Forest Service), but the indigenous community wanted full ownership. They wanted to prevent non-Indians from fishing in the lake and desecrating it with trash from their campsites. They wanted control over the lake so they would not need to justify their use of the lake with intermediary authorities. The authority of Taos Pueblo to control the lake came from their own creation story, and in their view, no other justification was required.

Taos Pueblo was successful in their quest when then-President Richard Nixon transferred ownership of Blue Lake back to Taos Pueblo in 1972. The reason the federal government acquiesced had little to do with acknowledging the demands of the tribe to freely practice their native religion. Rather, a fortuitous confluence of political interests rendered the land transfer expedient for all parties. The result was a sense of good will, but no greater understanding of the real significance of Blue Lake within the Taos Pueblo worldview (Nabokov 2006).

2. Participation in water planning

How can indigenous communities participate meaningfully in water planning conducted by agents of the mainstream society, when there are fundamentally different ideas about water itself? The short answer is that it requires real commitment on all sides to employ a planning process that is sensitive to the cultural challenges (Groenfeldt 2003b). A common pitfall on the indigenous side is that their representatives in the water planning process may be technically knowledgeable but culturally weak; the very fact that they have acquired technical skills in the outside world is sometimes a clue that they have become disconnected from their community's cultural values. The case of Cochiti Dam cited in Chapter 2 is a good example. The supporters of the dam within the indigenous community were those who had substantial experience in the outside world (in this case, the men who had fought in World War II) and they were swayed by the economic arguments offered by the dam's sponsors, the US Army Corps of Engineers (Pecos 2007). The community faction opposing the dam tended to be those whose worldview was more traditional, and to whom the economic justifications had little cultural relevance.

Perhaps the most common pitfall among the non-indigenous side of water planning (typically a corporation or a government water agency) is making too many assumptions about how water is perceived. Jackson (2006) notes that even such basic terms as "cultural values" and "social values" are not easily agreed upon among regional planners in Australia. In a planning effort to capture the cultural values of indigenous aboriginal groups along the Daly River, the term "cultural values" served as a gloss for "indigenous values" while "social values" was the term used for what an anthropologist would call the cultural values of the non-indigenous (mostly Euro-Australian) population. This situation underscores the challenges in cross-cultural communication with Indigenous Peoples.

Members of a dominant culture tend to overlook the values dimension of their own worldview. What an outside observer might label as a "cultural value" is perceived from inside the culture as simply the way things are, a basic piece of reality unencumbered with any overlay or underlay of values. Indigenous Peoples, on the other hand are keenly aware of their own culture, to the extent that they are sometimes accused of exaggerating their cultural uniqueness as a negotiating strategy. In the Australian and American contexts especially, Indigenous Peoples are very much aware that they have "culture" whereas the hydrologists, engineers, and economists driving the water planning process from the government side can afford to overlook their own cultural values. Their dominant culture has set the terms within which the indigenous community is being invited to comment. In the words of anthropologist Arturo Escobar (1995), this is a case of "semiotic hegemony." The dominant society has usurped not only the land and water, but the very code by which indigenous communities conceptualize their natural resources.

Water plans and strategies have become essential documents in the water literature of most countries and international agencies. The World Bank regularly updates its institutional Water Policy, the European Union has a Water Framework Directive, and the United States, though shying away from developing a national water policy, is rife with water plans at the state and project levels, and increasingly at the level of river basins and watersheds. Water planning by indigenous communities, however, remains very much the exception rather than the rule. Aside from Australia, where there has been a government-led effort to work with indigenous communities in developing water strategies (Jackson 2009), there are very few comprehensive water resources management plans developed by, or even for, indigenous communities. Instead, the more common form of indigenous big-picture water perspectives is a declaration of the fundamental principles and "ethics" describing their relationship to water.

There have been a considerable number of indigenous water statements and declarations, over the past decade, with very consistent messages. The Indigenous Peoples Kyoto Water Declaration is perhaps the best known. The Declaration was drafted during the 3rd World Water Forum held in Kyoto in 2003, by the indigenous participants. The key drafters were Tom Goldtooth, president of Indigenous Environmental Network, and Victoria Taupi-Cruz, the Executive Director of Tebtebba. The declaration was partly modeled on an indigenous statement to the UN Sustainable Development Conference held in Johannesburg in 2002, the Kimberley Declaration, which some of the same people had also been involved in drafting. The Kyoto Declaration was initially communicated to the World Water Forum through an unofficial march through the conference center with the indigenous participants speaking the declaration out loud, followed by a press conference. Later the Declaration was posted on various websites[5] and is also included in the UNESCO publication, *Water and Indigenous Peoples* (Chibba et al. 2006).

Box 7.3 Indigenous Peoples Kyoto Declaration on Water

Two sections of the Declaration outline a set of ethics for water governance. The first section, entitled, "Relationship to Water" (paragraphs 1–3) explains why Indigenous Peoples feel a responsibility to protect water ecosystems. Another section is labeled, "Right to Water and Self Determination" (paragraphs 9–12) and describes the rights and responsibilities of Indigenous Peoples to protect their cultural way of life.

Relationship to Water

1. We, the Indigenous Peoples from all parts of the world assembled here, reaffirm our relationship to Mother Earth and responsibility to future generations to raise our voices in solidarity to speak for the protection of water. We were placed in a sacred

manner on this earth, each in our own sacred and traditional lands and territories to care for all of creation and to care for water.

2. We recognize, honor and respect water as sacred and sustains all life. Our traditional knowledge, laws and ways of life teach us to be responsible in caring for this sacred gift that connects all life.

3. Our relationship with our lands, territories and water is the fundamental physical cultural and spiritual basis for our existence. This relationship to our Mother Earth requires us to conserve our freshwaters and oceans for the survival of present and future generations. We assert our role as caretakers with rights and responsibilities to defend and ensure the protection, availability and purity of water. We stand united to follow and implement our knowledge and traditional laws and exercise our right of self-determination to preserve water, and to preserve life. ...

Right to Water and Self Determination

9. We Indigenous Peoples have the right to self-determination. By virtue of that right we have the right to freely exercise full authority and control of our natural resources including water. We also refer to our right of permanent sovereignty over our natural resources, including water.

10. Self-determination for Indigenous Peoples includes the right to control our institutions, territories, resources, social orders, and cultures without external domination or interference.

11. Self-determination includes the practice of our cultural and spiritual relationships with water, and the exercise of authority to govern, use, manage, regulate, recover, conserve, enhance and renew our water sources, without interference.

12. International law recognizes the rights of Indigenous Peoples to:

- Self-determination
- Ownership, control and management of our traditional territories, lands and natural resources
- Exercise our customary law
- Represent ourselves through our own institutions
- Require free prior and informed consent to developments on our land
- Control and share in the benefits of the use of, our traditional knowledge.

If Indigenous Peoples hold such righteous ethics, why do we see such inconsistencies in the real world? And why does indigenous water planning seem to stop at the level of lofty declarations rather than addressing the practical details needed to ensure that their rivers are indeed protected? There is always a tension between ethical values and practical action, of course, and not only among Indigenous Peoples. The gap between ethics and practice, however, does not deny the importance of ethics in motivating practical behavior; it merely indicates that there are other influences, besides ethics, which contribute to practical outcomes.

Whether and how these big-picture ethics of indigenous relatedness with water is integrated into actual plans and policies depends very much on who is driving the planning process, and with what intentions and, in a word, "ethics." The government of Australia and the individual states are committed to "recognising Indigenous relationships with water for spiritual, cultural and economic purposes ... [and] have committed to include Indigenous representation in water planning, incorporate Indigenous social, spiritual and customary objectives and strategies [and to] take account of the possible existence of native title rights to water."[6] As an outgrowth of this position, the government supports indigenous planning capacity and has invested in both research and action programs to incorporate meaningful indigenous representation (Jackson 2009).

In the Andean region, indigenous communities maintain a water culture that goes back to the Incas but which is today challenged by state-sponsored water governance forms and values (Boelens et al. 2010). From a planning perspective, however, the struggle for water governance can be seen as a potential pathway for indigenous participation in the planning process. Through activism (e.g. protest marches demanding water rights), dialogue, and even through violence, messages about water values and ethics are communicated to the authorities who control water policies and planning.

In both the Australian and Andean cases, the practical expressions of indigenous engagement – whether through participation in planning workshops or street demonstrations – are informed by vision statements or declarations.[7] In other cases, where indigenous communities lack effective organizations, and where government agencies fail to invite indigenous representation, water planning proceeds without input from Indigenous Peoples' interests. Such has been the case in Chhattisgarh, India, where new pressures on water resources from mining, industry, and agriculture, are impinging on customary uses by indigenous communities. Without making a concerted effort to incorporate indigenous representation into water planning, development assistance projects are unlikely to represent indigenous interests. Rather, in a continuation of the Colonial legacy, development projects reflect the priorities of the outside donors and local elites who have input into the planning process (see e.g. Anderson and Huber 1988).

3. Customary rights vs. "legal" rights

Under the Doctrine of Discovery proclaimed by the Vatican during the 15th Century, the Portuguese and Spanish Crown adopted a very explicit policy of ignoring the customary land and water rights of Indigenous Peoples. From both a legal and religious perspective, the Doctrine of Discovery justified the enslavement of Indigenous Peoples and the seizing of their lands, including the water flowing through those lands. The Doctrine was later invoked by the US Supreme Court in 1823. Not only has the doctrine never been formally repealed (though this process is ongoing at the United Nations), but contemporary legal frameworks, including US law, still incorporates references to the Doctrine as a justification for state expansion into traditional indigenous territory (Miller 2005:2–3).

The moral legacy of this ethic is seen today in the general absence of state recognition of customary water rights (van Koppen et al. 2007). The Pyramid Lake Paiute Tribe in the state of Nevada have relied on the once plentiful fish from Pyramid Lake for some 4,000 years. The lake is fed by the Truckee River which flows out of the Sierra Nevada mountains. Shortly after 1900, the US government constructed a dam on this river, upstream of the lake, to divert water into an irrigation canal destined for Euro-American farmers some distance away. The dam diverted about half the flow of the river, launching a cascade of ecological interactions: the lake level dropped, salinity increased, and fish could no longer reach the upper river to spawn. The result was the near decimation of the Indian tribe, bereft of its primary source of subsistence (Wilkinson 2010). Court rulings during the 1970s to 1990s found that the US government had acted wrongly in ignoring the customary water rights of the tribe, but ruled that since so much time had elapsed, there was no practical way to compensate the tribe for their degraded lake (Wilkinson 2010:220–2).

Similar cases abound where indigenous communities relied on water supplies that were later wrested from their control. In the northwestern United States, the coastal Indian tribes who relied traditionally on salmon, have seen fish populations collapse from water diversions and hydroelectric dams (Fisher 2012). This is also the struggle that Andean farmers are currently engaged in: the irrigation canals first constructed by their indigenous Incan ancestors have recently been expropriated by state agricultural or irrigation agencies (Boelens et al. 2007).

Where the dominant state authorities choose to respect customary law, as in Australia, the two sides can enter into a discussion or a negotiating process to find a mutually acceptable solution. However, because of the unequal power relations, the final agreement is normally couched in the terminology of the more powerful side. Strategies of "water diplomacy" (Islam and Susskind 2013), which presume a negotiation process among roughly equal partners, are less useful when one side holds the power to force a settlement. And even when the powerful party has the best of intentions (e.g. Australia, we presume) the cultural values and ethics implicit in the language and categories (e.g. the concept of water "resources") skews the discussion towards the powerful side.

Two strategies offer a solution to the dilemma of skewed water diplomacy. One solution is to not try for negotiation or diplomacy within a context of assimilation, but rather agree to disagree and aim for convivial separation. By treating water management as a political (and ethical) issue, Indigenous

Peoples become more free to create their own relationship to water without trying to fit the categories of the dominant society (Palmer 2006). The cultural differences are too great to bridge, nor is there any good reason to try; just embrace diversity!

The other approach to dealing with the uneven "playing field" facing representatives from indigenous vs. mainstream society is for the indigenous players to embrace the mainstream "rules" (i.e. the Western legal framework) without embracing the values and ethics implicit in those laws. Thus we find Maori attorneys arguing successfully in New Zealand that the Whanganui River should be accorded legal standing as a person. This legal fiction has a basis in both the Western legal framework and in Maori customary law; both legal systems recognize that "personhood" can be applied to things other than human people.

Box 7.4 Rivers as People[8]

The Whanganui River will become a legal entity and have a legal voice under a preliminary agreement signed between Whanganui River iwi and the Crown.

This is the first time a river has been given a legal identity. A spokesman for the Minister of Treaty Negotiations said Whanganui River will be recognized as a person when it comes to the law – "in the same way a company is, which will give it rights and interests."

The agreement was signed on behalf of Whanganui iwi by Brendan Puketapu of the Whanganui River Maori Trust, which represents a group of iwi along the river, and the Crown in Parliament.

Under the agreement the river is given legal status under the name Te Awa Tupua – two guardians, one from the Crown and one from a Whanganui River iwi, will be given the role of protecting the river. An agreement between the Crown and local iwi on what the values will be in protecting the river are yet to be decided. A whole river strategy, in collaboration with iwi, local government, and commercial and recreational users is still being decided. An eventual settlement will also include monetary compensation for historical claims.

The Minister for Treaty for Waitangi Negotiations, Christopher Finlayson, said the signing was an historic event. "Whanganui River iwi have sought to protect the river and have their interests acknowledged by the Crown through the legal system since 1873. They pursued this objective in one of New Zealand's longest running court cases." Today's agreement which recognizes the status of the river as Te Awa Tupua (an integrated, living whole) and the inextricable relationship of iwi with the river is a major step towards the resolution of the historical grievances of Whanganui iwi and is important nationally.

"The agreement does not signify the end of the settlement, but it is a significant step towards settlement. Matters of detail and additional redress will be to be negotiated between the parties," said Mr Finlayson. "Whanganui Iwi also recognise the value others place on the river and wanted to ensure that all stakeholders and the river community as a whole are actively engaged in developing the long-term future of the river and ensuring its wellbeing," said Mr Finlayson.

The legal term for the art of seeing the same things from two very different perspectives is "legal pluralism." If we are serious about embracing cultural diversity then embracing legal pluralism offers a way of operationalizing that diversity. The Western legal system and the water ethics that underlie the laws and – the word fits: customs – of that legal system are not going to disappear very soon. In order to retain their cultural integrity, Indigenous groups will need to find ways of accommodating their customary water behavior and ethics, within that Western reality. *Legal pluralism* offers a ready-made label that can legitimize indigenous water ethics to a Western audience, and relax the pressure on Indigenous worldviews.

4. Indigenous perspectives on water contamination

The right to be able to drink water directly from the river is not yet recognized by the United Nations as a human right, but for many indigenous communities, that is the water quality standard they aspire to. This measure is far simpler than the "total maximum daily loads" (TMDLs) of the US Environmental Protection Agency, or the goal of "fishable and swimmable" rivers cited in the 1972 National Environmental Protection Act (National Research Council 2001). Many countries recognize the rights of their citizens to enjoy a healthy environment, including healthy rivers (Boyd 2012), yet the practical significance of this ethic is often overwhelmed by competing values, particularly economic values.

Pollution, the contamination of water ecosystems, is generally regarded in the sustainability literature as an economic issue more than a moral or ethical one. The principle of "polluter pays" is seen as central to social and economic justice. Ethics comes into play in setting the fees for pollution high enough to have some bearing on behavior. But from an indigenous perspective, money, even a lot of money, is not necessarily adequate. Though speaking of forests, this observation by Griffiths (2007:111) applies equally to water: "Many reject the principle that industrial and corporate polluters can buy permission to continue polluting by trading in forest carbon credits. They also dismiss the notion that the value of forests can be reduced to the monetary value of their carbon stocks, and stress that for their peoples the non-monetary cultural and spiritual values of their forest are of utmost importance and must be respected."

The sticking point in using monetary valuation to restore justice from environmental degradation is a matter of both incommensurability of values (Trainor 2006) as well as a basic sense of fairness. At the 2003 World Water Forum in Kyoto, Pablo Solon, who would later become the Bolivian ambassador to the United Nations, noted that pollution is a crime, and the "polluter pays" principle is an attempt by governments and corporate interests to legalize a crime by offering compensation (Groenfeldt 2003a). Nonetheless, when compensation or no compensation are the only two choices (as in the case of compensating for past CO_2 pollution into the atmosphere) fairness would suggest that compensation does have a role. During the December 2010 climate negotiations in Copenhagen, Mr Solon as an Ambassador, suggested, in reference to the United States as the biggest contributor to global CO_2 levels, that "The polluter should pay ... If you break it, you buy it!"[9]

When a river or lake is already polluted, what can be done besides restoration on one hand or compensation on the other? In the worldview of Indigenous Peoples there is still more that can be done. Ceremonies can be offered to help heal nature, while also helping heal the spirits of people as well. Since 2003, Grandmother Josephine Mandamin, a member of the Ojibway First Nation in Ontario, Canada, has been walking around the Great Lakes. Her reasons are a combination of raising awareness to motivate human action, and spiritual healing of the Great Lakes water. The consciousness of both realms – people and water – are linked, and must be healed together (see Box 7.5).

Box 7.5 Grandmother Walks to Protect Water[10]

Grandmother Josephine Mandamin of Thunder Bay, Ontario, a member of the Anishinabekwe (Ojibway) First Nation, along with her sister Melvina Flamand, initiated the Mother Earth Water Walk to pray for water's health and promote awareness that water needs protection. They, along with a group of Anishinabe women, plus other supporters, walked around Lake Superior in Spring 2003, around Lake Michigan in 2004, Lake Huron in 2005, Lake Ontario in 2006, Lake Erie in 2007, Lake Michigan again in 2008, then around the St. Lawrence River in 2009.

While she was walking throughout North America, Mandamin said she was "collecting consciousness." Mandamin says, "Collecting consciousness is not easy to explain. But when we are walking with the water, we are also collecting thoughts with that water. And in the collecting of thoughts, we are also collecting consciousness of people's minds. The minds, hopefully, will be of one, sometime."

Through her walks of awareness, Grandmother Mandamin is trying to get the attention of leadership and corporations. "The main thing that I'm trying to raise consciousness for, is that the people that are destroying everything, and the powers that be, like the presidents and the prime ministers, really need to step forward and really protect the water just like endangered animal species."

To really understand the importance of water, Grandmother Mandamin recommends people learn to have a deep appreciation of it by fasting to know what it's like to be without water, and to use it in a good way. Mandamin says using water in a good way means thinking consciously about how water is being used. She says people need to question how they are using it and whether they are working at conserving water. But, Grandmother Mandamin says it's not her place to tell people how to protect the water, and instead, she poses a question, "What are you going to do about it?"

Protecting the Waters of the Rio Grande

The indigenous community of Isleta Pueblo is located on the Rio Grande in central New Mexico, just downstream from Albuquerque, a city of 450,000 people. In 1992, the tiny pueblo of 2,500 people gained the legal right to set its own water quality standards for the river, forcing the much larger upstream city of Albuquerque to clean its effluent water to a higher standard.[11] The city had already been in compliance with the standards established by the state of New Mexico, but those were based on water to be used for irrigation and recreational boating. The Pueblo of Isleta, however, wanted to perform traditional ceremonies in the river, which included wading in the river and drinking small amounts. In 1987 when the US Congress amended the Clean Water Act, it gave Indian Tribes the option of setting their own water quality standards rather than being subject to the standards set by the states, in this case, the state of New Mexico. Isleta Pueblo jumped at the chance to set its own standards for the Rio Grande and adopted much stricter standards for arsenic and ammonia, in particular, forcing the upstream city to upgrade its water treatment facility to meet the new standards. The city of Albuquerque appealed, but in 1998 a court ruling settled the issue in favor of Isleta Pueblo. This was a legal decision which recognized the ethical principles of the Tribe. Writing in a Law Review article that same year, Allison Dussias (1998:1–659 to 1–660) discusses the significance of the case:

> The very fact that the Pueblo would officially establish ceremonial use of the Rio Grande waters as a designated use indicates the different perspective that the Pueblo brings to its role as environmental regulator. The river is not seen as merely a venue for fishing and recreational activities. For the Pueblo, protection of the quality of the river's water

has a religious and cultural motivation. The water plays an important role in tribal ceremonies, which, the district court noted, members of the Pueblo were reluctant to describe in detail because it is considered inappropriate to reveal the nature of the ceremonies to outsiders. By approving the ceremonial use designation, EPA, in effect, allowed the Pueblo to use its own understanding of the importance of water as a basis for establishing standards under a federal regulatory program. Clearly this is a great departure from the efforts of earlier federal government officials to eradicate the nature-based religious beliefs and practices of Native Americans and replace them with an understanding of natural resources as mere commodities readily available for exploitation. Moreover, the Pueblo's promulgation of strict water quality standards demonstrated its willingness to use its sovereign authority to protect the purity of the river water beyond the level of protection that the state was interested in providing.

Penokee Mine, Wisconsin

A proposed $1.5 billion taconite mine in northern Wisconsin, six miles upstream from the reservation of the Bad River Band of Lake Superior Chippewa Tribe, is threatening the water that the indigenous communities depend upon.[12] Unlike the case of Isleta Pueblo, the indigenous communities in Wisconsin lack a legal basis for controlling water quality from the mine. State laws define what the mine can or cannot do, and neither indigenous values of sacred waters, nor international designation as a Ramsar Site,[13] is enough to protect the tribal waters. To tribal chairman, Mike Wiggins, this is a question of environmental justice: "The fact that our reservation is situated next to a bunch of metal in the ground should not inherently doom my people to negative consequences in our homeland." The economic arguments put forward by the mine's proponents are not persuasive. In the words of Wiggins describing his tribal territory, "What you'll notice is essentially what our ancestors saw when they looked down the shoreline. You don't see condos, casinos, hotels, anything. That's important to us and our value system, and it trumps economic development … it allows future generations to have what we have. And there are places to go if our tribal members want to be corporate CEOs or if they want to live their lives on concrete. But we have to think ahead seven generations and remember that it really manifests itself in our environmental stewardship … it is a sacred place here. We take that stuff very seriously."[14]

Where legal protections are absent, can moral protection have an effect? This is where governance comes into play. By framing water as a material resource whose value derives from exploitation, it makes economic sense to sacrifice water quality in favor of a $1.5 billion mine. A different cultural frame which recognizes water as a sacred trust to be conveyed to future generations is what Chairman Wiggins is proposing. Whose ethics will prevail?

Conclusions: Water Ethics and Cultural Diversity

When indigenous views about water use or water protection are at odds with the ethics and/or laws of the dominant society, what happens? With few exceptions, the dominant society prevails. It is, after all, dominant, and can usually enforce the unstated principle of "Might makes right." Cases where indigenous groups prevail against these odds, such as Isleta Pueblo's successful dispute with the city of Albuquerque, point to the importance of a legal system that gives recognition to indigenous rights. In this instance, the legal basis was a 1987 amendment to an existing federal law establishing the governance arrangements over water quality. But that pre-existing law is itself tied to a colonial legal framework imposed on the Pueblo Indian tribes through a long history of Spanish rule followed by American military interventions that brought the Pueblo lands under American control in the 19th Century.

Legal rights, including human rights, are fundamentally important to people as individuals and to the cultures of social groups, but laws do not create cultures, they only enable cultures to flourish within those legal protections. As intruders onto the landscapes and waterscapes of Indigenous Peoples, our responsibility to respect their cultural rights does not stop with delineating their legal rights to water of a certain quantity or quality, by saying, in effect, "OK; this is yours and this is ours." That was the logic underlying the countless treaty agreements between American Indian tribes and the United States government during the 19th Century. Those treaties reflected the values of the dominant society's culture. The legal agreements today do effectively the same thing; they are cross-cultural negotiations but through a legal process set by the dominant society and reflecting the values and ethics of that society.

How should we view Indigenous Peoples' ethics about water? I am suggesting that we (and the "we" in this case means non-indigenous and indigenous people alike) should view those ethics seriously and respectfully. Those values are not anachronisms from another era that will inevitably be replaced by the more evolved values of Western materialism. Not only do Indigenous Peoples have (in theory) an individual right to be different, but they also have a cultural right to participate in their collective culture (Engle 2010). As individuals they are protected by human rights, and as members of an indigenous culture they are (again, in theory) protected by cultural rights, most recently expressed in the UN Declaration on the Rights of Indigenous Peoples.

The new opportunities that international aid programs offer to the developing world in general, and to the indigenous world in particular, need to be examined through an ethical lens. What are the values that are implicitly designed into those development programs of a village water supply or irrigation system or micro-credit options? Are those programs part of an unwitting stealth attack on the cultural principles of the people we claim to be helping? Or do the development programs consciously try to incorporate the cultural ethics of the communities concerned?

Attending to the ethics imbedded in water projects and policies is especially important in indigenous contexts for three basic reasons. First, because indigenous and traditional cultures possess philosophical wisdom as well as practical techniques for peaceful coexistence with the natural world. The second reason is that Indigenous Peoples bear a disproportional impact from water development and water pollution (e.g. from mining) that disrupts their lives, livelihoods, and cultures. For traditional fishing cultures displaced by dams along the Narmada River in India, or the Mekong River in Laos, the disruption is not confined to looking for a new job; it is an entire way of living and a way of knowing. And the third reason is that it is our "duty to learn" (Finch 2012); it is our reciprocal duty to try to understand the water ethics of Indigenous Peoples, and to promote water policies which respect their ethical principles.

The injustices suffered by Indigenous Peoples, such as displacement of entire communities and cultures in the name of water development, is now generally accepted as a moral issue and not simply an economic or legal issue. As a global society, we are making ethical progress even to establish these concepts. But our newly evolved concepts of cultural rights need to be operationalized with corresponding moral tools of analysis. This is precisely what ethics analysis can offer, and how it can help address seemingly intractable issues. Rather than using an understanding of indigenous ethics to try to induce indigenous communities to comply with external plans for water development, we can adopt a learning attitude to explore with our indigenous counterparts what their own ethical principles would suggest for a water future.

Water strategies which blend indigenous ethics with the latest global thinking on sustainable water policies are not nearly as far-fetched an idea as might have been the case two decades ago. In the next chapter we consider how the ethical assumptions of global water thinking is evolving. Might we become so advanced in our globalized concepts that we find ourselves aligned with the worldviews of Indigenous Peoples?

Notes

1 Further details about the conference where this talk was presented (but not the talk itself) can be found at the website for the Continuing Legal Education Society of British Columbia, http://www.cle.bc.ca/onlinestore/productdetails.aspx?cid=648.

2 From the World Water Forum session report, http://www.worldwaterforum4.org.mx/files/SessionSummaries/FT1_15_SESSION%20REPORT.pdf.

3 The full text of the *United Nations Declaration on the Rights of Indigenous Peoples* is available on the UN website, http://www.un.org/esa/socdev/unpfii/docu ments/ DRIPS_en.pdf.

4 See Nabokov 2006:73–90 for a discussion of indigenous religion among the Taos Pueblo Indians in northern New Mexico, and a comparison with Christianity.

5 The Declaration can be viewed or downloaded from the website of the Water-Culture Institute at http://www.waterculture.org/KyotoDeclaration.html.

6 Source: Australian National Water Commission webpage on Indigenous Water Management, http://web.archive.org/web/20120121015952/http://www.nwc.gov.au/ planning/indigenous.

7 See (1) "A Policy Statement on North Australian Indigenous Water Rights" issued by the North Australian Indigenous Land and Sea Management Alliance and the Indigenous Water Policy Group, November 2009, http://www.nailsma. org.au/sites/default/files/Water-Policy-Statement-web-view.pdf#overlay-context= water-resource-management/indigenous-water-policy-group-iwpg, and (2) the "Andean Vision of Water" issued in 2003, http://www.condesan.org/memoria/agua/Andean VisionWater.pdf.

8 Source: *New Zealand Herald*, August 30, 2012 http://www.nzherald.co.nz/nz/news/ article.cfm?c_id=1&objectid=10830586.

9 Source: Climate Justice Now website, http://www.climate-justice-now.org/bolivia- responds-to-us-on-climate-debt-if-you-break-it-you-buy-it/.

10 Source: *Ontario Birchbark* (online newspaper) article by Jennifer Ashawasegai, http://www.ammsa.com/publications/ontario-birchbark/grandmother-walks-protect- water.

11 Source: "A tiny tribe wins big on clean water," *High Country News*, February 2, 1998, http://www.hcn.org/issues/123/3922.

12 Source: Wisconsin Network for Peace and Justice (website), http://wnpj.org/ penokeemine.

13 The Kakagon and Bad River Sloughs, part of the Bad River Reservation, was designated as the 31st Ramsar Site in the United States, in 2012, http://www. badriver-nsn.gov/tribal-news/200-kakagon-and-bad-river-sloughs-recognized-as-a- wetland-of-international-importance.

14 Source: Interview with Mike Wiggins, posted on *Wisconsin Voices*, August 14, 2012, http://wivoices.areavoices.com/2012/08/15/404/.

8   Towards a New Water Ethic

Calls for a new water ethic are not new. Sandra Postel raised the alarm in the concluding chapter of her 1992 book, *Last Oasis*:

> We have been quick to assume rights to use water, but slow to recognize obligations to preserve and protect it. ... [We] need a set of guidelines and responsibilities that stops us from chipping away at natural systems until nothing is left of their life-sustaining functions. ... In short, we need a water ethic – a guide to right conduct in the face of complex decisions about natural systems we do not and cannot fully understand (Postel 1997:184–5).

What Postel does not point our very explicitly, however, is that we already have a water ethic; every society does. What we really need is a *new* water ethic to replace the water ethic that is currently in effect, and which constitutes the hidden root cause of our all-too-obvious water crisis.

The challenge of replacing an existing water ethic with a new one implies a very different strategy than would be the case of introducing a water ethic *de novo*. To be fair, Postel recognizes that the water ethic she is talking about would involve some deconstruction, as well as construction: "Adopting such an ethic would represent a historic philosophical shift away from the strictly utilitarian, divide-and-conquer approach to water management and toward an integrated, holistic approach that views people and water as related parts of a greater whole" (Postel 1997:185).

As a social scientist, perhaps I am overly awed by the powerful inertia of socio-cultural systems. Anthropologists study those systems on the premise culture makes a difference; it has staying power and does not change overnight, except, of course, when cultures *do* change overnight. But we have special terms for these unusual events: revolution, social upheaval, the Arab Spring, the Cultural Revolution. And we also know from history that even when changes are quick and dramatic, there are important elements of the old order that persist into the new. The French Revolution did not eliminate the aristocracy, nor did the Industrial Revolution totally eliminate a spiritual perception of nature.

What is important to appreciate about the process of introducing a "new water ethic" is that its introduction needs to address the presence of the old water ethics. Those old ethics have co-evolved with the society, the economy, and the culture of which those water ethics form a part. Just as John Muir advised caution in tugging too hard on one part of the integrated ecosystem, lest the whole system unravel, the challenge of introducing a new ethic of water needs to address the many interconnections that bind the existing ethics so firmly into the fabric of our way of life.

The good news for water ethics reformers is that the dominant water ethic is not really monolithic; the arena of water management is full of interesting exceptions and inconsistencies. From Indigenous Peoples' declarations to innovative river restoration projects to environmentally and socially progressive national legislation, there are more than enough examples of new water ethics from which we can learn and take inspiration.

The other piece of good news is that many aspects of the dominant water ethic are already supportive of the broad goals of sustainability, but tend to be expressed in high level meetings and reports. Nonetheless, there is an increasingly rich set of globally supported guidance on water management which reflects, albeit rather vaguely, the very ethics we need. This global consensus offers the starting point(s) for a "global water ethic" which can be used as a basis for building more explicit ethical frameworks at local and national levels.

The Global Water Ethic

Is there really any doubt about what kind of water management we want? Isn't there very clear consensus that we want water management that is sustainable, that does not continually "chip away" at natural systems, leaving us with lifeless rivers and dried up lakes and aquifers? And isn't there also a consensus, articulated into a UN Resolution, that everyone on the planet has access to clean water and sanitation? And to ensure that the basic needs of people and ecosystems are being met, aren't we also committed to participatory forms of water governance?

A careful assessment of the water policy statements from the UN General Assembly and the many UN-related water organizations would suggest that we already have a strong set of principles and guidelines that can lead us to sustainable management, simply by following their prescriptions. Unfortunately the operational world of water decision-makers give little attention to the gratuitous directives coming from UN institutes. It is precisely at this operational level, far removed from international mandates, that there is the greatest need for clarifying ethical principles, because it is at this level where actions happen.

The value of the policy directives of UN agencies and global conferences is that they are there to guide us if we feel a need to ask for guidance. Transboundary disputes are the most common context where the value of global standards and ethical principles can be appreciated. It is for this reason that so much of the IWRM literature deals with transboundary situations, even though IWRM principles apply just as well to local and national scales. And as the recent experience with the 2010 UN Declaration on the Right to Water and Sanitation has shown, global standards can empower local communities in advocating through local political processes. For example, WASH (Water and Sanitation for Health) programs in Moldova and also in India are basing their outreach campaigns on the UN-designated right to water and sanitation. By spreading the message that clean water is a human right, they are mobilizing local citizens to clean up trash from the river banks, and to put pressure on local government officials for toilets.[1]

The emerging global ethic provides a frame within which debates about operational specifics can take place. Should the dam be built? Should water quality standards be tightened? Can we afford the costs of a water conservation education program? The global ethic which guides water resources policies is an outgrowth of the concept of Integrated Water Resources Management (IWRM) which became defined at the 1977 Mar Del Plata conference and further refined at the Dublin conference of 1992 (see Box 8.1). IWRM became a professional standard for the water sector, incorporating a holistic view of water which gives recognition to environmental sustainability, social welfare, and governance arrangements. The definition of IWRM, according to the Global Water Partnership, is as follows: "IWRM is a process which promotes the coordinated development and management of water, land and related resources, in order to maximize the resultant economic and social welfare in an equitable manner without compromising the sustainability of vital ecosystems" (GWP 2000:22).

How can IWRM be operationalized? "In pursuing IWRM there is a need to recognize some overriding criteria that take account of social, economic and natural conditions." The GWP guidance identifies three "overriding criteria" of IWRM: (1) efficiency: water must be used with maximum possible efficiency, (2) equity: the basic right for all people to have access to water of adequate quantity and quality for the sustenance of human well-being must be universally recognized, and (3) sustainability: so that the present use of the resource does not compromise its use by future generations (GWP 2000:30).

Box 8.1 Dublin Principles

The International Conference on Water and the Environment was held in Dublin in January 1992 as a preparatory meeting for the UN Conference on Sustainable Development held in Rio later that same year. The Dublin delegates agreed to the following four "guiding principles," in order "to reverse the present trends of overconsumption, pollution, and rising threats from drought and floods."

Principle No. 1 – Fresh water is a finite and vulnerable resource, essential to sustain life, development and the environment. Since water sustains life, effective management of water resources demands a holistic approach, linking social and economic development with protection of natural ecosystems. Effective management links land and water uses across the whole of a catchment area or groundwater aquifer.

Principle No. 2 – Water development and management should be based on a participatory approach, involving users, planners, and policy-makers at all levels. The participatory approach involves raising awareness of the importance of water among policy-makers and the general public. It means that decisions are taken at the lowest appropriate level, with full public consultation and involvement of users in the planning and implementation of water projects.

Principle No. 3 – Women play a central part in the provision, management, and safeguarding of water This pivotal role of women as providers and users of water and guardians of the living environment has seldom been reflected in institutional arrangements for the development and management of water resources. Acceptance and implementation of this principle requires positive policies to address women's specific needs and to equip and empower women to participate at all levels in water resources programs, including decision-making and implementation, in ways defined by them.

Principle No. 4 – Water has an economic value in all its competing uses and should be recognized as an economic good. Within this principle, it is vital to recognize first the basic right of all human beings to have access to clean water and sanitation at an affordable price. Past failure to recognize the economic value of water has led to wasteful and environmentally damaging uses of the resource. Managing water as an economic good is an important way of achieving efficient and equitable use, and of encouraging conservation and protection of water resources.[2]

From my reading of the Dublin Principles and the GWP statements about IWRM, I deduce my own four statements which I believe are a fair representation of the concepts, but in more straightforward language: (1) nature needs to be kept alive (ecological function); (2) everyone has a right to water and sanitation (social justice); (3) water should be used responsibly in agriculture and industry (responsible use); and (4) stakeholders should be involved in decision-making (participation).[3] These four principles constitute a conceptual foundation for envisioning a broader set of water ethics, whether globally or locally:

1. *Keeping nature alive.* The notion that restoring natural ecological functions is desirable is a central tenet of IWRM generally. IWRM assumes that

ecosystem services have value, and healthier ecosystems generally have more of those values than unhealthy ones. A recent UNEP report equates healthy water ecosystems with water security (UNEP 2009). Since society relies on nature's services, ensuring that the ecosystem is able to provide those services is central to security. The overwhelming consensus about our water future, whether from businesses, governments, or environmentalists, is that functioning natural ecosystems must be part of the solution. The details about how to do this are, of course, full of controversy, but the overarching principle that some degree of natural ecological function is necessary for a sustainable water future is a central tenet of IWRM.

The consensus that nature is indispensible, and will remain so into the foreseeable future, may come as a surprise to jaded observers of actual water development. Blasting rivers into submission, inundating irreplaceable global heritage under deep reservoirs, and turning lakes into toxic waste dumps has become such a routine part of what passes for modern water management, that we might easily overlook the ethic of respect for nature which has persisted, at least as a minority view.

The "frame" of sustainable water management based on functioning natural ecosystems provides an important dimension of the global water ethic from which we can consider the pesky operational details. Just about everyone can agree that we need to balance the needs of nature with the needs of people. The argument is not about the principle of balance, but the operational issue of determining the balance point in any given situation. The principle of "functioning natural ecosystems are indispensible" is not quite of the same order as "rivers have a right to exist" but the two concepts are logically linked, and an exploration of the former principle can lead, I believe, to support for the latter principle, as is discussed later in this chapter.

2. *Human right to water and sanitation.* Granting priority to drinking water over any other competing use is a standard, and perhaps universal, principle during times of drought. The logic seems obvious: access to drinking water is a matter of life or death. This prioritization has been reflected in numerous declarations of principle. The crowning moment for endorsing the human right to water and sanitation was its adoption as a UN Resolution in 2010. This event solidified the stature of the human right to water as having a basis in international law, even though there is no provision for enforcing the standard.

3. *Responsible use.* The intuitive concept of using water carefully has been given an economic interpretation in the IWRM literature, starting with the Dublin statement that, "Water has an economic value in all its competing uses and should be recognized as an economic good," (see Box 8.1). According to the GWP criteria, "water must be used with maximum possible efficiency." The language chosen emphasizes the challenges of finding enough water to produce food, or provide jobs, and shies away from

commitments to do more with less. The GWP cites "securing water for food production" as a main challenge, along with finding water for "developing other job creating activities" (GWP 2000:10). In contrast, the International Water Management Institute made an institutional commitment to increasing the agricultural productivity of water through the "More Crop Per Drop" program.

In the private sector, business associations are usually careful to avoid specific commitments. In a recent overview of analytical water tools for businesses, the World Business Council for Sustainable Development (WBCSD) explained their purpose in making these tools available as the following: "Our purpose is to help businesses and key stakeholders identify the water tools and initiatives that will best meet their specific needs, and to preserve the sustainability of our water resources" (WBCSD 2012:3). Individual companies, on the other hand, seem proud to publicize their commitments to using less water. For example, Coca-Cola has pledged to be water neutral in its full range of global operations by 2020, through a combination of water efficiencies and "replenish" programs, incurring water savings through community projects (Sarni 2011:194).

4. *Participatory water governance.* The Dublin Principles are often cited critically by social progressives for promoting an overly economic valuation of water, but even those same critics (myself included) are appreciative for the language advocating a participatory approach "at the lowest appropriate level." The importance placed on stakeholder participation, local community consultations, and especially the inclusion of women in all phases and aspects of water planning (Dublin Principle 3, above) clearly define an ethic of broad-based participatory governance. While both Indigenous Peoples' organizations and environmental groups are missing from the early descriptions of participation within IWRM documents, both groups are generally (but not always) included in contemporary lists of "who's who" among stakeholders. This is an example of the "social learning" taking place within the IWRM approach (Pahl-Wostl et al. 2007).

From Global Ethics to Operational Ethics

The shortcoming of globally accepted ethical prescriptions about water, however, is that they can be easily ignored. In the absence of concerted global outreach, local water decisions are usually made on the basis of locally held cultural principles and ethics, not to mention local power politics and economic incentives. It is within this messy context of practical water decisions that we need to apply water ethics. The basic strategy I am suggesting is the following: By forging a clear set of ethical principles, or simply clarifying the ethics that are already in place but hidden in the background, local decisions about water can be guided, or at least informed, by those ethics. This does not mean that the decisions actually taken will be consistent with those ethics, since power, politics, and greed also exert influences that may be counteractive. But going to the trouble of articulating the ethics can at least enhance the likelihood that those ethics will have at least some influence on the final outcome.

Global standards about water management can help us in establishing principles of best practice which local management strategies can invoke. For example, a commonly held goal for urban water supply systems is to ensure the sustainability of the natural water ecosystems which serve as the water source. To meet that goal, the sustainable yield of the natural water sources (groundwater and surface water) would need to be calculated and would then serve as the frame within which operational management would be carried out. The question for water planning then turns to the definition of sustainable yield and the assumptions underlying the concept of "sustainable." Is the frame of sustainability limited to the physical water in the environment that serves as the source of the urban water supply system, or are we also concerned about the sustainability of the water-dependent natural ecosystem, including vegetation, fish, insects, and other wildlife?

Can we build on the shared principles already incorporated into the IWRM concept, and then pull in some of the not-so-shared ethics already being applied in some cases, and then add some additional principles, and come up with a new, sustainable water ethic for the 21st Century and beyond? I think we can, and have written this book based on a belief that designing and implementing that ethic is the most important challenge for water stakeholders – all of us – to undertake. All the rest, the behavioral changes implied by a new ethic, depend on getting the ethics right first. Otherwise we are back to trying to reverse global warming by replacing our light bulbs. While changing light bulbs and shower heads can help raise awareness, it is too little too late, and may serve only to lull us into dangerous complacency. We need big changes quickly and we need to adopt a new set of ethics that will support that change.

Elements of a New Water Ethic

What's new and exciting in the world of water, and particularly in water ethics? This section reviews some promising initiatives that incorporate innovative water ethics and that provide the building blocks for a new ethics framework. We will consider these initiatives according to the same categories used elsewhere in this book:

Managing water ecosystems
1. Water for food
2. Water for people
3. Water for industry
4. Water rights of Indigenous Peoples
5. Water governance

1. Managing water ecosystems

Managing rivers for ecological health, as mandated in the EU's Water Framework Directive, is a promising application of the economic principle of ecosystem services. But it is an ethical development as well. Whether the ecological status of a river is classified as normal, modified, or heavily modified (EU terminology), the prescription of the Water Framework Directive is to take steps to improve that status. The classification determines what benchmarks to apply, but the direction of effort is to invest in improvement to whatever the current status is deemed to be. In considering an intervention to the river, such as new levees along the bank to prevent flooding, analysis as to whether this is a good idea or not proceeds on the basis of ecological as well as economic analysis. Not merely, "Do the economic benefits warrant the economic costs?" but also, "will the ecological benefits outweigh any ecological costs?" (Johnson 2012).

The application of environmental flow standards in many countries has been especially influential in shifting the expectations about water development. Instead of expecting a new project – a wastewater treatment plant, or a river diversion – to inflict ecological harm on the river, projects can also be seen as opportunities for investing in ecological restoration (Brierley and Fryirs 2008). A wastewater treatment plant, for example, might improve downstream water quality, and a river diversion project, which would certainly leave the river in a less healthy state than before, could be amended to include a restoration component such as an area of floodplain reconnection, or removal of a dam from an upstream tributary. Indeed, the growing movement to remove some of the least useful dams is motivated by ethics that place a high value on re-naturalizing rivers both for human enjoyment (tourism and recreation) as well as for the rivers themselves (Grossman 2002).

Ecologically based management strategies for water ecosystems, whether rivers, lakes, wetlands, or aquifers, harness nature's own methods to serve the interests of society. As discussed in Chapter 2, non-structural methods of flood management have been adopted in the Napa River Valley in California and engineers in the Netherlands are investing billions of euros in "making room for rivers" to allow for managed flooding between widely spaced levees. The river's ecology becomes more dynamic and healthier, while society benefits from decreased risk of major flooding. The terminology alone marks an evolution of ethics about what constitutes management best practice. The term "management" has replaced "control" in discussions of flood strategies, along with "non-structural" and "vegetative barriers" when concrete and steel were the former construction materials of choice. Command-and-control may finally be giving way to a kinder, gentler approach of "guide and manage."

2. Water for food

Of all the uses of water, none is as quantitatively important as agriculture, which uses some two-thirds of the fresh water abstracted from nature.[4]

Of course, agriculture is also part of the environment, and has the potential for providing ecosystem services on a par with natural ecosystems. The type and magnitude of agriculture's environmental services, however, depend on the type of farming practiced. When a broad set of ecological, social, and cultural functions are incorporated into the valuation, along with the economic considerations, the greatest returns per drop of water are likely to come from small-scale, agroecological farming strategies. The Common Agricultural Policy of the EU, as well as the national agricultural strategy of Japan have explicitly endorsed the multifunctional character of farming, and provide subsidies and other incentives to promote modes of agriculture that deliver a broad spectrum of benefits (Renting et al. 2009).

3. Water for people

It is hardly surprising that people take priority over any other competing uses, whether for agriculture, industry, or even nature. The Millennium Development Goal of reducing by half the number of people without access to safe water and sanitation by 2015, and the formal UN decision in 2010 to recognize water as a human right, has spawned a huge response from the international community and local governments and NGOs. There is a strong underlay of ethical principles motivating these efforts. The concern is primarily about protecting the health of people who currently lack regular access to safe drinking water and sanitation. Without that access, they will continue to be victims of diseases picked up in their drinking water, often through fecal contamination of that water. The ethical motivations are primarily social (human welfare) and economic (human productivity), while environmental and cultural ethics play supporting roles.

The ethical significance of the global movement to ensure safe drinking water is its embrace of an expanded community of ethical concern. Not only do we feel a responsibility to the welfare of our family members, village, or nation. The appeals for action on safe drinking water invite an emotional response, rooted in our existing ethical principles, to help people half way around the world, living, and in danger of dying, in places we have never seen. This expansion of our ethical sphere of responsibility offers hope that our ethical space might be enlarged yet further, to include environmental and cultural justice as well.

4. Water for industry

Ethics is an acknowledged topic of concern in industry, though traditionally relegated to the realm of conducting business deals or employee relations. Corporate water ethics falls under the category of Corporate Social Responsibility (CSR), an interesting framework for action where for-profit companies have adopted varying kinds of ethical positions that can go well beyond the economic bottom line. Indeed, the standard model for describing CSR is the triple bottom line of economic, social, and environmental "profit." Companies like Coca-Cola and Unilever, who have made explicit strategic commitments to water stewardship, use this in their advertising, and clearly expect to derive some economic advantage from their ethically progressive positions on water issues.

While the methods of "water footprinting" along with standardization of reporting water use, have enhanced the overall water awareness of corporations and their investors and customers, the most promising new development in my view is the concept of "water stewardship." Defined and promoted through the Alliance for Water Stewardship, which itself consists of a mix of companies, water research institutes, and environmental NGOs, the Alliance is raising the bar for corporate water responsibility, by inviting various industries to suggest the standards they would like to meet and then holding the individual companies within those industries accountable through a public reporting process. The beauty of the stewardship concept is that it is open-ended and well suited to the real-world dynamics of social-environmental-economic concerns (see discussion in Chapter 1).

5. Water rights of Indigenous Peoples

Indigenous Peoples' statements about water invariably allude to how their cultural and social rights and identities are intertwined with the water ecosystems they have long depended upon. Their articulations of their relationship with their land and waters provide powerful teachings that can guide the formulation of water ethics for the non-indigenous world as well (Sandford and Phare 2011). This is one contribution of Indigenous Peoples to the emerging discipline of water ethics. The second contribution stems from the process of struggles over water and land rights linked to proposed water development (e.g. dams) or extractive industries (mining and oil and gas). The concept of "free, prior, and informed consent" has emerged as an international standard of ethical conduct between outsiders' proposals and Indigenous Peoples' interests. This standard is written into the UN Declaration on the Rights of Indigenous Peoples, and has been adopted by some of the major development agencies (e.g. Asian Development Bank) and even some transnational corporations.

6. Water governance

Global standards of water governance have steadily evolved over the past few decades, the cumulative result of deliberate capacity-building initiatives, advances in social theory and its application, and the maturity of national and international regimes of political governance (Conca 2006, Groenfeldt and Schmidt 2013). Two important trends, which together offer an opening for applying a new set of ethical principles, are (1) legitimizing a governance role for everyone within a water basin, and (2) applying a broad ecological frame to water use and management. Both trends were stimulated by the concept of IWRM, but go further, fueled by new ideas from feminist studies and deep ecology (Brown and Schmidt 2010) as well as CSR. The tangible expression of these trends is the pervasive establishment of new governance institutions at the basin level. Such institutions may be legally mandated, as in the EU Water Framework Directive which requires river basin councils to be established in major rivers, or South Africa's system of catchment committees, or the institutions may be optional, as in the United States, but the overall trend is unmistakable. Stakeholders – people, organizations, and businesses – are getting increasingly involved (Sabatier et al. 2005).

The water ethics that we need are already here, to some extent; they are expressed in active projects, programs, and in the swirl of ideas about people and nature, what we are doing to the planet, and how we can change the pattern of ecosystem exploitation. It is very easy to become (or remain) discouraged, resigned to the inevitable loss of an ecologically healthy world, and trying to prepare ourselves for what Bill McKibben calls, a "tough new planet" (McKibben 2010). Indeed, the changes in climate that have been brought about through human production of CO_2 do seem inevitable, and preparing for life on a hotter planet is the reasonable thing to do. But while the health of water ecosystems is certainly connected to rainfall and temperature patterns, the internal dynamics of water ecosystems are surprisingly resilient. There are many active measures we can take to restore ecological function to the lakes and rivers that we have ruined through our past behaviors (Brierley and Fryirs 2008).

The key to reversing the damage to water ecosystems, however, is not through finding clever ways to fix specific ecological problems, or even by conserving more water. These things are important, but only when orchestrated into a coherent and effective strategy. We need to win the overall "war" and not necessarily each and every little battle along the way. Our vision is a world where the interests of humans and nature are recognized as, if not entirely co-equal, still very much co-dependent.

How Can We Change Our Water Ethics?

How can we build upon the rich and growing set of progressive water management practices, and the ethics driving those practices, to shape a new standard – a new water ethic? How can the ethics of ecological, social, and cultural respect expand from isolated exceptions to become the norm of water policy and practice? This section considers five mutually beneficial strategies for reforming the water ethics we have inherited, and transforming them to the new water ethic(s) we wish to bequeath to future generations: (a) broaden water governance, (b) reframe water education, (c) apply new types of water knowledge, (d) create new water experiences, and (e) analyze water ethics.

(a) Broadening water governance

While contemporary water governance already reflects a broader set of concerns than was perhaps even imaginable half a century ago, there is still much room for improvement. When water decisions are made by the powerful elite, they will rarely reflect the needs of society as a whole, not to mention the future generations of society. We need broader water governance for some of the same reasons that we need democratic governance of our political systems. But the importance of democratic water governance faces particular challenges because we are dealing with the governance of nature (water and water ecosystems) by people. How will nature be represented in this governance?

Water governance needs to become broader in two ways: (1) geographically, we need to consider the whole dynamic of water at the basin level and beyond, to include groundwater and coastal zones where fresh water interacts with the oceans, and (2) conceptually we need input from a diversity of perspectives beyond the conventional water disciplines of hydrology, engineering, law, and economics. In particular, water governance needs to be informed by the biological and social sciences, and by the humanities. In addition to diversity of disciplines, water governance needs diversity of people, including Indigenous Peoples, women, and youth. Both dimensions of an expanded water governance are accepted in theory by proponents of IWRM, but the actual practice of water governance remains the domain of an overly narrow set of disciplines. How can water governance "loosen up" and bring in more diversity?

Part of the governance solution will come from welcoming a diversity of values and cultures into the governance circle. One pathway to a new water ethic, in other words, is to adopt a new institutional ethic of valuing diversity. Meanwhile, the institutional mechanisms that can engender broad, diverse stakeholder participation in water governance are well known: watershed and river basin councils, stakeholder committees attached to large basin commissions (e.g. the Murray Darling River Commission), or networks of organizations along a river basin.[5] While it is certainly preferable for such organizations to have legal sanction and some executive authority over water management, voluntary organizations which rely on influence through persuasion can also be effective. This is the case in most of the United States, where state and federal agencies facilitate (and partially finance) local voluntary groups, but rarely invest them with any statutory authority. Voluntary river and watershed associations rely, ultimately, on being able to mobilize the ethics of local stakeholders.

(b) Reframing water education

Just as the concept of governance needs to be stretched in order to encompass diverse perspectives and values, the "frame" of water education needs to be expanded to include new categories of knowledge. It will always be important to teach children the basics of the water cycle and stream dynamics, but if that is where water education stops, the lesson becomes one of limiting the concept of water management to the physical manipulation of water, and there is no room for an ethical appreciation of water or water ecosystems. Schools serve to socialize children, as well as to educate them, and socializing them into the belief that water management is a technical subject better left to the experts is the kiss of death for inculcating a new water ethic for the next generation. There is a tremendous opportunity, and challenge, to rethink water education at all levels – from elementary and secondary schools to university and graduate degree courses.

Nearly every discipline can offer a unique contribution to our understanding of water management and the underlying water ethics: water law is its own field of study in most universities of the American West, where water use is tied up in complex legal frameworks that require specialists to unravel. Yet while water management is also bound in cultural values and beliefs, which are only partly reflected in those laws, the study of "water culture" remains a niche specialty, the subject of a growing number of books and case studies,[6] but not (yet) a recognized field of study in its own right.[7]

In my own educational evolution, I was drawn to water management during graduate work in anthropology because it offered interesting social and cultural problems that could shed light on cultural dynamics.[8] Prodding me in this research direction was a flurry of social science interest in irrigation management at the time (see Chapter 3). The influx of social scientists into the formerly technical topic of irrigation management helped bring about a paradigm shift from irrigation as a purely engineering topic to a broader view that invited inter-disciplinary expertise under the broad banner of "management" applied to irrigation.

The opportunity for bringing ethics into the mainstream of water education and governance might follow a similar course to the "socializing" of irrigation. Ethics, when applied to both water governance and water education, constitutes a broadening of conventional categories, inviting the application of new disciplinary perspectives (Groenfeldt and Schmidt 2013). The task for ethics (or for ethicists) is to demonstrate the ways that ethical principles are already influencing water decisions, understanding how those ethics are functioning, and analyzing how new ethics might be applied to the challenges of water sustainability.

(c) Applying new water knowledge

How do we decide what knowledge is relevant to water management in addition to hydrology, engineering, biology, law, and economics (to name a few)? This is where the frames which we construct around the topic of water management take on practical importance. To explain how people behave around water, we need to understand political science and economics, and perhaps psychology, sociology, and anthropology as well. An understanding of the values and ethics underlying human behavior around water requires many complementary perspectives. Psychologists, political scientists, environmental historians, sociologists, geographers, and others analyze the social and political dynamics around water. Anthropologists, philosophers, and theologians can apply their perspectives to the cultural dimensions.

These and other diverse disciplinary insights about what water is and how it is managed can contribute to a deeper understanding of the underlying values/ethics, and their roles in motivating particular water decisions and policies. We also need to invite perspectives from different cultures, especially those of Indigenous Peoples who retain distinctly unique cultural understandings of nature and water ecosystems. This indigenous knowledge about water is not readily reducible to descriptions by researchers, but needs to be derived directly from indigenous "wisdom keepers" (Armstrong 2006). What outside researchers can contribute, however, is an interpretation of the significance and cultural meaning of this Indigenous knowledge. Together, these two types of new water knowledge can contribute to a broader understanding of water management from an ethical perspective, and to a deeper understanding of particular water ethics within a cultural context.

(d) Experiencing water directly and indirectly

The visceral experience of water and water ecosystems is probably a necessary though not in itself sufficient condition for appreciating and valuing water, and developing an ethical sensibility about that water. A better understanding of nature allows us to appreciate her all the more (Carlson 2010), and what better way to understand water than through experiencing it?

Environmental artists work professionally to bring people in contact with representations of nature, but people can also engage with nature directly. The standard awareness-building approach to connect people with water ecosystems is through recreation (e.g. river rafting, swimming, sailing), fishing, and hikes or community clean-ups along the river banks. During my tenure with the Santa Fe Watershed Association, we used all these methods (though recreational use was limited to wading in the ankle-deep water of our tiny stream) and encountered enthusiastic responses from grateful residents, seemingly out or proportion to the very modest level of water contact which the activities provided.

While there is no question in my own mind that such activities are much appreciated by the participants, the same people who bonded with the river on clean-up days were unlikely to testify in support of the river when water policy measures came before the local government. The connection with the river was authentic, perhaps, but they were not seeing the broader picture of how that river is connected to a larger system of water, of which they (as water users) are also an integral part. It is the classic dilemma of not seeing the forest because we are focusing too much on the individual trees.

But it is not only that they don't see the larger forest (the overall water system) they also don't fully see themselves as creatures living in that forest. They don't really feel, in a deep and intimate way, that the forest, the river, the water world around them, is "home."

Those direct experiences help, but they are not strong enough to counter the opposing indoctrination from society that a river is an unruly ribbon of water that needs to be carefully controlled. How can people experience and interact with water more consistently in their everyday lives? In fact, we already do! Each of us experiences water multiple times every day in our domestic lives (household water use) and in our civic and professional lives as we move around our local landscape/cityscape and see rivers, canals, drainage ditches, fountains, puddles or nameless stagnant pools of water. These micro-interactions with water offer opportunities for consciousness raising about what water is and how we are connected to it. We only need to be prepared to notice the water dimensions of our daily world.

Box 8.2 Learning to "see" the water around us

One of the best ways to raise awareness about water it to become involved in conserving water within our own households and gardens, and within our communities. From an ethics development perspective, the important outcome of water conservation efforts is not the tangible saving of water, but the conceptual capacity-building of greater water awareness. This point is illustrated in the "vital signs" initiative by Brad Lancaster in Tucson, Arizona. Lancaster distributes small but noticeable signs to install near the entrance of homes, to indicate which forms of water conservation are being used, e.g. rainwater harvesting, gray water harvesting, solar hot water, etc. The aim is not only to save water, but also to raise awareness.

Though water conservation programs are all the rage in strategies to ensure urban water security, the ethical opportunities in these efforts are typically overlooked.[9] Indeed, the emphasis on the technological fixes, such as low-flow faucets and shower heads, and more efficient toilets and washing machines, can serve to reinforce the concept of water as a commodity. One of the intangible benefits of rainwater harvesting and permaculture practices in inculcating ethical awareness is that these practices help connect us to nature, through attending to rainfall and the drainage patterns within our neighborhoods. When we become aware of the water dynamics around us, we will also have a deeper awareness in the mundane acts of washing our hands or pouring a glass of water.

The other side of water awareness is the "supply side." We need to have a regular supply of water representations on which we can place our attention. This is where urban design makes a difference. When we walk to work and pass over a stream, is that stream channel visible or is it buried beneath the pavement in a concrete culvert (as so many urban streams are)? The practice of "daylighting" urban streams, and sometimes whole rivers (e.g. in Los Angeles) brings benefits not only to urban ecosystems, but also to the emotional life of local citizens. Intelligent urban design can integrate both natural and created water features to create visual, sensual, auditory, and even olfactory experiences of water that enhance our enjoyment while reminding us of water's multifarious values. In Freiburg, Germany, the ancient small drainage canals (*Bächle*) that were covered over during the drive for modernity following World War II have been revived as a major design element in the urban center.[10]

Art and artists have a critical role in deepening our aesthetic and emotional appreciation of water, along with conveying factual information which we might not take in without the attractive packaging. Eco-artists contribute to building an ethical sensibility through "critiquing the ways we frame nature" (Boetzkes 2010:2). While art is not very good at providing answers about what should be done, it is very good at offering questions: "Is this right?" "Might there be some other way of doing this?" Two basic ways that art and artists can contribute to the development of our water ethics is (1) through representing water, water bodies (e.g. a lake) or water infrastructure (e.g. pipes, dams, etc.) and showing these to us in a way that might play with our assumptions about how we view water, and (2) through earth art, where the artist intervenes directly in the landscape or waterscape.

Box 8.3 Three water artists

Basia Irland describes herself as a "water and eco-artist." One of her projects is creating "ice books" which are ice sculptures in the shape of an open book. She etches out little holes on the open page and inserts native seeds from whatever river she is working on, then adds water to the holes, and refreezes the book so the seeds are embedded in a form that looks like text. Then she ceremonially launches the ice book into the river, where it floats downstream, the ice melts, releasing the seeds which, she hopes, will find a suitable spot along the banks to grow and flourish. It's a rather indirect way of restoring riparian vegetation, but that's not the point, or at least it's not the only point (Irland 2007).

The photographer, Victoria Sambunaris,[11] produces big landscapes and waterscapes to show others what nature looks like, how we've modified that landscape. Through her photographs what is normally perceived as ugly (e.g. a coal mine) becomes hauntingly beautiful, or at least neutral. From an activist's perspective, her work might seem annoyingly non-judgmental; we are free to form our own opinions of, for example, the stark beauty of the pool of toxic water in an abandoned copper mine.

"Viewing her photographs is a bit like watching the dogs in an animal shelter. Their endearing faces bear the scars of abuse, evoking a mix of emotions from pity to anger to compassion, and perhaps to action."[12]

The painter, Clyde Aspevig,[13] brings a more activist intent. He wants to inspire us to conserve the natural beauty of the land and water-scapes that he paints: "By listening to the non-silence of the desert, we are able to hear it as a non-empty landscape, not a void but rather a profound presence" he writes in an article entitled, "The nature of art, the art of conservation" (Aspevig 2010).

Representations of water may be as old as art itself and water motifs and symbolism continue to hold a prominent place in contemporary art. Earth art provides a different sort of experience. Whereas representational art helps us see water (and rivers, etc.) in new ways, earth art is more about relationships: how water is related to and connected with the rest of nature, and to us. When Basia Irland launches an ice book into the river (see Box 8.3), she is helping us see the context of that river as we imagine the book floating downstream, releasing its buried seeds into the water and eventually to take root along the banks. When Christo constructs a cover over the Arkansas River in Colorado for his "Over the River" project,[14] we have an opportunity to rethink our own relationship to that river, to rivers in general and "to sense this deep relationship between topography and human experience" (Schama 2008).

(e) Analyzing ethics directly

The methods outlined above rely on indirect processes (art, education, governance, science) to create enabling conditions for transforming the ethical principles held by individuals and communities. Might it also be possible to address the ethics directly? Are water ethics subject to direct management interventions? Along with managing physical water, or social institutions, could the intangible ethical principles also be managed? The premise of this book is that an understanding of the nature of water ethics – what they are and how they function in decisions about water – will help improve decision-making about water. It stands to reason that a deeper understanding of water ethics might also lead to changes – improvements – in the ethics themselves. The following steps outline a proposed methodology for identifying and analyzing the current ethics, and evaluating and proposing alternatives.

Step #1 – Identify the prevailing ethics about water. Identifying the operative values underlying current behavior is the first logical step in the process of harmonizing values with desirable behavior outcomes. Until we identify the existing ethics, our attempts to change that behavior directly will be clumsy and inefficient, though not necessarily ineffective.

Step #2 – Analyze the values. Once identified, the existing ethics can be analyzed and debated. The inconsistencies between the values embedded in water laws and the values of society as a whole, or of particular interest groups (e.g. environmentalists) can serve as a basis for debate and, hopefully, eventual consensus.

Step #3 – Evaluate alternatives. Alternative ways of valuing water and water ecosystems involve concepts (alternative ethics) as well as technologies and practices (e.g. rooftop water harvesting). Principles of the soft-path approach (Brooks et al. 2009) can be particularly useful at this stage in setting aside the consideration of ethics, for the moment, and focusing on the pragmatic issue of identifying alternative pathways to arrive at a desired end.

Step #4 – Propose new policies. When there is clarity about the desired end results (the vision) and the values and attitudes that the stakeholder community wish to inculcate (the ethics), then there can be constructive discussion about the specific policies that would be consistent with those ethical principles and lead to the shared vision.

The practical application of this direct analysis of ethics would be in combination with the indirect methods discussed earlier – governance arrangements, education, applied science, and water experiences (including art). The direct analysis could be conducted in a workshop setting, while the other approaches require real activities in the real world. Both the workshop process and the more practical activities could be integrated into broader programs covering various aspects of water management, and not only ethics. But maintaining an awareness of ethics as a distinct dimension of water management will be critical. With that awareness, ethics analysis can be integrated into standard planning approaches.

Box 8.4 Water Ethics Network

The Water Ethics Network was launched in 2011 as an information network to harness the expertise and creativity of the many people already working on water ethics issues. The Network helps connect the dots to reveal new alternatives for managing rivers, lakes, springs, wetlands, and aquifers that bring social, cultural, environmental, as well as economic benefits to local communities. Through a website (http:// waterethics.org), e-newsletter, and social media, the Network shares information about issues, research, campaigns, and people that are applying ethics principles to water policies and practices.

The Network's agenda is not only the passive sharing of information. Through that function, the network's aim is to influence the water agenda by promoting ethics discourse within the water profession and water discourse among those who work on ethics, not only religious organizations and philosophers, but also social, cultural, and environmental activists.

Conclusions

The good news is that we already have many elements of the new water ethic that we need. We are actually overloaded with good ethical principles to apply, and there are many examples of programs and initiatives which are putting those ethics into practice. In my view this is a very significant "fact" which deserves to be celebrated. The glass is at least half full. While it is important not to make light of the environmental tragedies that we have become inured to in the water world, there is a wealth of ideas and experiences that can be applied to address the problems.

The "real" problem is not a lack of ideas, concepts, or even intentions. And in my view, the real problem is not even social inequities, corruption, or power struggles, though I don't want to underplay these as major factors. In my view the real problem is one of paradigms, and the analysis and application of ethics offers a way to reform and reframe those paradigms. We have seen that many of the pieces from which the new paradigm, the new water ethic, can be constructed, are already available. We only need to find a way to assemble the puzzle and draw enough attention to it that the new paradigm will be adopted by enough people, organizations, companies, and governments. This is the idea behind the Water Ethics Network (see Box 8.4) which I founded in 2011 after coming to the realization that cultural values and ethics about water seem to lie at the heart of the water crisis.

The thesis of the Water Ethics Network is that enough lessons have already been learned, and relevant new experience is continuously being gained and reported on. What is most needed is a way to connect the people and organizations who are already applying the lessons and gaining that experience. By giving exposure to their work and publicizing the topic of water ethics, perhaps more "buzz" can be created about the values dimensions of water management. If the problem is values, then let's work on those values, and let's find as many new ideas as possible to help move the work forward.

Notes

1 These examples come from the 6th World Water Forum's "Solutions for Water" website, http://www.solutionsforwater.org.

2 Source: http://www.wmo.int/pages/prog/hwrp/documents/english/icwedece.html.
3 The first three of these themes correspond to the four "combs" of water use categories within the IWRM concept (water for nature, water for people, water for food, and water for industry), while the fourth theme (participation) corresponds to the "integrated" part of IWRM, i.e. integrated governance (GWP 2000:29).
4 Global estimates of the proportion of total available water used in agriculture vary widely from source to source, but the figure given is invariably greater than 70%, so regardless of the precise number it is large and very significant.
5 An example of such a network is OneMississippi, http://1mississippi.org/.
6 See especially, Johnston et al. 2012.
7 The absence of "water culture" as a recognized field of study motivated me to establish the Water-Culture Institute in 2010, http://www.waterculture.org.
8 My PhD Dissertation was entitled, "Change, Persistence, and the Impact of Irrigation: A Controlled Comparison of Two North Indian Villages," University of Arizona, 1984.
9 The emphasis on organizational culture that is commonplace in corporate strategies has been somehow missed by urban planners and water experts alike.
10 For a discussion and photographs of the *bächle*, see the website of EcoCity Builders, http://www.ecocitybuilders.org/freiburg-germany-city-of-the-future-continued/.
11 See http://victoriasambunaris.com.
12 Blogpost by D. Groenfeldt, 12 November 2010, http://blog.waterculture.org/2010/11/12/how-art-helps-us-help-rivers-a.aspx.
13 See http://www.clydeaspevig.com.
14 See http://www.overtheriverinfo.com/.

9 Conclusions

One of my favorite aphorisms attributed to Abraham Lincoln is "Not to decide is to decide." Something similar could be said about ethics. Not to explore the ethical content of a course of action is itself an ethical choice. Claiming that a decision is value-neutral reflects an (incorrect) assumption that there are no values underlying a particular decision or course of action. Since there is overwhelming evidence that values really do influence just about everything we do and how we do it (the disciplines of psychology, anthropology, sociology, and culture studies are part of the evidence), a refusal to explore those values could be interpreted as irresponsible, or "unethical," reflecting an ethic of ignorance, similar to the child's perspective that "What I can't see won't hurt me."

If we accept that values and ethics really are bubbling about just below the surface of water decisions, then we have a responsibility to find out what they are, and how those bubbles are influencing the decisions which, ultimately, might affect all of us, as well as our descendants and the rest of nature. Discovering what our ethics really are requires some tools of discovery. We have made use of a very simple conceptual tool, a framework of four categories of ethics on one axis, and four domains of water management on the other (Chapter 1, Table 1.1). This framework can help us identify the values we hold within each of the ethics categories: economic, environmental, social, and cultural ethics.

We might feel that we don't really have an opinion about some of these ethics when applied to particular water management issues. How could, or should, cultural ethics relate to urban water supply? Isn't that a technical issue? The example of the Orangi community-managed sanitation project in Karachi, Pakistan (Chapter 4) shows how community governance of technical infrastructure (toilets and sewer lines) can do double duty of building the institutional capacity of that community. This dynamic takes on cultural significance where the community is culturally distinctive and governance autonomy empowers the community's "right to be different."

This book has emphasized ethics analysis as a tool for making decisions about water management options: Should we build the dam, build a different kind of dam, or build no dam at all? An analysis of the costs and benefits of each option can be informed by an understanding of the values and ethics held by the diverse stakeholders. At this level, ethics analysis can serve as a complement to an ecosystems services perspective. Though I personally cringe at the idea of monetizing every kind of value, the principle that there are real values provided by natural ecosystems, fits nicely with ethics analysis. A fishing community along the Mekong River, who view the river as a sacred living being, derives real value from an undammed, healthy riparian ecosystem, whether that value can be converted into cash equivalents or not. The importance of applying economic analysis to diverse values is that it draws our attention to the value categories. We can expect highly divergent views about how much value to accord to, say, the aesthetic enjoyment of seeing irrigated rice terraces as opposed to bare fields, but we can expect reasonable people to agree that seeing those rice terraces can be a valued experience for at least some people.

It is the discovery of new kinds of value that we had not been aware of before, and new levels of appreciation for those values, that offer hope for our water ecosystems, and our water future. Just as littering was once socially accepted but is now viewed as socially, environmentally, and legally wrong, a similar shift in attitudes is taking place regarding water pollution. We have made tremendous progress in caring about visible pollution of our rivers and lakes, but we have become stymied on the non-point source, the invisible pollution of agrochemicals, in particular. Ethics analysis offers a way of making that hidden pollution more visible by drawing attention to the ethical ramifications of passive-aggressive pollution.

Analyzing and publicizing the collateral damage from mountaintop removal, however, has had surprisingly little impact on the egregious behavior of the mining companies. Why not? Without a clear sense of the importance of their mountain streams, not to mention the mountains themselves, local residents are not able to connect the dots. So long as they live in economic trauma and see no recourse other than competing for the few remaining jobs in coal mining, the dots will remain unconnected.

The stakes for our water future are incredibly high, and there are so many obvious disconnects between what needs to be done, and what is actually being done, to safeguard our water environment and the people and cultures whose fate is tied to that environment. Mountaintop removal mining is a sobering reminder of the dysfunctional policies that we need to contend with. Yet at the same time, we can see the glow on the horizon of an emerging global water ethic. Will we feel the heat of that sun before our water ecosystems succumb to the cold, dark night of ignorance?

What can we do? We can start by acknowledging that our ethics are out of control, i.e. they are not operating within a constructive framework of water governance. Major water decisions, about building dams, allowing irreparable contamination of rivers and groundwater, and diverting rivers to support unplanned urban growth, are being made without checking in with the ethical implications. How can we exert control over something that we don't, in fact, have control over?

We don't have control, but we have influence through the emerging standards of best practice and generally shared global water ethics, the most important of which is the ethic of stakeholder participation. In an analysis of stakeholder participation in water resources planning in Quebec, Cosgrove (2009) shows the outcome achieved high standards of environmentalism by including everybody's perspectives and finding a solution that would meet all reasonable needs. As we might expect from ecological theory, the long-term interests of people and nature are not usually at odds, but it takes a broad coalition of interests to realize this.

The level of participation needed to make an effective difference in the trajectory of water policies, however, will not be met simply by vague calls for more and better stakeholder participation, or even by offering examples of how it can work. Somehow we need to leverage the prevailing cultural values (ethics) about water governance so there is greater priority placed on participation, and then the magic of participatory democracy can do its work. When water decisions are understood as subjective decisions about ethics, and not only as technical decisions about the physical management of water, the value of broad stakeholder representation becomes apparent. Most stakeholders lack useful technical knowledge, but all stakeholders have an opinion! They all have values which they want to see represented in the water policies that will affect them.

The way that water ethics can solve the water crisis is by legitimizing a governance role for all stakeholders and accepting their ethics as important. The policy solutions that work for all stakeholders will also "work" for the environment, because some of those stakeholders will be representing nature's interests too. The solution, in other words, lies in the involvement of stakeholders, and the logic for involving those stakeholders rests on an appreciation of ethics. Everybody needs to be involved.

Messages for Water Advocates

The message for everyone concerned about water is, "Get involved!" Get involved in the water decisions that will affect you, or will affect your ethical sphere, which hopefully will include nature and at least seven generations of your descendants. Bring your values and ethics to the decision-making table, whether it's a board room table or a kitchen table, and offer your views and listen to other views. Values are often conflicting and need to be forged into a coherent system of values (i.e. an ethic) through discussion and debate. The related message to "Get involved!" is to find your gift; identify what unique perspective or experience or knowledge you can offer to the water discourse or activities.

Box 9.1 The Relevance of Victorian River Ethics

I was recently on a plane flying to Denver, seated next to two graduate students in English literature en route to their first professional conference where they were giving papers related to their PhD research on 19th-Century English literature. We exchanged our professional stories and I found myself suggesting that every discipline has something to offer to our understanding of water: my own field of anthropology, or geography, or history ... and I asked about their own subject. How was water perceived in 19th-Century England? How were the rivers used at that time; how did writers portray them? What did 19th-Century English water ethics look like?

They had never thought to ask such a question, and neither had I, but all three of us could see that it was not only an academically interesting question (perhaps the topic of their next conference paper!) but would have practical implications for both understanding the contemporary role of rivers in English life, and for developing policy recommendations for the future. How might an awareness about the historic use or even abuse of their rivers 200 years ago deepen the public's appreciation for their rivers today, and perhaps stimulate their imaginations for what their rivers could be in the future? Not even 19th-Century English Literature scholars are exempt from the moral responsibility to help improve water policies!

Just as artists who work on water issues see their role as one of raising the viewer's awareness, interest, and appreciation, through their art, we can all find ways to apply some creativity in our own water specialties. I debriefed with a hydrologist at a water conference recently after we had listened to a keynote address about water ethics. I thought it had been a great talk, particularly since it was "my" topic. He, on the other hand, was critical, feeling that the speaker had "talked down" to him, as if the subject of water ethics somehow excluded the involvement of hydrologists. He had gone into hydrology, he explained, precisely because he felt a moral responsibility to do something to help the natural world. He chose hydrology; I had chosen anthropology, and there we both were at the same meeting. We both self-identified as water ethicists. Are there others as well?

I am coming to realize that there are lots of others, both within the water profession, as well as people with a personal interest, who want to help "water" or the river, or the planet in some abstract way. We are all responding to the tug of our ethical sphere puffing out to include nature. We are the people Aldo Leopold imagined! How can we respond to that ethical tug? What can we do? Here are some suggestions.

What Water Professionals Can Do: People whose main professional work involves water issues, in public agencies, engineering businesses, universities, consulting firms, environmental NGOs, etc., are already responding to an ethical concern about water through their career choices. This is an important fact to acknowledge, and offers a path into the emotional memories of how this professional interest in water started, and to try to rekindle those emotions around your current professional tasks, whatever they are. Those memories provide a way of "harmonizing emotion and thought" to tap into the "emotional intelligence" needed for rational decision-making (Goleman 1995:27–8). If you are working on the supply side, finding more water to meet society's seemingly endless thirst, as an engineer, geologist, biologist, lawyer, economist, etc., you can look for creative solutions that serve nature's needs as well. If you are already working on water issues from "inside" nature, as a biologist, ecologist, or meteorologist, you can take inspiration from Rachel Carson and work to instill a sense of wonder and appreciation in yourself (first) and in the people around you.

What Non-Water Professionals Can Do: What if you chose another career path that was not connected to water? Your first step to get involved in water is to figure out how your own professional expertise and interests might connect in some way to the challenges of meeting the water crisis. You already know where your skills lie; you only need to explore the water crisis with a creative mind and you will be able to identify some low-hanging fruit. If you are a social scientist or a humanist attached to a university, have coffee with a colleague from the Water Resources Department, or anyone you know who is involved in water issues professionally or even peripherally, and brainstorm with them about how you might get involved. It could be writing an academic paper (see Box 8.1) or talking to a class of engineering students, or writing a guest blog post. If you are a health professional you could get involved in water quality issues from disposal of medical wastes and pharmaceuticals. If you are a social worker or psychologist you could explore how sensory experiences with water can support emotional balance (Kellert 2012).

What Businesses Can Do: If you are a business owner or worker interested in water, you probably already know about the water footprint tool for identifying how to reduce overall use and impact (see Chapter 1). You can use that tool as stepping stone to a proactive company policy to promote an ethic of water stewardship with your suppliers and business associates (see the case of Indiska in Chapter 5) as well as your customers, and local (or even non-local) government agencies. Working through the business associations that your company is already part of might be the most effective way to express your water ethic. The unique advantage of business, from a water ethics perspective, is that you have a well-established identity as being concerned with economic profit so when you "come out" in support of environmental, social, or cultural values that message carries extra legitimacy.

What Public Sector Professionals Can Do: If you are working in a government agency that has a water mandate, you can, of course, do a lot (see above: What Water Professionals Can Do). But what if you are among the other 99% of public sector professionals who do not have water in your job description? If you are in local government, consider sponsoring an initiative to develop a water stewardship standard for your city that would set out both the principles and target actions to protect the local water environment. You can find ideas on the Alliance for Water Stewardship website at http:// www.allianceforwaterstewardship.org. As with small businesses working through larger business associations, you work through the state or national associations that your city belongs to, or a national association representing your profession (e.g. tax accountants or land use planners) and get involved with water issues through them. Most directly and importantly is to simply be aware of water decisions that come up within your own work and analyze the ethics embedded those issues.

What Environmentalists Can Do: Water is a part of the environment that flows through everyone's home and everyone's body every day. Water is "living" proof that the environment is part of us. If you work for an environmental organization, or volunteer, or are a member of an environmental organization (WWF has 5 million members worldwide)[1] you can encourage the organization to develop a water program, or strengthen the ones that they have. Why? Because water decisions need more environmental input. Many environmental groups view water policies as too technical or too complicated, or as a distraction from their primary focus. But water is part of all life, and every environmental topic has inherent links to water issues. You can help your organization identify the most important links and explore how the organization's mission can be furthered by addressing those links.

What Regular Citizens Can Do: If you don't fit into any of the above categories, not to worry. There is an important role for you too! We can all be mindful of our individual water use, but don't stop there. Talking about water with your family, friends, and colleagues, and your political representatives, can have important multiplier effects. It can be empowering to realize that our water "crisis" is composed of so many little decisions which involve choices that reflect values. Your friends might be relieved to learn that they are not victims of mismanaged water ecosystems, but rather unwitting accomplices!

What Indigenous People Can Do: Your indigenous identity involves a relationship with the lands and waters of your native place. You can embrace that connection and help your community to protect the health of your local waters through ongoing local initiatives, or perhaps you can start a new initiative. Invite elders to talk to school children about water traditions. Get involved in natural resources plans and ensure that cultural values are incorporated. Help revive ceremonies related to water and agriculture. Participate in planning and monitoring business initiatives that will impact on water use, especially extractive industries. Most importantly, from the perspective of promoting sustainable water ethics, become a bridge between your culture and (1) other indigenous cultures and (2) the non-indigenous "mainstream" world. Look for opportunities both locally and internationally to present your understanding about water, water ecosystems, and the natural world. Those opportunities might take the form of legal actions, or political lobbying, or participating in conferences, or other forms of outreach.

What Members of Religious Organizations Can Do: Religions incorporate ethics as central features of doctrine. You can make three important contributions: (1) As a religious adherent, you have expertise in the application of ethics to everyday decisions, including water decisions. Through your involvement in water decisions at any level (local to global) you can help identify the implicit values in alternative proposals, which others may not see so clearly. (2) As a proponent of the particular ethics prescribed by your religion, you can help translate those precepts into practical terms that can be considered in water discussions. (3) As a member of an organization, you can lobby governments, businesses, etc., asking them to adopt water policies and practices which comply with the moral values of your religion.

What Artists Can Do: You can help us see the interplay of ethics and aesthetics in our relationship to water and the natural world (Carlson 2010). You can reveal the moral dilemmas of our impacts on water, whether from dams, mines, lawn chemicals, or industry. Whether through painting, photography, video, dance, sculpture, or film, you can convey the emotional dimensions of how we use, abuse, and feel about water ecosystems. But, as artists, you already know that. How can you do this more effectively in terms of practical influence on water policies? Collaboration with water activists could help direct your artistic expressions to current questions and controversies. Help us see and feel the meaning of the water controversies we usually only read about in news accounts or dry reports!

Ethics: Antidote to the Water Crisis

Working with ethics and paying attention to the many ways that we derive value from water is an affirmation about the big picture values which give meaning to our lives. When we deliberately focus on solutions that can meet both material needs as well as our social, cultural, and even emotional needs, and while protecting or perhaps restoring ecosystem health, we discover options that we would not have imagined through conventional economically driven planning processes. We consider artificial wetlands as substitutes for conventional wastewater treatment; we explore water-neutral landscape options that do not require diversions from rivers, and we favor urban plans that showcase the streams and rivers once buried under concrete.

There is an ethical dimension to water decisions, and to decisions that indirectly affect water. Denial that anything can be done prevents that ethical dimension from inflating into a space where things can happen. We need first of all to recognize the ethical dimension, and imbue it with our attention so it can grow into a space where we can debate with others who can also see that space. We cannot expect to agree with all the other views expressed in that space, but we can have a dialogue, we can explain our views, we can listen, we can argue and debate. It is a dialogue that can have great consequences. It is inside that ethical space that we can discover enough ethics in common that consensus can form around that seed of shared values.

We don't have to agree on every point, nor do we need to reach a consensus on every issue. Sometimes we will have to agree to disagree. We need only to reach enough consensus on the most essential issues that we can make a little progress on the health of our water ecosystems and the sustainability of our supplies. We only need to avert the water crisis a little longer. In the meantime we can be busy forging consensus on more and more issues. Ethics will not provide a single solution; but through working on the basis of ethical principles we can forge enough solutions enough of the time that the water crisis we see today can recede like a mirage into the future, inspiring us to move forward.

Note

1 Source: EarthShare, http://www.earthshare.org/2008/09/world-wildlife.html.

Bibliography

Acreman, M.C. and Ferguson, A.J.D. (2010) "Environmental flows and the European Water Framework Directive," *Freshwater Biology*, vol. 55, 32–48

Agarwal, A. and Narain, S. (1999) *Making Water Management Everybody's Business: Water Harvesting and Rural Development in India*, Gatekeeper Series no. 87, International Institute for Environment and Development, London

Altieri, Miguel (1985) *Agroecology: The Science of Sustainable Agriculture*, Westview Press, Boulder, CO

Anaya, J. (2000) *Indigenous Peoples in International Law*, Oxford University Press, New York

Anderson, F. and Engberg, R. (2006) "Water policy: present and future," *Water Resources Impact*, vol. 8, no. 6, 4

Anderson, R.S. and Huber, W. (1988) *The Hour of the Fox: Tropical Forests, the World Bank, and Indigenous People in Central India*, University of Washington Press, Seattle

Ariely, D. (2012) *The Honest Truth about Dishonesty*, HarperCollins, New York

Armstrong, A. (2009) "Viewpoint: further ideas towards a water ethic," *Water Alternatives*, vol. 2, no. 1, 138–47

Armstrong, J. (2006) "Water is Siwlkw" in M. Chibba, D. Nakashima, and R. Boelens (eds) *Water and Indigenous Peoples*, UNESCO, Paris

Arthington, A.H. (2012) *Environmental Flows: Saving Rivers in the Third Millennium*, University of California Press, Berkeley

Arthington, A.H., Bunn, S.E., Poff, L., and Naiman, R.J. (2006) "The challenge of providing environmental flow rules to sustain river ecosystems," *Ecological Applications*, vol. 16, no. 4, 1311–18

Aspevig, C. (2010) "The nature of art, the art of conservation," *Convergence*, winter 2010, 6–13

Association of State Floodplain Managers (ASFM) 2008, Natural and beneficial floodplain management, *ASFPM Whitepaper*, ASFM, Madison, Wisconsin, http://www.floods.org/PDF/WhitePaper/ASFPM_NBF%20White_Paper_%200908.pdf

Australian Human Rights Commission (2008) "'Indigenous peoples and water," *Native Title Report*, Chapter 6, http://www.hreoc.gov.au/social_justice/nt_report/ntreport08/index.html

Baghel, R. and Nüsser, M. (2010) "Discussing large dams in Asia after the World Commission on Dams: Is a political ecology approach the way forward?," *Water Alternatives*, vol. 3, no. 2, 231–48

Bahri, A. (2012) *Integrated Urban Water Management*, TEC Background Papers No. 16, Global Water Partnership, Stockholm

Bakker, K. (2010) *Privatizing Water: Governance Failure and the World's Urban Water Crisis*, Cornell University Press, Ithaca, NY

Bakker, K., Kooy, M., Shofiani, N.E., and Martijn, E.J. (2008) "Governance failure: rethinking the institutional dimensions of urban water supply to poor households," *World Development*, vol. 36, no. 10, 1891–1915

Barlow, M. (2012) "Foreword," in Sultana and Loftus (2012)

Barlow, M. and Clarke, T. (2002) *Blue Gold: The Fight to Stop Corporate Theft of the World's Water*, The New Press, New York

Barnett, C. (2011) *Blue Revolution: Unmaking America's Water Crisis*, Beacon Press, Boston

Berry, K. and Mollard, E. (2010) *Social Participation in Water Governance and Management: Critical and Global Perspectives*, Earthscan, London

Billington, D.P., Jackson, D.C., and Melosi, M.V. (2005) *The History of Large Federal Dams: Planning, Design, and Construction in the Era of Big Dams*, US Department of the Interior, Bureau of Reclamation, Denver Colorado

Binney, P., Donald, A., Elmer, V., Ewert, J., Phillis, O., Skinner, R., and Young, R. (2010) *IWA Cities of the Future Program: Spatial Planning and Institutional Reform*, Discussion Paper for the World Water Congress, September 2010, International Water Association, London

Biswas, A.K. (2004) "Integrated water resources management: a reassessment," *Water International*, vol. 29, no. 2, 248–56

Blackbourn, David (2006) *The Conquest of Nature: Water, Landscape, and the Making of Modern Germany*, New York, Norton

Boelens, R. (1998) "Equity and rule-making," in R. Boelens and G. Davila (eds) *Searching for Equity: Conceptions of Justice and Equity in Peasant Irrigation*, Van Gorcum, Assen, The Netherlands

Boelens, R., Bustamante, R., and de Vos, H. (2007) "Legal pluralism and the politics of inclusion: recognition and contestation of local water rights in the Andes," in B. van Koppen, M. Giordano, and J. Butterworth (eds) *Community-based Water Law and Water Resource Management Reform*, CAB International, London

Boelens, R., Getches, D., and Guevara-Gil, A. (eds) (2010) *Out of the Mainstream: Water Rights, Politics and Identity*, Earthscan, London

Boetzkes, A. (2010) *The Ethics of Earth Art*, University of Minnesota Press, MN

Bogardi, J., Dudgeon, D., Lawford, R., Flinkerbusch, E., Pahl-Wostl, C., Vielhauer, K., and Vorosmarty, C. (2011) "Water security for a planet under pressure: interconnected challenges of a changing world call for sustainable solutions," *Current Opinions in Environmental Sustainability*, vol. 4, 1–9

Bonnardeaux, D. (2012) *Linking Biodiversity Conservation and Water, Sanitation, and Hygiene: Experiences from sub-Saharan Africa*, Africa Biodiversity Collaborative Group, Washington, DC

Both ENDS and Gomukh (2005) *River Basin Management: A Negotiated Approach*, Both ENDS (Amsterdam) and Gomukh (Pune, India)

Boyd, D. (2012) "The constitutional right to a healthy environment," *Environment: Science and Policy for Sustainable Development*, vol. 54, no. 4, 3–15

Bray, F. (1986) *The Rice Economies: Technology and Development in Asian Societies*, University of California Press, Berkeley, CA

Brelet, C. and Selborne, J. (2004) "Best ethical practice in water use," *World Commission on the Ethics of Scientific Knowledge and Technology*, UNESCO, Paris

Brierley, G. and Fryirs, K. (2008) *River Futures: An Integrative Scientific Approach to River Repair*, Island Press, Washington, DC

Brookfield, H., Parsons, H., and Brookfield, M. (2003) *Agrodiversity: Learning from Farmers across the World*, United Nations University Press, Tokyo

Brooks, D.B., Brandes, O.M., and Gurman, S. (2009) *Making the Most of the Water We Have: The Soft Path Approach to Water Management*, Earthscan, London

Brown, A. (2010) "Reliable mine water technology," *Mine Water Environment*, vol. 29, 85–91

Brown, P.G. and Schmidt, J.J. (2010) *Water Ethics: Foundational Readings for Students and Professionals*, Island Press, Washington, DC

Cardwell, M. (2008) "Rural development in the European Community: charting a new course?" *Drake Journal of Agricultural Law*, spring 2008

Carlson, A. (2010) "Contemporary environmental aesthetics and the requirements of environmentalism," *Environmental Values*, vol. 19, 289–314

Cernea, M. (1991) *Putting People First: Sociological Variables in Rural Development*, Oxford University Press, New York

Cernea, M.M. (2003) "For a new economics of resettlement: a sociological critique of the compensation principle," *International Social Science Journal*, no. 175

Chambers, Robert (1986) "Normal professionalism, new paradigms and development," Unpublished Manuscript DP227, Institute of Development Studies, Sussex

Chambers, R. (2007) "From PRA to PLA and pluralism: practice and theory," Working Paper 286, Institute for Development Studies, Sussex

Chambers, R., Saxena, N.C., and Shah, T. (1989) *To the Hands of the Poor: Water and Trees*, Oxford and & IBH Publishing Co, New Delhi

Chibba, M., Nakashima, D., and Boelens, R. (eds) (2006) *Water and Indigenous Peoples*, UNESCO, Paris

Clark, C. (2012) "The centrality of community participation to the realization of the right to water: the illustrative case of South Africa," in Sultana and Loftus (2012)

Coca-Cola Company (2011) *The Water Stewardship and Replenish Report*, http://www.thecoca-colacompany.com/citizenship/pdf/replenish_2011.pdf

Conca, K. (2006) *Governing Water: Contentious Transnational Politics and Global Institution Building*, MIT Press, Cambridge, MA

Cooley, H., Hutchins-Cabibi, T., Cohen, M., Gleick, P.H., and Heberger, M. (2007) *Hidden Oasis: Water Conservation and Efficiency in Las Vegas*, Pacific Institute, Berkeley, CA and Western Resource Advocates, Boulder, CO

Cosgrove, W.J. (2009) "Public participation to promote water ethics and transparency," in M.R. Llamas, L. Martínez-Cortina, and A. Mukherj (eds) *Water Ethics: Marcelino Botín Water Forum 2007*, CRC Press/Balkema, Leiden, Netherlands

Cosgrove, W.J. and Rijsberman, F.R. (2000) *World Water Vision: Making Water Everybody's Business* (for the World Water Council), Earthscan, London

Coward, E.W. (1980) *Irrigation and Agricultural Development in Asia*, Cornell University Press, Ithaca, NY

Cowley, D. (2003) "Water requirements for endangered species in New Mexico," *Proceedings of the 47th Annual New Mexico Water Conference*, WRRI Report, no. 326, April 2003, 97–108, http://wrri.nmsu.edu/publish/watcon/proc47/contents.html

Curtis, M. (2012) *Asia at the Crossroads: Prioritising Conventional Farming or Sustainable Agriculture?* Action Aid, London, http://www.actionaid.org/sites/files/actionaid/asia_at_the_crossroads_full_report_2012.pdf

Daily, G. (ed.) (1997) *Nature's Services: Societal Dependence on Natural Ecosystems*, Island Press, Washington, DC

Danert, K. (2012) "Rural water for all: the river may be wide but it can be crossed," Final Report April 2012, Rural Water Supply Network, http://www.rural-water-supply.net/_ressources/documents/default/1-359-2-1341319418.pdf

deBuys, W. (ed.) (2001) *Seeing Things Whole: The Essential John Wesley Powell*, Island Press, Washington, DC

de Groot, M. and de Groot, W.T. (2009), "Room for river measures and public visions in the Netherlands: a survey on river perceptions among riverside residents," *Water Resources Research*, vol. 45, W07403, 1–11

Delli Priscoli, J., Dooge, J., and Llamas, R. (2004) *Water and Ethics: Overview*, UNESCO International Hydrological Programme & World Commission on the Ethics of Scientific Knowledge and Technology, Series on Water and Ethics, Essay 1, UNESCO, Paris

Delli Priscoli, J. (2012) "Introduction," *Water Policy*, vol. 14, 3–8

de Schutter, O. (2011) "Agroecology: a path to realizing the right to food," *Food First Backgrounder*, vol. 17, no. 2, 1–5

Dharmadhikary, S. (2005) *Unravelling Bhakra: Assessing the Temple of Resurgent India*, Manthan Adhyayana Kendra, Badwani, India

Diemer, G. and Slabbers, J. (eds) (1992) *Irrigators and Engineers*, Thesis Publishers, Amsterdam

Douglas, M. (2004) "Traditional culture; let's hear no more about it," in V. Rao and M. Walton (eds) *Culture and Public Action*, Stanford University Press, Stanford CA

Dussias, A.M. (1998) "Asserting a traditional environmental ethic: recent developments in environmental regulation involving Native American tribes," *New England Law Review*, vol. 33, no. 1, 1–653 to 1–667

Dyson, M., Bergkamp, G., and Scanlon, J. (eds) (2003) *Flow: The Essentials of Environmental Flows*, IUCN, Gland, Switzerland, http://www.waterandnature.org

El-Ashry, M.T. and Gibbons, D. (eds) (1988) *Water and Arid Lands of the Western United States* (A World Resources Institute book), Cambridge University Press, Cambridge

Engle, K. (2010) *The Elusive Promise of Indigenous Development: Rights, Culture, Strategy*, Duke University Press, Durham, NC

English, P.W. (1998) "Qanats and lifeworlds in Iranian Plateau villages," in *Transformations of Middle Eastern Natural Environments: Legacies and Lessons*, Bulletin series / Yale School of Forestry and Environmental Studies, no. 103, Yale University Press, New Haven

Escobar, A. (1995) *Encountering Development: The Making and Unmaking of the Third World*, Princeton University Press, NJ

Falkenmark, M. (2003) *Water Management and Ecosystems: Living with Change*, GWP Background Paper No. 9 (2003), http://www.gwptoolbox.org/images/stories/gwplibrary/background/tec_9_english.pdf

Falkenmark, M. and Rockström, J. (2006) "The new blue and green water paradigm: breaking new ground for water resources planning and management," *Journal of Water Resources Planning and Management*, May/June 2006, 129–32

Fazlur-Rahman (2007) "The role of Aga Khan Rural Support Programme in rural development in the Karakorum, Hindu Kush and Himalayan region: examples from the northern mountainous belt of Pakistan," *Journal of Mountain Science*, vol. 4, no. 4, 331–43

Feldman, D.L. (1991) *Water Resources Management: In Search of an Environmental Ethic*, Johns Hopkins University Press, Baltimore, MD

Finch, D.M. and Tainter, J.A. (1995) *Ecology, Diversity, and Sustainability of the Middle Rio Grande Basin*, USDA Forest Service General Technical Report RM-GTR-268, Fort Collins

Finch, L.S.G. (2012) "The duty to learn: taking account of indigenous legal orders in practice," Paper presented at Indigenous Legal Orders and the Common Law, Continuing Legal Education Society of British Columbia, November 15, Vancouver, BC

Finnegan, W. (2002) "Letter from Bolivia: Leasing the Rain," *The New Yorker*, April 8:45–53, http://www.newyorker.com/archive/2002/04/08/020408fa_FACT1

Fisher, A. (2012) "Spirit of the salmon: native religion, rights, and resource use in the Columbia River basin," in D. Gordon and S. Krech III (eds) *Indigenous Knowledge and the Environment in Africa and North America*, Ohio University Press, Athens, OH

Fleskens, L., Filomena, D., and Eicher, I. (2009) "A conceptual framework for the assessment of multiple functions of agro-ecosystems," *Journal of Rural Studies*, vol. 25, 144–55

Fletcher, R. (2010) "When environmental issues collide: climate change and the shifting political ecology of hydroelectric power," *Peace and Conflict Review*, vol. 5, no. 1

Food and Water Watch (2012) "Nevada's groundwater pipeline: shortsighted and unsustainable," *Fact Sheet*, February, http://documents.foodandwaterwatch.org/doc/NevadaPipeline.pdf

Fort, D. and Nelson, B. (2012) *Pipedreams: Water Supply Pipeline Projects in the West*, National Resources Defense Council, Washington, DC

Garces-Restrepo, C., Vermillion, D., and Muñoz, G. (2007) *Irrigation Management Transfer: Worldwide Efforts and Results*, FAO Water Reports 32, Rome

Giordano, M.A., Rijsberman, F.R., and Saleth, R.M. (2006) *"More Crop per Drop": Revising a Research Paradigm*, International Water Management Institute and IWA Publishing, London

Gittinger, J.P. (1982) *Economic Analysis of Agricultural Projects*, The World Bank, Washington, DC

Gleick, P.H. (2009) *The World's Water 2008–2009: The Biennial Report on Freshwater Resources*, Island Press, Washington, DC

Gleick, P.H. and Christian-Smith, J. (2012) *A Twenty-First Century US Water Policy*, Oxford University Press, New York

Glendenning, C.J. (2009) *Evaluating the Impacts of Rainwater Harvesting (RWG) in a Case Study Catchment: The Arvari River, Rajasthan, India*, PhD Thesis, University of Sydney

Glennon, R. (2002) *Water Follies: Groundwater Pumping and the Fate of America's Fresh Waters*, Island Press, Washington, DC

Global Compact (2011) *The CEO Water Mandate: An Initiative by Business Leaders in Partnership with the International Community*, The UN Global Compact, New York

Goleman, D. (1995) *Emotional Intelligence: Why It Can Matter More than IQ*, Bantam, New York

Gorriz, C. and Groenfeldt, D. (1995) *Proceedings of the International Seminar on Participatory Irrigation Management, Mexico, February 8–15, 1995*, World Bank Economic Development Institute, Washington, DC

Green, C.H., Parker, D.J., and Tunstall, S.M. (2000) "Assessment of flood control and management options," *WCD Thematic Reviews Options Assessment: IV.4*, World Commission on Dams Secretariat, Cape Town

Griffiths, T. (2007) "Seeing 'red': avoided deforestation and the rights of Indigenous Peoples and local communities," *Indigenous Perspectives*, vol. 9, nos. 1–2, 93–118

Groenfeldt, D. (1991) "Building on tradition: indigenous irrigation knowledge and agricultural development," *Agriculture and Human Values*, vol. 7, 114–20

Groenfeldt, D. (2003a) "Report on the March 2003 World Water Forum sessions on indigenous perspectives on water and development," Water-Culture Institute, http://www.waterculture.org/uploads/Indigenous_Sessions_Summary.pdf.

Groenfeldt, D. (2003b) "The future of indigenous values: cultural relativism in the face of economic development," *Futures*, vol. 35, 917–29

Groenfeldt, D. (2006a) "Multifunctionality of agricultural water: looking beyond food production and ecosystem services," *Irrigation and Drainage*, vol. 55, 1–11

Groenfeldt, D. (2006b) "Water development and spiritual values in western and indigenous societies," In M. Chibba, D. Nakashima, and R. Boelens (eds) *Water and Indigenous Peoples*, UNESCO, Paris

Groenfeldt, D. (2008) "Animism, economics, and sustainable water development," in S. Shaw, and A. Francis (eds) *Deep Blue: Critical Reflections on Nature, Religion, and Water*, Equinox, London, 237–52

Groenfeldt, D. and Schmidt, J. (2013) "Ethics and water governance," *Ecology and Society*, vol. 18, no. 1, 14, http://dx.doi.org/10.5751/ES-04629-180114

Groenfeldt, D. and Svendsen, M. (2000) *Case Studies in Participatory Irrigation Management*, World Bank Institute, Washington, DC

Grossman, E. (2002) *Watershed: The Undamming of America*, Counterpoint, New York

GWP (2000) *Integrated Water Resources Management*, TAC Background Papers No. 4, Global Water Partnership, Stockholm

GWP and INBO (2009) *A Handbook for Integrated Water Resources Management in Basins*, Global Water Partnership, Stockholm and the International Network of Basin Organizations, Paris, http://www.riob.org/IMG/pdf/GWP-INBOHandbook ForIWRMinBasins.pdf

Haberman, D.L. (2006) *River of Love in an Age of Pollution: The Yamuna River of Northern India*, University of California Press, Berkeley

Hanemann, W.M. (2002) *The Central Arizona Project*, Dept. of Agricultural and Resource Economics and Policy Working Paper No. 937, University of California, Berkeley, http://are.berkeley.edu/~gh082644/cap.pdf

Hecht, Susanna (1995) "The evolution of agroecological thought," in M. Altieri, *Agroecology: The Science of Sustainable Agriculture*, Westview Press, Boulder, CO, 1–20

Hefny, M.A. (2009) "Water management ethics in the framework of environmental and general ethics: The case of Islamic water ethics," in Llamas et al. (2009)

Hirsch, P. (2010) "The changing political dynamics of dam building on the Mekong," *Water Alternatives*, vol. 3, no. 2, 312–23

Hoekstra, A.Y. (2013) *The Water Footprint of Modern Consumer Society*, Routledge, Abingdon and New York

Hoekstra, A.Y., Chapagain, A.K., Aldaya, M.M., and Mekonnen, M.M. (2011) *The Water Footprint Assessment Manual: Setting the Global Standard*, Earthscan, London

Horst, L. (1996) "Intervention in irrigation water division in Bali, Indonesia: a case of farmers' circumvention of modern technology," in G. Diemer and F. Huibers (eds) *Crops, People and Irrigation: Water Allocation Practices of Farmers and Engineers*, Intermediate Technology Publications, London

Hundley, Norris Jr. (1988) "The great American Desert transformed: aridity, exploitation, and imperialism in the making of the modern American West," in El-Ashry and Gibbons (1988)

Hunt, R. and Hunt, E. (1976) "Canal irrigation and local social organization," *Current Anthropology*, vol. 17, no. 3, 389–412

IIMI (1987) *Public Intervention in Farmer-Managed Irrigation Systems*, International Irrigation Management Institute, Colombo, Sri Lanka

International Assessment of Agricultural Knowledge, Science and Technology for Development (IAASTD) (2009) *Agriculture at a Crossroads: Global Report*, Island Press, Washington, DC

Irland, Basia (2007) *Water Library*, University of New Mexico Press, Albuquerque, NM

Isdell, N. (2009) Remarks during the launch of the "Declaration on U.S. Policy and the Global Challenge of Water" at the Center for Strategic and International Studies, Washington, DC, March 18, http://csis.org/files/media/csis/events/090318_declaration_launch_summary.pdf

Islam, S. and Susskind, L.E. (2013) *Water Diplomacy: A Negotiated Approach to Managing Complex Water Networks*, RFF Press, New York

Jackson, S. (2006) "Compartmentalising culture: the articulation and consideration of Indigenous values in water resource management," *Australian Geographer*, vol. 37, no. 1, 19–31

Jackson, S. (2009) "National Indigenous Water Planning Forum: background paper on indigenous participation in water planning and access to water," CISRO, Australia

James, A.J. (2011) *Sri Lanka: Lessons for Rural Water Supply; Assessing Progress Towards Sustainable Service Delivery*, IRC International Water and Sanitation Centre, The Hague

Johnson, C. (2012) "Toward post-sovereign environmental governance? Politics, scale, and EU Water Framework Directive," *Water Alternatives*, vol. 5, no. 1, 83–97

Johnston, B.R. (ed.) (1994) *Who Pays the Price? The Sociocultural Context of Environmental Crisis*, Island Press, Washington, DC

Johnston, B.R., Hiwasaki, L., Klaver, I.J., Ramos Castillo, A., and Strang, V. (eds) (2012) *Water, Cultural Diversity, and Global Environmental Change: Emerging Trends, Sustainable Futures?* UNESCO, Paris and Springer, Dordrecht, Germany

Joint Steering Committee for Water Sensitive Cities (2009) *Evaluating Options for Water Sensitive Urban Design: A National Guide*, BMT WBM, Brisbane, Australia, http://www.environment.gov.au/water/publications/urban/pubs/wsud-guidelines.pdf

Jones, T., Newborne, P., and Phillips, B. (2006) *Applying the Principles of Integrated Water Resource and River Basin Management – An Introduction*, Report to WWF-UK, London, http://awsassets.panda.org/downloads/applying_the_principl es_of_integrated_water_resource_and_river_basin_management_aug_06_ver.pdf

Kellert, S. (2012) *Birthright: People and Nature in the Modern World*, Yale University Press, New Haven

Kellert, S., Heerwagen, J., and Mador, M. (2008) *Biophilic Design: The Theory, Science and Practice of Bringing Buildings to Life*, Wiley, New York

Kellert, S. and Wilson, E.O. (1995) *The Biophilia Hypothesis*, Island Press, Washington,DC

Khon Kaen University (1987) "Proceedings of the 1985 International Conference on Rapid Rural Appraisal. Rural Systems Research and Farming Systems Research Projects," Khon Kaen, Thailand

Kiser, M., Megdal, S., Stratton, M., Vasquez, V., and Zucker, C. (2011) *Report of the Regional Water Assessment Task Force "ThinkTank" Process Conducted in the Tucson Active*

Management Area, Pima County Association of Governments, Tucson, AZ, http://www.pagnet.org/documents/water/RWATFThinkTankReport-2011-08.pdf

Kloezen, W.H., Garcés-Restrepo, C., and Johnson, S.H. (1997) *Impact Assessment of Irrigation Management Transfer in the Alto Rio Lerma Irrigation District, Mexico*, Research Report 15, IIMI, Colombo, Sri Lanka

Korten, D. (1995) *When Corporations Rule the World*, Kumarian Press, West Harford, CT

Korten, F.E. and Siy, R.Y., Jr. (1989) *Transforming a Bureaucracy: The Experience of the Philippine National Irrigation Administration*, Kumarian Press, West Hartford, CT

Kreamer, D.K. (2010) "The meaning of hydrophilanthropy," *Water Resources Impact*, vol. 12, no. 5, 3–5

Lal, Rattan (2007) "Soil science and the carbon civilization," *Soil Science of America Journal*, vol. 71, no. 5, 1425–37

Lancaster, B. (2008) *Rainwater Harvesting for Drylands and Beyond, Volume 1: Guiding Principles to Welcome Rain into Your Life and Landscape*, Rainsource Press, Tucson, Arizona

Landen, E. and Propen, D. (2012) *Milking Nature's Bottom Line: A Full-Cost-Accounting of Proposed CAFO Operations in Jo Daviess County, Illinois*, Landen Consulting, Chicago, http://www.landenconsulting.com/downloads/Milking–Natures-Bottom-Line-20130212.pdf

Lansing, J.S. (1996) "Simulation modeling of Balinese irrigation," in J. Mabry (ed.) *Canals and Communities: Small-scale Irrigation Systems*, University of Arizona Press, Tucson, AZ

Leach, E. (1961) *Pul Eliya: A Village in Ceylon*, Cambridge University Press, London

Ledford, D. (2012) "Promoting environmental and wildlife wellbeing," *American Coal*, no. 1, 30–4

Lejon, A.G.C., Malm Renöfält, B., and Nilsson, C. (2009) "Conflicts associated with dam removal in Sweden," *Ecology and Society*, vol. 14, no. 2, 4, http://www.ecologyandsociety.org/vol14/iss2/art4/

Leopold, A. (1970 [1949]) *A Sand County Almanac*, Oxford University Press, New York

Leopold, L. (1977) "A reverence for rivers," *Geology*, vol. 5, 429–30

Leopold, L. and Maddock, T. (1954) *The Flood Control Controversy: Big Dams, Little Dams and Land Management*, Ronald Press, New York

Le Quesne, T., Kendy, E., and Weston, D. (2010) *The Implementation Challenge: Taking Stock of Government Policies to Protect and Restore Environmental Flows*, WWF-UK, Godalming, Surrey

Lewis, R.B. and Hestand, J.T. (2006) "Federal reserved water rights: Gila River Indian Community Settlement," *Journal of Contemporary Water Research and Education*, no. 133, 34–42 http://www.camelclimatechange.org/files/204101_2042 00/204113/lewis-and-hestand.pdf

Li, R., Van Beek, E., and Gijsbers, P. (2004) "Integrated water resources management for the Yellow River in China: a discussion of scientific and ethical approaches," in *The Basis of Civilization – Water Science? Proceedings of the UNESCO/IAIIS/IWTIA symposium held in Rome, December 2003*, IAHS Publ. 286, http://iahs.info/redbooks/a286/iahs_286_0150.pdf

Limerick, P.N. (1987) *The Legacy of Conquest: The Unbroken Past of the American West*, Norton, New York

Linton, J. (2012) "The human right to what? Water, rights, humans, and the relation of things," in Sultana and Loftus (2012)

Liu, J., Dorjderem, A., Fu, J., Lei, X., Liu, H., Macer, D., Qiao, Q., Sun, A., Tachiyama, K., Yu, L., and Zheng, Y. (2011) *Water Ethics and Water Resource Management*, UNESCO Ethics and Climate Change in Asia and the Pacific (ECCAP) Project Working Group 14 Report, UNESCO, Bangkok

Llamas, M.R., Martínez-Cortina, L., and Mukherj, A. (eds) (2009) *Water Ethics: Marcelino Botín Water Forum 2007*, CRC Press/Balkema, Leiden, Netherlands

Llamas, M.R. (2012) "Foreword: the role of the Botín Foundation to support the analysis of issues on water ethics," *Water Policy*, vol. 14, 1–2

Mander, J. and Tauli-Corpuz, V. (eds) (2006) *Paradigm Wars: Indigenous Peoples' Resistance to Globalization*, Sierra Club Books, San Francisco

Martinez Austria, P. and van Hofwegen, P. (eds) (2006) *Synthesis of the 4th World Water Forum*, Comisión Nacional de Agua, Mexico, http://www.worldwater council.org/fileadmin/wwc/World_Water_Forum/WWF4/synthesis_sept06.pdf

McCool, D. (2012) *River Republic: The Fall and Rise of America's Rivers*, Columbia University Press, New York

McGranahan, G. and Satterthwaite, D. (2006) "Governance and getting the private sector to provide better water and sanitation services to the urban poor," IIED Human Settlements Discussion Paper Series

McKibben, B. (2010) Eaarth: *Making a Life on a Tough New Planet*, Times Books, NY

Meinzen-Dick, R. (1997) "Farmers participation in irrigation, 20 years of experience and lessons for the future." *Irrigation and Drainage Systems*, vol. 11, 103–18

Merchant, C. (2010) "Fish first! The changing ethics of ecosystem management," in P.G. Brown and J.J. Schmidt (eds) *Water Ethics: Foundational Readings for Students and Professionals*, Island Press, Washington, DC

Mehta, L., Veldwisch, G.J., and Franco, J. (2012), "Introduction to the special issue: water grabbing? Focus on the (re)appropriation of finite water resources," *Water Alternatives*, vol. 5, no. 2, 193–207

Mellor, J. (1966) *The Economics of Agricultural Development*, Cornell University Press, Ithaca, NY

Miller, R. (2005) "The Doctrine of Discovery in American Indian Law," *Idaho Law Review*, vol 42, 1–122

Molden, D. (ed.) (2007) *Water for Food, Water for Life: A Comprehensive Assessment of Water Management in Agriculture*, Earthscan, London

Molle, F. (2008) "Nirvana concepts, narratives and policy models: insights from the water sector," *Water Alternatives*, vol. 1, no. 1

Molle, F. and Berkoff, J. (2009) "Cities vs. agriculture: a review of intersectoral water re-allocation," *Natural Resources Forum*, vol. 33, 6–18

Molle, F., Wester, P., and Hirsch, P. (2007) "River basin development and management," in D. Molden (ed.), *Water for Food, Water for Life: A Comprehensive Assessment of Water Management in Agriculture*, Earthscan, London

Moore, D., Dore, J., and Gyawali, D. (2010) "The World Commission on Dams +10: revisiting the large dam controversy," *Water Alternatives*, vol. 3, no. 2, 3–13

Morrison, J., Postel, S. and Gleick, P. (1996) *The Sustainable Use of Water in the Lower Colorado River Basin*, Pacific Institute, Oakland, CA, Executive Summary, http://www.pacinst.org/reports/sustainable_co_river/sustainable_co_river_es.pdf

Mosher, A.T. (1966) *Getting Agriculture Moving: Essentials for Development and Modernization*, Praeger, New York

Muir, J. (1911) *My First Summer in the Sierra*, Houghton Mifflin Co, Boston

Muir, J. (1912) *The Yosemite*, Century, New York

Nabokov, P. (2006) *Where the Lightning Strikes: The Lives of American Indian Sacred Places*, Penguin Books, New York

Nadeau, J., Megdal, S.B., Rupprecht, C., and Choate, B. (2012) "Testing the waters: Tucson links water conservation with environmental benefits," *American Water Works Association Journal*, vol. 104, no. 2, 76–9

Nash, R.F. (1989) *The Rights of Nature: A History of Environmental Ethics*, University of Wisconsin Press, Madison, WI

National Research Council (1989) *Alternative Agriculture*, National Academy Press, Washington, DC

National Research Council (1991) *Colorado River Ecology and Dam Management: Proceedings of a Symposium May 24–25, 1990 Santa Fe, New Mexico*, National Academies Press, Washington, DC, http://www.nap.edu/catalog/1832.html

National Research Council (2001) *Assessing the TMDL Approach to Water Quality Management*, National Academy Press, Washington, DC

Nelson, B. et al. (2007) *In Hot Water: Water Management Strategies to Weather the Effects of Global Warming*, National Resources Defense Council, Washington, DC

Netting, R.McC. (1993) *Smallholders, Householders: Farm Families and the Ecology of Intensive, Sustainable Agriculture*, Stanford University Press, CA

Oblitas, K. and Peter, R. (1999) *Transferring Irrigation Management to Farmers in Andhra Pradesh, India*, World Bank Technical Paper 449, Washington, DC

OECD (2001) *Multifunctionality: Towards an Analytical Framework*, OECD, Paris

OECD (2011) *Benefits of Investing in Water and Sanitation: An OECD Perspective*, OECD Studies on Water, OECD Publishing, Paris

Orr, S. (2013) "Dams on the Mekong," GWF Discussion Paper 1302, Global Water Forum, Canberra, Australia, http://www.globalwaterforum.org/2013/01/15/dams-on-the-mekong/

Ostrom, E. (1965) *Public Entrepreneurship: A Case Study in Ground Water Basin Management*, PhD Dissertation, University of California, Los Angeles

Ostrom, E. (1990) *Governing the Commons: The Evolution of Institutions for Collective Action*, Cambridge University Press, New York

Ostrom, E. (1992) *Crafting Institutions for Self-Governing Irrigation Systems*, ICS Press, San Francisco

Padre, S. (2000) "Harvesting the monsoon: livelihoods reborn," *ILEIA Newsletter*, March 2000

Pahl-Wostl, C., Craps, M., Dewulf, A., Mostert, E., Tabara, D., and Taillieu, T. (2007) "Social learning and water resources management," *Ecology and Society*, vol. 12, no. 2, 5, http://www.ecologyandsociety.org/vol12/iss2/art5/

Pahl-Wostl, C., Gupta, J., and Petry, D. (2008) "Governance and the global water system: a theoretical exploration," *Global Governance*, vol. 14, 419–35

Palacios, E. (2000) "Benefits and second-generation problems of irrigation management transfer in Mexico," in Groenfeldt and Svendsen (2000)

Palmer, L. (2006) "'Nature', place and the recognition of indigenous polities," *Australian Geographer*, vol. 37, no. 1, 33–43

Pecos, R. (2007) "The history of Cochiti Lake from the Pueblo perspective," *Natural Resources Journal*, vol. 47, no. 3, 639–52

Petts, G.E. (2009) "Instream flow science for sustainable river management," *Journal of the American Water Resources Association*, vol. 45, no. 5, 1071–86

Pollan, M. (2006) *The Omnivore's Dilemma: A Natural History of Four Meals*, Penguin, New York

Pollan, M. (2008) *In Defense of Food: An Eater's Manifesto*, Penguin, London

Postel, S. (1997) *Last Oasis: Facing Water Scarcity*, Norton, New York

Postel, S. and Richter, B. (2003) *Rivers for Life: Managing Water for People and Nature*, Island Press, Washington, DC

Pretty, Jules (2002) *Agri-Culture: Reconnecting People, Land and Nature*, Earthscan, London

Pretty, J. (2006) "Agroecological Approaches to Agricultural Development," Background Paper for the World Development Report 2008, http://siteresources. worldbank.org/INTWDR2008/Resources/2795087–1191427986785/PrettyJ_Agroec ologicalApproachesToAgriDevt[1].pdf

Putnam, R. (2000) *Bowling Alone: The Collapse and Revival of American Community*, Simon & Schuster, New York

Quevauviller, P. (2010) "Is IWRM achievable in practice? Attempts to break disciplinary and sectoral walls through a science-policy interfacing framework in the context of the EU Water Framework Directive," *Irrigation and Drainage Systems*, vol. 24, 177–89

Raby, N. (2000) "Participatory irrigation management in the Philippines: national irrigation systems," in Groenfeldt and Svendsen (2000)

Rao, V. and Walton, M. (eds) (2004) *Culture and Public Action*, Stanford University Press, Stanford, CA

Ravnborg, H.M., Bustamante, R., Cissé, A., Cold-Ravnkilde, S.M., Cossio, V., Djiré, M., Funder, M., Gómez, L.I., Le, P., Mweemba, C., Nyambe, I., Paz, T., Pham, H., Rivas, R., Skielboe, T., and Yen, N.T.B. (2012) "Challenges of local water governance: the extent, nature and intensity of local water-related conflict and cooperation," *Water Policy*, vol. 14, 336–57

Reece E. (2005) *Lost Mountain: A Year in the Vanishing Wilderness Radical Strip Mining and the Devastation of Appalachia*, Penguin, New York

Reisner, M. (1993) *Cadillac Desert: The American West and its Disappearing Water* (original 1986) Penguin Books, New York

Reisner, M. and Bates, S. (1990) *Overtapped Oasis: Reform or Revolution for Western Water*, Island Press, Washington, DC

Renting, H., Rossing, W.A.H., Groot, J.C.J., Van der Ploeg, J.D., Laurent, C., Perraud, D., Stobbelaar, D.J., and Van Ittersum, M.K. (2009) "Exploring multifunctional agriculture. A review of conceptual approaches and prospects for an integrative transitional framework," *Journal of Environmental Management*, vol. 90, 112–23

Revi, A. (2008) "Climate change risk: an adaptation and mitigation agenda for Indian cities," *Environment and Urbanization*, vol. 20, no. 1, 207–29.

Revkin, A.C. (2009) "Peeling back pavement to expose watery havens," *The New York Times*, July 16, 2009, http://www.nytimes.com/2009/07/17/world/asia/17daylight. html?pagewanted=all&_r=0

Richards, P. (1987) *Indigenous Agricultural Revolution: Ecology and Food Production in West Africa*, Westview Press, Boulder, CO

Richter, B., Mathews, R., Harrison, D., and Wigington, R. (2003) "Ecologically sustainable water management: managing river flows for ecological integrity," *Ecological Applications*, vol. 13, no. 1, 206–24

Rijsberman, F. (2008) "Every last drop: managing our way out of the water crisis," *Boston Review*, September/October 2008

Rokeach, M. (2000) *Understanding Human Values*, 2nd edn, Simon and Schuster, New York

Roszak, T. (1992) *The Voice of the Earth*, Simon & Schuster, New York

Sabatier, P.A., Focht, W., Lubell, M., Trachtenberg, Z., Vedlitz, A., and Matlock, M. (eds) (2005) *Swimming Upstream: Collaborative Approaches to Watershed Management*, MIT Press, Cambridge, MA

Sandford, R.W. and Phare, M.A. (2011) *Ethical Water: Learning to Value What Matters Most*, Rocky Mountain Books, Toronto

Saravanan, V.S., McDonald, G.T., and Mollinga, P.P. (2009) 'Critical review of Integrated Water Resources Management: moving beyond polarised discourse," *Natural Resources Forum*, vol. 33, 76–86

Sarni, W. (2011) *Corporate Water Strategies*, Earthscan, London

Satterthwaite, D., McGranahan, G., and Mitlin, D. (2005) "Community-driven development for water and sanitation in urban areas," Report produced by the International Institute for Environment and Development for the Water Supply and Sanitation Council, Geneva

Scarborough, V.L. (2003) *The Flow of Power: Ancient Water Systems and Landscapes*, SAR Press, Santa Fe, New Mexico

Schama, S. (2008) "Over the River," in Christo and Jeanne-Claude, *Over the River: Project for the Arkansas River, State of Colorado*, Taschen, Cologne, 9

Schmidt, J. (2012) "Secure or insecure? The right to water and the ethics of global water governance," in Sultana and Loftus (2012)

Schultz, J. (2008) "The Cochabamba water revolt and its aftermath," in J. Schultz and M. Draper (eds) *Dignity and Defiance: Stories from Bolivia's Challenge to Gobalization*, University of California Press, Berkeley

Scott, J.C. (1998) *Seeing Like a State: How Certain Schemes to Improve the Human Condition Have Failed*, Yale University Press, New Haven, CT

Scudder, T. (2006) *The Future of Large Dams: Dealing with Social, Environmental, Institutional and Political Costs*, Earthscan, London

Seavy, N., Gardali, T., Golet, G., Griggs, F.T., Howell, C., Kelsey, R., Small, S., Viers, J., and Weigand, J. (2009) "Why climate change makes riparian restoration more important than ever: recommendations for practice and research," *Ecological Restoration*, vol. 27, no. 3, 330–38

Selborne, J. (2000). "The Ethics of Freshwater Use: A Survey," Report of the Commission on the Ethics of Science and Technology (COMEST), UNESCO, Paris, http://unesdoc.unesco.org/images/0012/001220/122049e.pdf

Shiva, V. (1991) *The Violence of the Green Revolution: Third World Agriculture, Ecology and Politics*, Zed Books, London

Shivamohan, M.V.K. and Scott, C. (2005) "Coalition building for participatory irrigation management under changing water resources trends: reflections on reforms in Andhra Pradesh, India," in G. Shivakoti, D. Vermillion, W.F. Lam, E. Ostrom, U. Pradhan, and R. Yoder (eds) *Asian Irrigation in Transition: Responding to Challenges*, Sage Publications, New Delhi

Smith, P. (1988) Improving the project identification process in agricultural development, *Public Administration and Development*, vol. 8, 15–26

Smith, M. and Barchiesi, S. (2009) *Environment as Infrastructure: Resilience to Climate Change Impacts on Water through Investments in Nature*, IUCN Perspectives on Water and Climate Change Adaptation, IUCN, Gland, Switzerland

Soderbaum, P. (2008) *Understanding Sustainability Economics: Towards Pluralism in Economics*, Earthscan, London

Sophocleous, M. (2005) "Groundwater recharge and sustainability in the High Plains aquifer in Kansas, USA," *Hydrogeology Journal*, vol. 13, 351–65

Sohail, M. and Cavill, S. (2006) "Ethics: making it the heart of water supply," *Civil Engineering*, vol. 159, 11–15 Paper 14264

Stanbury, P. (1987) *Processes of Village Community Formation in an Agricultural Settlement Scheme: The Indira Gandhi Nahar Project, India*, PhD Dissertation, Department of Anthropology, University of Arizona, http://arizona.openrepository.com/arizona/handle/10150/184165

Steyaert, P. and Ollivier, G. (2007) "The European Water Framework Directive: how ecological assumptions frame technical and social change," *Ecology and Society*, vol. 12, no. 1, art. 25, http://www.ecologyandsociety.org/vol12/iss1/art25/

Strang, V. (2004) *The Meaning of Water*, Berg, Oxford

STWI (2012) *Swedish Textile Water Initiative Guidelines*, STWI, Stockholm, http://www.swedishwaterhouse.se/galleries/documents/STWI/STWI_Guidelines_-Short_version_webb.pdf

Sultana, F. and Loftus, A. (eds) (2012) *The Right to Water: Politics, Governance and Social Struggles*, Earthscan/Routledge, London

Sura, A. (2010) "The Cloaca Maxima: draining disease from Rome," *Vertices*, vol. 23, 22–7

Suzuki, D. and Knudtson, P. (1992) *Wisdom of the Elders: Honoring Sacred Native Visions of Nature*, Bantam Books, New York

Svendsen, M. and Nott, G. (2000) "Irrigation management transfer in Turkey: Process and outcomes," in D. Groenfeldt and M. Svendsen (eds) Case Studies in Participatory Irrigation Management, World Bank Institute, Washington, DC

Taylor, B. 2010, *Dark Green Religion: Nature, Spirituality and the Planetary Future*, University of California Press, Berkeley, CA

Todaro, M. and Smith, S. (2003) *Economic Development*, Addison Wesley, Boston

Trainor, S.F. (2006) "Realms of value: conflicting natural resource values and incommensurability," *Environmental Values*, vol. 15, 3–29

Transparency International and Water Integrity Network (2008) *Global Corruption Report 2008: Corruption in the Water Sector*, Cambridge University Press, Cambridge, UK

Tullos, D., Brown, P.H., Kibler, K., Magee, D., Tilt, B., and Wolf, A.T. (2010) "Perspectives on the salience and magnitude of dam impacts for hydro development scenarios in China," *Water Alternatives*, vol. 3, no. 2, 71–90

UNEP (2009) *Water Security and Ecosystem Services: The Critical Connection*, United Nations Environment Programme, Nairobi

UNESCO (2011) *Water Ethics and Water Resource Management, Ethics and Climate Change in Asia and the Pacific (ECCAP) Project Working Group 14 Report*, UNESCO, Bangkok

UN Global Compact and Rockefeller Foundation (2012), "A framework for action: social enterprise and impact investing," http://www.unglobalcompact.org/docs/issues_doc/development/Framework_Social_Enterprise_Impact_Investing.pdf

United Nations (2008) "United Nations Declaration on the Rights of Indigenous Peoples," United Nations, New York, http://www.un.org/esa/socdev/unpfii/documents/DRIPS_en.pdf

United Nations General Assembly (2010) "The human right to water and sanitation," United Nations A/64/L.63/Rev.1, July 26, 2010

Uphoff, N. (1986) *Improving International Irrigation Management with Farmer Participation: Getting the Process Right*, Westview Press, Boulder, CO

van Koppen, B. (2007) "Dispossession at the interface of community-based water law and permit systems," in van Koppen et al. (2007)

van Koppen, B., Giordano, M., and Butterworth, J. (eds) (2007) *Community-based Water Law and Water Resource Management Reform*, CAB International, London

van Koppen, B., Cossio Rojas, V., and Skielboe, T. (2012) "Project politics, priorities and participation in rural water schemes," *Water Alternatives*, vol. 5, no. 1, 15

Varady, R., Meehan, K., and McGovern, E. (2009) "Charting the emergence of 'global water initiatives' in world water governance," *Physics and Chemistry of the Earth*, vol. 34, 150–5

Vermillion, D. (1997) "Impacts of irrigation management transfer: a review of the evidence," *IWMI Res. Rep.*, vol. 11, 1–35

Wade R. (1982) "The system of administrative and political corruption: canal irrigation in South India," *The Journal of Development Studies*, vol. 18, no. 3, 287–328

Warner, J., Wester, P., and Bolding, A. (2008) "Going with the flow: river basins as the natural units for water management?" *Water Policy*, vol. 10, suppl. 2, 121–38

Water and Sanitation Program (2011) *Lessons in Urban Sanitation Development: Indonesia Sanitation Sector Development Program 2006–10*, World Bank, Washington, DC

Water Resources Group (2012) *Background, Impact and the Way Forward*, Briefing report prepared for the World Economic Forum Annual Meeting 2012 in Davos-Klosters, Switzerland, January 26, 2012

WBCSD (2012) *Water for Business: Initiatives Guiding Sustainable Water Management in the Private Sector*, World Business Council for Sustainable Development, Geneva

WCD (World Commission on Dams) (2000) *Dams and Development: A New Framework for Decision-Making*, Earthscan, London

Wilkinson, C.F. (2010) "Indian water rights in conflict with state water rights: the case of the Pyramid Lake Paiute tribe in Nevada, US," in R. Boelens, D. Getches, and A. Guerva-Gil (eds), *Out of the Mainstream: Water Rights, Politics and Identity*, Earthscan, London

Williams, D.R. (2002) "When voluntary, incentive-based controls fail: structuring a regulatory response to agricultural nonpoint source water pollution," *Washington University Journal of Law and Policy*, vol. 9, 21–121

Wittfogel, K. (1957) *Oriental Despotism*, Yale University Press, New Haven

WMO (World Meteorological Organization) (2009) *Integrated Flood Management Concept Paper*, WMO no. 1047, World Meteorological Organization, Geneva

Woodhouse, P. 2010. "Beyond industrial agriculture? Some questions about farm size, productivity and sustainability," *Journal of Agrarian Change*, vol. 10, no. 3, July 2010, 437–53

Wittfogel, K. (1957) *Oriental Despotism*, Yale University Press, New Haven

World Bank (2000) *World Development Report 2000/2001: Attacking Poverty*, Oxford University Press, New York

World Commission on Environment and Development (1987), *Our Common Future*, Oxford University Press, New York

Worster, D. (1985) *Rivers of Empire: Water, Aridity, and the Growth of the American West*, Pantheon, New York

Worster, D. (1992) *Under Western Skies: Nature and History in the American West*, Oxford University Press, New York

WWF (2004) *Living with Floods: Achieving Ecologically Sustainable Flood Management in Europe*, Brussels: WWF European Policy Office, July 2004

Yamaoka, K., Groenfeldt, D., Asan, K., and Sugiura, M. (2009) "Social capital accumulation through building up irrigation water governance in monsoon Asia: comparative analysis of policy measures," in G. Tripp, M. Payne, and D. Diodorus (eds) *Social Capital*, Nova Science Publishers, New York

Index

Aga Khan Rural Support Programme 116
agricultural heritage 66
Agriculture at a Crossroads (report by IAASTD) 54
agroecology 60–2
Alliance for Water Stewardship, 9, 89, 97, 103, 164, 180
Amazon River 35
American Coal Council 91, 99
ancient engineering 18
anti-nature ethic 20
artists 84, 168, 170, 178,181
Aspevig, Clyde 171
Aswan Dam 34
Avari River Pariliament (Rajasthan) 129–30, 133

Bali Irrigation Improvement Project 136
beneficial use vii, 22
biophilic design 84
Black Mesa (Arizona) 141
Blankenship, Don 97–100
Blue Lake (New Mexico) 141
Borlaug, Norman 56
Botin Foundation, 7

Cadillac Desert 23
Carson, Rachel 44, 179
CEO Water Mandate 87, 89, 96–7, 103–4
Cernea, Michael 57
Chambers, Robert 61–2
Chhattisgarh (India) 145
Christianity 35
climate change x, 9, 18, 23, 27, 34, 41, 45–6, 50, 62, 64, 87, 89, 94, 96–7, 100, 119
Cloaca Maxima (Rome) 19

Coca-Cola Company 88, 94, 160
Cochabamba (Bolivia) 121–2
Cochiti Dam 29, 40, 47, 139, 142
Colorado River 28, 80
Comission Nacional del Agua, CNA (Mexico) 117
command-and-control approach 24, 38, 42, 162
community development 61, 124
Comprehensive Assessment of Water Management in Agriculture 51
Concentrated Animal Feeding Operations (CAFOs) 44, 66
Conserve to Enhance program 81–2
Corporate Social Responsibility 104, 163–4
corruption 16, 113, 173
cost-benefit analysis, 2, 18, 23, 27, 53
cultural heritage 33, 52, 64, 66
cultural values 133, 136–7, 139, 142, 167, 173, 177, 179 see also: Frames
customary law 144–7

dams 17, 19–20, 23–4, 25–8, 31, 33–37, 47, and Narmada River 25 and World Bank 24–25, and climate change 45–6, and Indigenous Peoples 153, dam removal 162
Delli Priscoli, J. 7
demand management 81
Dublin Principles 157–8, 160
Dujian irrigation project (China) 19

Echo Park Dam 23
ecological status 23, 42, 162
ecological water management 23–4, 42, 46
ecosystem services, 2, 9, 37, 42, 47, 53, 65, 127, 176

emotional intelligence 179
engineering ethic 20
engineering hubris, 16
environmental flow 42–4, 162
environmental organizations 9, 127, 180
ethical space 182
ethics (and values, 3; applied to water, 4; ethics categories, 5, 18, 47 economic ethics, 5, 43, social ethics 32, 132; cultural ethics 32; water use ethics 41, 48; environmental ethics 43, 127, 132; methodological ethics 79; ethics analysis 120, 171; stewardship ethic 129;
European Model of Agriculture 63

Fatehpur Sikri (India) 68, 81
Feldman, David, 7
fish ladders 31, 47
fisheries 31, 130
flood control 34–7, 39–40
flood management 38–9, 41, 162
food security 51–2, 63, 65, 113
Foote, Mary Hallock 21
Frames 136, 167
free, prior, and informed consent 26–7, 32, 135, 164

Gleick, Peter, 9
Glen Canyon Dam 23, 37
Global Water Partnership 109
Global Water System Project 46
Green Business [model] 93, 104
Green Revolution 54–7, 62, 113
groundwater management 59, 129

Hetch Hetchy Valley (California) 21
Hoover Dam 28
Hopi tribe 137, 141
human right to a healthy environment 44
human right to water (UN resolution) 68, 109, 111, 157, 159

Ickes, Harold 28
impact investing 58
Indigenous Environment Network, 7, 143
Indigenous Peoples 135–45, 149, 152–53
Indigenous Peoples Kyoto Water Declaration 143
Indiska 91–2, 101–2
industrial agriculture 53–4, 60
integrated flood management 38–9

Integrated Urban Water Resources Management (IUWM) 125–26
Integrated Water Resources Management (IWRM), 13, 50, 126–7, 157–61, 165–66
Intel Corporation 90
International Assessment of Agricultural Knowledge Science and Technology for Development (IAASTD), 54
International Water Management Institute (IWMI) 113
Irland, Basia 170–171
Irrigation: community-based 115; irrigation development 55–57, 114, 133; irrigation governance 112–14, 117, 119–20; irrigation management transfer 118; irrigation systems 55–57, 64, 113–16, 119, 133; See also: participatory irrigation management
Isleta Pueblo (New Mexico) 150

Kennedy, Bobby, Jr. 97–8, 100
Khan, Shoab Sultan 116
Kissimmee River (Florida) 17, 47

Lancaster, Brad 169
Land Ethic, 1, 8
Las Vegas (Nevada) 81, 84
legal pluralism 148
Leopold, Aldo 1, 2, 3, 8, 70, 178
Leopold, Luna, 8, 37
LIFELINK project 77
Linton, Jamie, 14
Los Angeles River 82–83

Manantali dam 37
Mandamin, Grandmother Josephine 149
Massey Energy 97–8, 102–3, 109
Mekong River 31, 34
Merchant, Caroline, 6
mercury (in mining), 12
Millennium Development Goals (MDGs) 69, 72, 94, 163
Mississippi River 35, 39
Missouri River 36
Mosher, Arthur 55
mountaintop removal (of coal) 97–100, 176
Muir, John, 13, 21
multifunctional agriculture 53, 62–3, 65

National Irrigation Administration
(Philippines) 114–15
negotiated approach 132
Nehru (Prime Minister of India) 28
Nile River 19, 34

Oder River 36
Ogallala Aquifer 59
options assessment 30
Orangi Pilot Research and Training
Institute 123
Ostrom, Elinor 59, 106–7

Pacific Institute, 9
paddy (rice) agriculture 37, 52
Pape, Louise, 13
participation 177; in irrigation 57, 107,
112, 114–17, 119–20, in IUWM 125;
in IWRM 127–28, 158; in river basins
131–32, 166; in water planning 142,
145, 177; participatory irrigation
management 57, 117
Pecos, Regis 29
Penokee Mine (Wisconsin) 151
PepsiCo 88, 90
Phoenix (Arizona) 14, 80
polluter pays (principle) 45, 110, 148–9
pollution 5–6, 41–44, 78, 101–103, 176;
from agriculture 53, 59–60, 66; from
coal mining 98–100; from sewage 70,
from textile factories 91–2,
and Indigenous cultures 141,
148, 153
Postel, Sandra, 8, 155
Powell, John Wesley 21
precautionary principle 44
prior appropriation 22
privatiization (of water services)
121–2
Pyramid Lake Paiute Tribe
(Nevada) 146

rational choice theory 108
rectification (of river channels) 20, 35
Reducing Emissions from Deforestation
and Degradation (REDD) 62
Reisner, Marc 23
religious organizations 181
resettlement 26–7, 32, 47
resilience (and climate adaptation) 45,
66, 119
Rhine River 20, 39
Rights of Nature, 9, 10, 43
rights of rivers 42

Rio Grande 29, 40–1
room for the river (Dutch
program) 38, 162
Roosevelt, Franklin 28

sacred water 140–1
Sambunaris, Victoria 170
San Antonio (Texas) 83
Santa Fe (New Mexico) 10, 14, 78,
125–6,
Santa Fe Natural Tobacco Company 95
Santa Fe River *vii*, 95, 128,
Santa Fe Watershed Association
128–9, 168
Schmidt, Jeremy, 13, 14
semiotic hegemony 142
Seoul (South Korea) 82–83
Singh, Rajendra 130–31
Slow Food 53
social equity 57, 69–70, 73, 75–6, 112,
soft path (concept), 9, 29, 172
South African National Water
Act 42
Stockholm International Water
Institute 92
supply management, 14–15
sustainable agriculture 53, 58, 61

Taos Pueblo (New Mexico) 141 see also,
Blue Lake
Tebtebba, 7, 143
triple bottom line 24, 100, 126, 164
Tucson (Arizona) 79–81
Tulla, Johann Gottfried 20

UN Declaration on the Rights of
Indigenous Peoples 32, 140,
152, 164
UNESCO, 7
Unilever 90, 92–3, 164
United Nations General Assembly
69–70,
US Army Corps of Engineers 20, 29,
35, 38–40, 142
US Bureau of Reclamation 20
US Clean Water Act 44, 60, 150
US Environmental Protection Agency
(EPA) 98–9, 128–9, 148

values (definition), 3
Via Campesina 53, 64
Vikas (Indian NGO) 75–6, 112
virtual water 50
Vision for Water and Nature 24

wastewater treatment 44, 181
water conservation, 10–11, 14–15, 81, 84, 87, 89, 169,
water diplomacy 111, 146
Water Ethics Network 172–3
water footprint (concept), 8, 9, 86–8, 179
Water Footprint Network, 8
Water Framework Directive (EU) 23, 42, 107, 162
water governance 3, 95, 106–12, 124, 126–29, 132–33, 160, 164–67, 176–77; and indigenous issues:143–45,
water grabs 50
water harvesting 70, 81, 130, 169
water hubris 80
water planning 160–61, 172; in Indigenous contexts 142–5, 180
water quality standards 43–5, related to industry: 91–92, 99, 101; and governance: 108; indigenous perspectives: 148, 150–52
water rights *viii–ix*, 77; groundwater rights 79–81; customary rights *vii*, 18, 145–46; of Indigenous Peoples 164
water scarcity *x*, 13–15, 46, 81, 133,
water security 78, 81, 159, 169; of companies 94,
water sensitive urban design 70, 82

water stewardship, 9–10, 90, 95–7, 124, 164, 179–80
water use 4, 8, 11–13, 41, 48, 109, 164–65, 180; in agriculture 50–51, 65–7; urban and domestic use 68ff; industrial use 86ff; indigenous views 152
water users association (WUA) 115, 119
watersheds (and governance) 21, 90, 94–5, 104, 111, 128–32, 138, 143, 166,
West Virginia Coal Association 99
Whanganui River (New Zealand) 147–48
Wittfogel, Karl 35
World Bank 114, 118, 121–2
World Business Council for Sustainable Development 89, 160
World Commission on Dams (WCD) 26–7, 30–32, 34, 135,
World Commission on Dams 26 (see also: WCD report)
World Water Commission 109
World Water Council 109–10
World Water Forum, 8, 24, 110
World Water Vision 109–10
Worster, D. 20

Yamuna River, 6, 141